To Hugh Woodcock
    and the D.C.P.S...

    with warm good wishes,

    from David Evans
    and all at D.C.

5: vi: 81.

By the same author

Above All Nations (with Vera Brittain and George Catlin)

Gollancz: The Story of a Publishing House

Frontispiece   Edward Alleyn (after the painting by an unknown artist)

God's Gift

A Living History of Dulwich College

Sheila Hodges

HEINEMANN · LONDON

Published by Heinemann Educational Books Ltd
22 Bedford Square, London WC1B 3HH

LONDON   EDINBURGH   MELBOURNE   AUCKLAND
HONG KONG   SINGAPORE   KUALA LUMPUR   NEW DELHI
IBADAN   NAIROBI   JOHANNESBURG
EXETER (NH)   KINGSTON   PORT OF SPAIN

British Library Cataloguing in Publication Data

Hodges, Sheila
    God's gift.
    I. Title
    373.421′64   LF795.D8

    ISBN 0-435-32450-0

Filmset in 'Monophoto' Baskerville by Eta Services (Typesetters)
Ltd., Beccles, Suffolk and printed by Butler & Tanner Ltd., Frome.

Contents

List of Illustrations

Introduction

by Lord Wolfenden, Chairman of the Board of Governors

THIS 'living history' is of direct personal interest to anybody who has any connection with Dulwich College. It tells the story of the past three hundred and sixty years of that part of the Foundation of Alleyn's College of God's Gift which we know as Dulwich College. That story is told here with scholarship without tedium, accuracy without pedantry, sympathy without sentimentality, crispness without cynicism. It includes not only the stately procession of Masters, with their individual ideals and changing problems, but also histories of the Picture Gallery, the Library, games and societies, Old Alleynian activities, and an appropriate sprinkling of anecdotes, all spiced with first-hand contemporary quotations. It is a fascinating narrative of ups and downs—yes, there have been downs as well as ups—at the College right through three-and-a-half centuries.

But this book is of interest and importance in a much wider context. The history of Dulwich forms part of the kaleidoscopic picture of English secondary education. That part is a distinctive one; for down those centuries Dulwich, essentially a day school, has held its unchallenged place among 'the public schools', which were essentially boarding schools. So the College was throughout this time an integral part of a local community—as it still is—as well as being part of the national picture.

This, then, is the living story of the first three hundred and sixty years of an educational institution which scores of thousands of men throughout the world call their own. There will be hundreds of thousands more of them in the centuries to come. Because, make no mistake about it, there will be boys coming to, and growing up in, and leaving Dulwich College for a long time yet. Of course it will change, as it has changed, many times and in many ways, since Edward Alleyn's first group of beneficiaries moved in. It is ignorant caricature which represents these places as unchanging antediluvian relics untouched by any breath of fresh air. But the point is that there is an 'it' which changes, an abiding and continuing entity with a life and character of its own. And as the pace of the outside world's changes increases, so the pressures on any school grow. The wisdom of those who manage its affairs will be judged by the extent to which the changes they make enrich the life of each individual boy and of the 'it' which is his background.

The College Governors are delighted and proud that this book has been written by Sheila Hodges, and deeply grateful to her for the devotion which shines through it.

Preface

In February 1941 a letter appeared in the *Alleynian* expressing surprise that no recent history of Dulwich College had appeared. 'I appeal to some Old Alleynian,' the writer said, 'to begin this great work which, while sketching the history of the whole foundation, would concentrate on the College itself.'

Since the country was then at war, it is not to be wondered at that this suggestion fell on barren soil. It is, however, quite puzzling that there has been no full-length book about the college since William Young's indispensable two-volume work, which was privately printed in 1882—though in effect it covered the years only from Edward Alleyn's foundation of his charity until the Act of Reconstitution of 1857. Two accounts were begun, but neither was completed. The first was written by R. J. Mackenzie, a relation by marriage of Alfred Carver, Master from 1858–83; this took the story up to shortly before the 1914–18 war, but was never finished or published because of the author's death. The second was written by William Darby, whose association with the college as pupil and master lasted for some thirty years. Again, his account was still unrevised when he died in 1968.

The history of this remarkable school should, it goes without saying, have been written by an Old Alleynian. But none has come forward—which is my excuse for embarking on the task. I have been privileged, thanks to the kindness of David Emms, virtually to pitch my tent within the school walls, as surely no outsider has ever been able to do before, sitting in on masters' meetings, prefects' meetings, classes, enjoying the freedom of the buildings and observing what went on inside them. For this I am deeply grateful, as I am to the many members of the teaching and administrative staff who have dealt so kindly and so patiently with my constant presence and endless questions.

Perhaps the scope and aims of the book should be explained. Since Young's book covers the pre-Reconstitution era exhaustively and interestingly, this period of the school's history has been dealt with quite briefly in the first chapter. On the other hand, it seemed important that the chronicle should be brought right up to date, for Dulwich is such a vital school, and so many changes are taking place, that it would have been nonsensical to cut the story short at, say, a respectful twenty years ago. This has its perils. For one thing, many of the people concerned are (fortunately!) still living; for another, it means that I, coming fresh to the college, am writing of matters about which many others know infinitely more than I could ever do. It also has the disadvantage that to some extent events may overtake the story; however, this is a risk that must be taken. So far as Chapter 7, which deals with the present, is concerned, since it would have been invidious to mention some masters and boys and not others, when so many contribute such a lot to the well-being of the school and have been immensely helpful to me personally, it seemed best to refer by name only to the present Master, David Emms.

No attempt has been made to include the history of the other two schools within the Foundation, Alleyn's and James Allen's Girls' School, since there is more than enough material for a book purely about the college.

In his autobiography G. C. Coulton quotes Benedetto Croce's remark that 'history is experience'. 'The letter of thanks we write after a visit,' Coulton goes on, 'recounting briefly our journey home and what we found there, is as truly history as a chronicle of the Norman Conquest.' This has, as it were, been my motto in writing this book, which tries to be above all a 'living history', portraying a faithful picture of life within the school walls: the formal history, perhaps, has yet to be written. But a school is like a pachyderm, as a former assistant master remarked: 'No one knows what is happening inside. And it's like a pachyderm inside too, with each class remaining private to the master.' A visitor to Dulwich during working hours would find barely a living soul visible over the whole vast area: all the life is going on within. So this book is not only for present and past Alleynians—who I hope will forgive the fact that it has not been written by one of their number—but also for parents, who through it may learn a little more of the school where their boys spend such a large part of their childhood.

Attending, as a privileged observer, so many meetings over the past two years, I have become vividly aware of the immense pull which such a school as Dulwich exercises over boys and masters alike. It has been a fascinating experience, during which I have grown to love and admire the college. I hope that my book will convey something of this feeling, and will repay in some small measure my debt of gratitude for having been allowed to write it.

Dulwich–Montreal–Tuscany   SHEILA HODGES
March 1978–October 1980

1 Edward Alleyn's Charity

1619–1857

'Two equal small rolls of paper to be indifferently made and rolled up in one of which rolls the words "God's Gift" are to be written, and the other roll is to be left blank . . .' (The Statutes)

F I V E miles south of Westminster as the crow flies, surrounded by an urban wasteland with little to delight the mind or eye, there lies an area remarkable for its luxuriance of trees, parks, well-designed housing estates, and for the impression that it gives of careful planning and concern. This small island of greenery owes its existence to a sixteenth-century actor, Edward Alleyn, who on 1 September 1566 was born in Bishopsgate, where his father had an inn.

Perhaps, in accordance with contemporary usage, plays were performed in the inn-yard, and Alleyn, while still a small boy, watched entranced as the players declaimed the melo-dramas of Lyly, Kyd, and other dramatists of the age. In any event, his own gifts as an actor were soon plain to see: prob-ably before he was eighteen he joined the Earl of Worcester's company of players, and here he stayed for some years, transferring to the Lord Admiral's men in 1589. Before long he was renowned as the greatest actor of his day, his very name 'able to make an ill matter good', and chief rival to Burbage, whom he antedated by a few years.

Though John Evelyn described him as a famous comedian, he was admired above all for his interpretation of Marlowe's plays, his greatest parts being Doctor Faustus, Tamburlaine, and Barabbas in *The Jew of Malta* (there is a statue of him in this last role in Canterbury cathedral). It is often claimed that he acted in Shakespeare's plays, but there is no evidence of this; in fact, Shakespeare is said to have poked fun at him, in the speech where Hamlet refers to the 'bellowing and strutting' of a certain type of contemporary acting. Nor can it actually be proved that the two men ever met, though it would have been strange if their paths had never crossed. The only established connection between them is Alleyn's purchase for fivepence of the *Sonnets* in 1609, the year of their publication.

It was not in Alleyn's destiny to follow for long the career of an actor, as precarious in the sixteenth and seventeenth centuries as it is today. In 1592 he married Joan Woodward, stepdaughter of Philip Henslowe, who owned and managed the Rose Theatre on Bankside, the district south of the Thames where the Elizabethans sought their amusement, rather as the Victorians sought theirs at the Crystal Palace. Alleyn went into partnership with his father-in-law, and gradually began to acquire property and amass a considerable fortune. Among their more lucrative purchases were the Paris Bear Garden, also on Bankside, and the much sought-after post of Master of the King's Games of Bulls and Bears. In 1600 they built the Fortune Theatre, in Golden Lane, Cripplegate, which was later to produce a substantial income for Dulwich College.

At the end of 1597 Alleyn went to stay with friends at Brill, in Sussex, and here for a while he enjoyed a quiet rural existence with his 'Mouse', as he called Joan, with whom he had a very loving relationship, as their tender letters to one another show. Three years later—it is said at the express wish of Queen Elizabeth—he returned briefly to the theatre, but after about 1603 he acted no more. His last recorded appearance in this context was on 15 March 1604, when, as the Genius of London and Thamesis, and 'with excellent action and a well-tuned, audible voice', he delivered an address of welcome to James I at the monarch's reception by the City.

He continued to accumulate property, and in 1605, for £5,000, bought the Manor of Dulwich from Sir Francis Calton, an impoverished knight—'£1,000 more than any other man would have given for it,' he is reputed to have said. Other 'small parcels of land' in the neighbourhood cost him a further £5,000 or so. In 1606 he is referred to in a bond as Lord of the Manor of Dulwich, a description that must have riled some of his contemporaries, who felt that an actor had no business aping his betters, for one anonymous satirist of the day wrote:

> With mouthing words that better wits have framed,
> They purchase lands and now esquires are made.

For some years, however, he appears to have continued to live in Southwark, and in 1610 succeeded his father-in-law as churchwarden of the liberty of the Clink.[1] This appointment involved many duties, among them the task of trying to introduce some respectability into this unsavoury neighbourhood.

He moved to Hall Place, the manor house of Dulwich, in about 1613. At the same time he entered into a contract with John Benson of Westminster, bricklayer, for the erection on Dulwich Green of a chapel, a schoolhouse, and twelve almshouses. Alleyn provided the bricks, wood, scaffolding, and other materials needed, while Benson furnished the labour. His price was forty shillings a rod, and he was a poor bargain, as was soon to be shown.

It is not known when Alleyn first had the idea of establishing a college or hospital for poor people and the education of poor boys, but it may have been in his mind from the time when he bought the manor. The foundation of charitable

---

[1] Once part of the estates of the Abbey of Bermondsey, but apparently granted in the twelfth century to the Bishop of Winchester. It became known as the Bishop of Winchester's Liberty, and later as the Clink Liberty, after the prison which stood within it. The City had no judicial rights within these liberties, and in this particular case the Bishop of Winchester exercised manorial discretion.

institutions of this kind had been popular throughout the sixteenth century: St Paul's School, Christ's Hospital, Repton, Westminster, Merchant Taylors', Rugby, Uppingham, and Harrow all came into existence then; Croydon Hospital (Whitgift) was founded in 1596, and Sutton's Hospital (Charterhouse) in 1611. England's endowed schools were admired and copied in many European countries, including Holland, Switzerland, Prussia, Saxony, and even as far afield as 'Muscovy'. Perhaps too Alleyn, who had no children by either of his marriages, wished to perpetuate his name through such a foundation. (His second wife, whom he married a few months after Joan's death in 1623, was Constance, the oldest daughter of John Donne. She was thirty-seven years younger than her husband, who was, indeed, a good deal senior to his new father-in-law. Though the two men had dined together, and had apparently been on friendly terms, while Joan Alleyn was alive, Donne deeply disapproved of his daughter's marriage, and wrote about it in very sour terms.)

By the autumn of 1616 the building was finished. It stood, as it still does today, between Gallery Road and College Road, though neither was then more than a rough track. Frequent rebuilding over the centuries has been necessary, but in appearance it was then very much as it is now, forming three sides of a grassy quadrangle, but with a wall enclosing the fourth side at the end of the two wings. The chapel was consecrated on Sunday 1 September, Alleyn's fiftieth birthday, by the Archbishop of Canterbury, who became the official Visitor, 'with full power and lawful authority . . . to visit, order, and punish according to the ecclesiastical laws and constitutions of this our realm of England'.

The first group of beneficiaries—a chaplain, six poor brothers and six poor sisters—moved into the college soon afterwards. The college register records as the first entry the enrolment of 'Cornelius Lymour of Christchurch in Oxford, fellow'. During the following year they were gradually joined by twelve poor scholars.

Not for some time, however, was the necessary patent of incorporation granted. Francis Bacon, the Lord Chancellor, greatly disliked these foundations. By ancient law, when property was given *in perpetuity* for charitable purposes it became exempt from the dues which would otherwise have accrued from it to the Crown, thus depriving the king of profitable revenues from rents and wardships, which he could have claimed if it had remained in private hands. 'I like well that Alleyn playeth the last act of his life so well,' Bacon wrote to the King's favourite, Buckingham; but, he went on, not only would the proposed foundation impoverish the royal coffers, but it would be much better if some of the money that Alleyn wanted to use to endow his college could be diverted to provide two lectureships at Oxford and Cambridge, 'foundations of singular honour to his Majesty and of which there is great want, whereas hospitals abound, and beggars abound never the less'.

Alleyn persisted, pleading his case on various occasions in person before the Lord Chancellor; and Bacon—who had raised exactly the same objections when Thomas Sutton asked permission to endow Charterhouse—at last gave way. On 21 June 1619, now celebrated as Founder's Day, James I granted letters patent to 'our trusty and well-beloved servant Edward Alleyn . . . Chief Master Ruler and Overseer of all and singular our games of Beares, Bulls, Mastive Doggs and Mastive Bitches', authorizing him to establish a college in Dulwich 'to endure and remain for ever', and to be called the College of God's Gift, in Dulwich in Surrey. On 13 September, three months after the Great Seal had been affixed (it cost Alleyn £18 16s 10d, including 17s 6d for 'vellome and strings'), the college was formally opened in the presence of the Lord Chancellor, the Earl of Arundel, Inigo Jones—the King's Surveyor and a friend of Alleyn's—and many other notables, whom Alleyn afterwards entertained to dinner.

The charity which he set up was to consist of a Master, a Warden, four fellows, six poor brothers, six poor sisters, and twelve poor scholars, who jointly became legal owners of his endowment of the manor of Dulwich, together with the extensive lands in which it was set. It was this act of incorporation by letters patent, continuing for ever and creating an entity that could be recognized in the courts as immortal persons capable of suing and being sued, that entitled the Foundation to the status of a college. The beneficiaries were to be chosen from the four parishes with which Alleyn was closely associated: St Botolph's, Bishopsgate, where he was born; St Saviour's, Southwark,[1] where he had lived and been churchwarden; that part of the parish of St Giles, Cripplegate, where the Fortune Theatre was situated; and the parish of Camberwell, in which lay his manor. (In 1773, when the population of Cripplegate became too big for its needs to be met by one church, another was built, St Luke's, and this parish became the beneficiary of Alleyn's endowment in place of St Giles.)

Alleyn did far more than provide the buildings and finance to keep the college going; though the first Master and Warden had duly been appointed, not only did he personally manage the affairs of the college, but for the rest of his life he minutely examined the many great institutions on which he wished to model his own, taking from each what seemed to him most in tune with his vision. He visited Winchester College and borrowed a copy of their statutes; he twice went to St Paul's School, visited Croydon Hospital, and journeyed by river, with his 'Mouse' and two friends, to inspect Thomas Sutton's Hospital—the first entry in his diary, in fact, records his trip there, on 29 October 1617, at a cost of one shilling. Speech days were to be modelled on those at Westminster and Merchant Taylors', and for the chapel services his Foundation was to look to King's Chapel and the Collegiate Church of St Peter at Westminster; while for the boys' instruction the books used in the 'free grammar schools of Westminster and Paul's' were to be followed. He sent to Amsterdam for the statutes and plans of an Orphanocomium and Gerontocomium which a wealthy Dutchwoman had founded there in 1550. There seems little doubt, in fact, that John Benson's building was modelled on this latter establishment, for there is a striking

[1] In 1905 St Saviour's Church became Southwark Cathedral.

resemblance between early prints of the college and contemporary engraving of the Gerontocomium.[1]

From all accounts Alleyn was a man of charm and affability, tall, handsome, religious and philanthropic, with a wide circle of friends whom he loved to entertain. He often rode to London to dine and talk, and never lost his connection with his one-time colleagues, whom he was always ready to help in case of need.

> His life was one of dignified ease and comfort. At various times he was the guest of, or dined in company with, the Archbishop of Canterbury, the Bishops of London and Winchester, Lord Treasurer Montague, Sir Julius Caesar, Master of the Rolls, the Countess of Kildare, the Ambassadors Count Gondomar and Sir Noel Caron, Sir Edward Sackville, Dr John Donne, and many more.

He was greatly interested in medicine, and counted many doctors among his friends, including Harvey, discoverer of the circulation of the blood. He evidently fancied himself as an amateur physician, for if any of his almspeople fell ill he liked to prescribe for them from among his own 'precious balms'.

In 1626, not long before he died, Alleyn signed a document which, in 123 statutes and ordinances, extended his original scheme; it is probable that this document had been drawn up some time before but not signed. Among other provisions, the statutes laid down that the Master and Warden should be 'of my blood and surname', or, if the former was impossible, then at least of his surname. Since he had no children, the stipulation with regard to blood relationship was unlikely to endure for long—in fact, the only men to hold office who fulfilled this qualification were the first three Masters and probably the fifth. The fourth asserted that he too was related to the Founder, but his claim was set aside. Strict rules of conduct were laid down, and all the beneficiaries had to be

---

[1] This engraving was reproduced in J. I. Pontanus' *Rerum et Urbis Amstelodamensium*, published in 1611. There is a translation of the statutes among the manuscripts in the college library.

unmarried, on pain of instantly forfeiting any right to a place in the college.

The poor brothers and sisters were to be of excellent character, and not less than sixty years of age. It would be the duty of the brothers to sweep and keep clean the inner and outer courts and cloisters, while the sisters were to weed and keep clean the gardens in front of the college, except for one of their number who was charged with looking after the welfare of the poor scholars.

These scholars were to be 'between the age of six or eight years or thereabouts' at the time of entry, and they were entitled to stay until they were eighteen. They were to be taught 'in good and sound learning, writing, reading, grammar, music and good manners [and] to write a fair hand', so that they might be prepared for university or for 'good and sweet trades and occupations'. As we learn from a later document, they inhabited the Long Chamber in the west wing, over the organist's two chambers. There they slept, two in a bed, with feather mattresses and feather pillows.

Alleyn also decreed that the people of Dulwich should be able to have their 'men children' instructed at the school, though they had to pay for the privilege: 'two shillings for every child's admittance, and sixpence a quarter to the schoolmaster towards brooms and rods, and every year at Michaelmas a pound of good candles for the use of the school'. 'Foreigners' children'—that is to say, children from outside Dulwich—could also attend the college, on payment of a fee to be determined by the Master and Warden. The total number of children, including the poor scholars, was not to exceed eighty at any one time.

Of the many other statutes, several specified the diet to be provided; this sounds remarkably wholesome and generous, with plenty of mutton, roast and boiled beef, 'pottage', bread in abundance, apple pies, fish, and other appetising dishes, as well as unlimited beer, all to be 'sweet and good'. No 'timber trees fit for shadow or shelter' must be cut or felled 'in any of the grounds adjoining or lying near to the west, south, and southwest parts of the said college', and no timber trees whatsoever should be cut unless they were needed for building purposes—a restriction that largely holds good today, for the Estates Governors still exercise rigorous control over the felling of trees.

The collegiates were to be chosen by lot, although 'mr doctor Love', the headmaster of Winchester, on the advice of his Warden had counselled against this, preferring election, 'not so much in respect of avoiding partiality and corruption, which might rather be avoided by lot than election, but that in divinity he [the Warden] conceiveth it not so lawful by lot to implore the immediate assistance of God in ordinary causes as this is, which he finds never to have been used but in cases of necessity'.

The most controversial clauses—which were to cause end-less trouble in the years to come—were those in which Alleyn enlarged the original number of beneficiaries to include six chanters, two churchwardens from each of the 'outside' parishes of St Saviour's, St Botolph's, and St Giles', and ten elderly pensioners from each of these parishes, who were first to be lodged in almshouses in each district, 'that from thence they may be admitted into the college as places fall void'. The chanters and churchwardens were to have the status of fellows, 'every one of them to have his voice' in the ordering of affairs as the senior fellows did. In addition, the chanters were to be sufficiently skilled in music and a variety of trades to be able to teach the scholars.

For two-and-a-half centuries the legality of these amending statutes was hotly contested in and out of the courts by the various interested parties, the point at issue being whether Alleyn was entitled to alter the original patent of incorpor-ation granted by James I. The bitter disputes that ensued were to continue almost uninterrupted, bedevilling the whole advancement of the college until its reconstitution in 1857, and even long afterwards.

In the summer of 1626 Alleyn journeyed to the north of England to visit an estate which he had recently bought there. Perhaps, like Bacon, he caught a fatal chill. All we know for certain is that soon after he returned he set about tidying up his affairs. On 29 September he signed the college statutes and ordinances, on 13 November he drew up a new will, and a

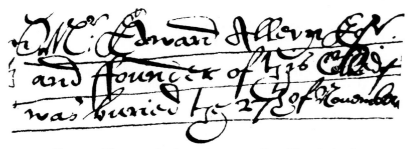

Fig. 1.1   The entry in the register recording Alleyn's death

week later he added two clauses to the statutes. He died on 25 November. The event is recorded in an entry in the college register which is all the more touching because it is so laconic, given no more prominence than the other, much humbler, entries: 'Mr Edward Alleyn Gov. and Founder of this College was buried the 27th of November', and lower down, beneath a roughly drawn line, 'The Founder died and was buried as above Novr 27, 1626'. His remains were laid in the college chapel, but at a point unspecified by history his tombstone came to light in the skittle-ground of the Half Moon public house in Lordship Lane, whence, around the middle of the nineteenth century, it was removed to its present position in the cloisters of the old college.

Alleyn bequeathed to the Foundation his staff and his seal ring with his arms, to be worn by the Master and his successors, as well as all his furniture and furnishings in the college, including his horses, oxen, and farm implements, books, pictures, musical instruments (including a lute, a pandora, a cythera, and six viols), and six pewter chamber-pots. The ring is still among the college possessions, but the staff, though its existence is recorded by one of the poor scholars in 1836 or thereabouts, has disappeared, and it is thought that most of the silver and plate which Alleyn left was stolen. The original seal, though no longer used, is still in existence, a heavy, elaborate metal cylinder with two pad-locks and keys—clearly no single individual was trusted to have sole access to it.

*   *   *

With a faith in the immutability of things that no one setting up such an institution would dare to show nowadays—and also, no doubt, because the provision for eternity was necessary if the endowment was to escape the predatory clutches of the Crown—many of the statutes which Alleyn laid down are prefaced by the words 'for ever', 'for all succeeding times to come', and similar phrases. But in this case 'eternity' lasted a very short while indeed, for no sooner was the founder dead than his legatees started to squabble over their share of the cake.

Anyone of a superstitious nature would have had good reason to feel that the college had been conceived under a star of ill-omen when, twelve years after Alleyn's death, John Benson's gimcrack building started to fall down, beginning with the steeple. The Foundation was by now in grave financial straits, for the annual income of £800 that Alleyn had left, provided out of rents from the property which the college had inherited, was soon inadequate for such a large number of pensioners. Part of this revenue came from the takings of the Fortune Theatre and rents from the buildings around it. A bad piece of drafting in Alleyn's will made it difficult for the college to assert their claim to the latter; while the Fortune Theatre itself, 'the fairest playhouse in this town', was closed down in 1643. Subsequently it fell into decay and provided no further revenue.

Another part of the college income must also have come to an end around the mid-seventeenth century. This issued from a source which, however we should regard it today, at the time when Alleyn lived was considered perfectly respectable—the establishments known as the Bankside stews, or brothels. No one can tell when they first sprang up, but they had been in existence long before the reign of Henry II, when the customs and regulations regarding their administration were consolidated into law. The proprietors of many of these places had unimpeachable pedigrees, including, over the centuries, kings of England and lord mayors of London, as well as successive bishops of Winchester, who, as lords of the manor in which these houses lay, had the additional duty of exercising jurisdiction over them. It was quite common for these brothels to be bequeathed to charities, and for what was called the 'bawds' rent' to be paid to the local churchwardens. At an earlier date the nuns of Stratford-at-Bow had carried on their charitable work on the proceeds of the brothel which they owned, and, further afield, a great Dublin hospital was entirely built from the takings in such houses. It was Henry VIII, of all people, who in 1545 repealed the legislation licensing the stews, which thus became illegal, but they continued to flourish, until in 1644 Parliament closed them down, together with the theatres and the gambling houses (though no doubt they continued to function in a clandestine way). Alleyn owned a number of these brothels, and in his will he bequeathed four of them—the Unicorn, the Barge, the Bell, and the Cock—to the corporation of the college, 'as an augmentation unto them . . . to be employed current according to the intent of the statutes'.

In 1638 the Visitor, the Archbishop of Canterbury, whose function it was to see that the founder's statutes were obeyed, decreed that the corporation should be dissolved for six months, and the money thus saved used to repair the damaged building. But this was by no means the end of the trouble. A few years later one wing and part of another collapsed; and on Friday 25 May 1703 'the college porch with the treasury chamber, etc., tumbled down to the ground'. Throughout the years there are many unkind references to Benson's unfortunate piece of jerry-building.

The college was vexed, too, by internal strife, especially by difficulties arising out of the ambivalent relationship between the Master and Warden on the one hand and the four fellows on the other. The fellows were in general educated men, for Alleyn had laid down that the two senior of them were to be Masters of Arts of Oxford or Cambridge, the third a graduate and divine, and the fourth 'a sufficient scholar to be usher of the school'. (In practice he became the organist, while the other three—at least in theory—occupied respectively the positions of preacher, schoolmaster, and usher.) So far as the Master and Warden were concerned Alleyn had, it is true, specified that they must be respectable, 'of learning, judgment, understanding, sufficient to discharge their places in the

college'. Their functions were, however, chiefly administrative, the Master's being to supervise the establishment, oversee
the accounts, defend and prosecute the college lawsuits, see
that the statutes were obeyed, and keep an eye on the well-
being of the pensioners; while the Warden was responsible for
the college finances and was in charge during the Master's
absence. Neither of them was required to have any academic
qualifications, and in hard practical terms they needed only to
be eternally celibate and to bear the founder's surname. This
combination of demands made it almost impossible to find
applicants of calibre: though some of the contestants were
men of culture, over the centuries they formed a bizarre
collection, including a vintner, peruke-maker, cooper, sea-
captain, dyer, carpenter, grocer, timber-merchant, linen-
merchant, hosier, malt-factor, and trooper.

Small wonder that, though nominally the Master was 'the
chiefest person' in the college, he and the Warden were apt to
be despised by the fellows, who were reported, by a committee
set up by Archbishop Sheldon, as 'petulant and saucy . . .
Whereas the fellows come to the chapel in surplices and hoods
according to their degrees and the Master and Warden barely
in surplices, which makes them appear to these young fellows
but as singing men.'

The role of the various Archbishop Visitors in the smooth
running of the college was anything but a sinecure, judging
from the number of occasions when they were called in to sort
out angry disagreements between Alleyn's disputatious pensioners. On one occasion the college solicitor commented that
the Archbishop had been 'put to a great deal of trouble to lay
the waves raised in this bottle'. The quarrels were endless and
bitter and over every possible and impossible issue, from
major problems about how the income should be spent and
who was entitled to benefit from it to petty squabbles about
whether or not the schoolmaster should keep his hat on in the
presence of the Master. There seem to have been few periods
when the foundation was free from lawsuits—which might be
said to have carried on the tradition of the founder, who was
perpetually going to law, and had various suits pending at the
time of his death.

At the outbreak of the Civil War all the fellows departed, probably to join the King's army, since they are styled 'delinquents' by Parliament. The college was virtually derelict, and in 1647 a company of Cromwell's soldiers was quartered there. They paid 19s 8d for the privilege—poor recompense, it would appear, for all the damage they did. Perhaps it was during their occupancy that 'the organ broke to pieces and was carried away'. The Long Parliament appointed a preacher and schoolmaster in place of the four absentees, and these men took up residence, but the Master and Warden, enraged that their prerogative had been usurped, retaliated by refusing to pay their salaries. Even when threatened with arrest they went on protesting, until in 1658 the interlopers were replaced by fellows chosen in the prescribed way, and matters returned to normal.

The Master and Warden were acting in accordance with the statutes in insisting that the election of the fellows, as of the other beneficiaries, was the business of the corporation. Alleyn had laid down careful instructions for the procedure, which began by whittling down the various candidates for any vacancy to two, who then drew lots. The most important offices, of course, were those of Master and Warden; and it was decreed that, when the Master died, the Warden should be immediately promoted to his place and a new Warden elected soon afterwards. There are several descriptions of these occasions, one of them relating to the election which took place in 1775, when four candidates offered themselves for the post of Warden.

On Monday morning, the 10th of July, the day of decision, there appeared at Dulwich a large concourse of people to be spectators of the ceremony, as well as those who were concerned in the election. The Chapel of God's Gift was opened, Divine Service was performed . . . and an excellent Sermon was preached . . . The Electors then proceeded to choose two from among the Candidates, by marking with a pen against the names of those they thought best qualified for Warden. The number of Electors is eleven, five within the house, and six without, consisting of the Master, three Clergymen, and an Organist, and the two Churchwardens of St Luke's, two of St Saviour's, and two of St

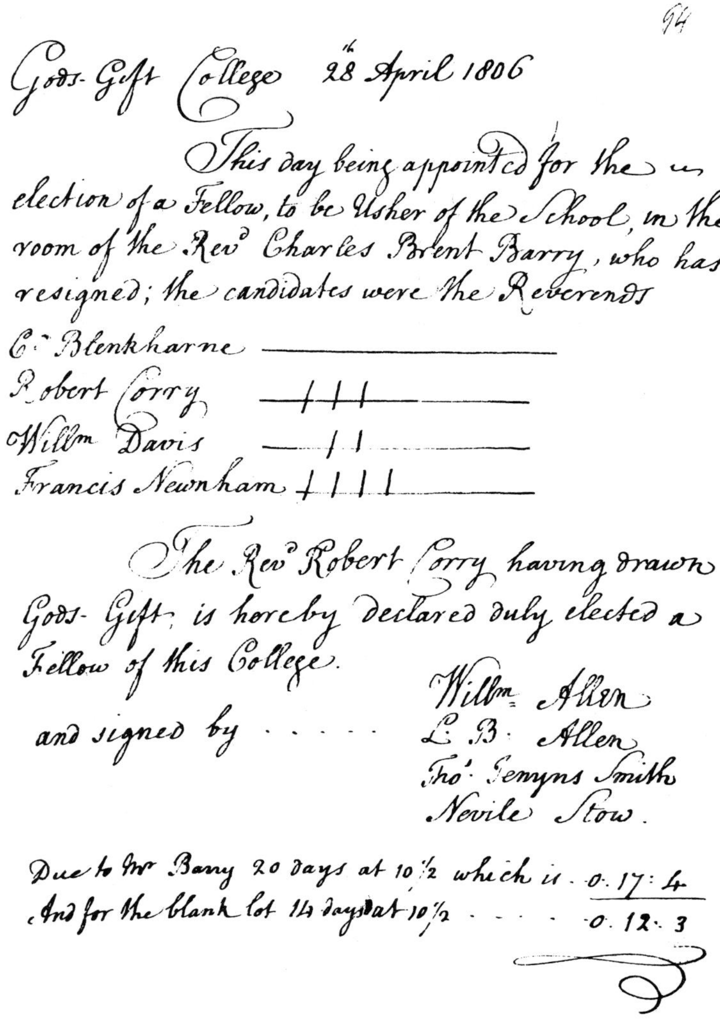

94

God's-Gift College   28th April 1806

This day being appointed for the election of a Fellow, to be Usher of the School, in the room of the Rev'd Charles Brent Barry, who has resigned; the candidates were the Reverends

C. Blenkharne _____

Robert Corry — +++ ———————

Will'm Davis — / / ———

Francis Newnham + | | | _____

The Rev'd Robert Corry having drawn God's-Gift; is hereby declared duly elected a Fellow of this College.

and signed by . . . . .
Will'm. Allen
L. B. Allen
Tho'. Jemyns Smith
Nevile Stow.

Due to Mr Barry 20 days at 10½ which is . 0. 17: 4
And for the blank lot 14 days at 10½ 0. 12. 3

Fig. 1.2 Entry from the *Private Sittings*: the election of the Rev. Robert Corry

Botolph, Bishopsgate, each of which has two suffrages for two
different Candidates ... A majority of votes was declared in
favour of Mr Henry and Mr William Allen; and these two
gentlemen were pronounced elected to the box ...

Previous to this, the Master had provided two Gentlemen of
known Character, Honour, and Fidelity, to inspect the two
above-named tickets, and to witness that every thing was conducted with the utmost Rectitude, Justice, and Impartiality. The
Gentlemen were Dr Allen, the late worthy master,[1] and Mr
Durnford, a person of eminence. Then the Master produced the
tin-box, which contained the tickets[2]; he shook them three times,
and opening the box, presented the two tickets to Mr William
Allen, just in his reach, but above his line of vision; then in the
decisive moment, Mr William Allen chose one, and Mr Henry
Allen the other. An awful pause ensued! Silence held the
spectators in deep suspense, and hope with mingled fear, sat
visible in the countenance of the two, on which all eyes were
fixed.

At length Dr Allen opened the ticket presented to him by Mr
William Allen, and finding God's Gift in the hands of Mr Wm.
Allen, of Lord Dartmouth's office, he was accordingly, amidst the
murmurs of applause, proclaimed Warden of the College of God's
Gift.

The Warden, in addition to being respectable and celibate,
had also to be a man of some substance. As he was in charge
of the finances of the college, he was obliged to give a security
in his own person of £1,000 (as time went on this sum was
increased considerably), and when finances became particularly rocky he sometimes lent the coffers money. He also
had to provide a banquet for the whole college to mark his
appointment. In 1731, when the new Warden was a grocer,
the menu consisted of hams, boiled fowls with cabbage,
carrots, French beans and artichokes, venison pie, a large
sirloin of beef, larded turkeys, codlin tarts, geese with gravy
and apple sauce, marrow puddings, fruit, lobsters, custards
and florentines (a kind of pie or tart), melons, pickles, prawns,
and salad. The poor brothers and sisters and the scholars

---

[1] This was Joseph Allen, the previous incumbent, who had not died, but
had married and was therefore obliged to resign.

[2] One was a blank piece of paper; the other bore the words 'God's Gift'.

came off badly as their betters were eating this sumptuous meal, for all they received were four large fowls and sauce and a plum pudding.

Once ensconsed, the chief object of Master, Warden, and fellows was to lead the pleasantest life possible. They did virtually nothing to further Alleyn's directions that every poor scholar should be adequately prepared for going out into the world, whether to university or to a satisfactory apprenticeship. There were, however, a few exceptions to this sad procession of nonentities.

The first was James Hume of Edinburgh, who became schoolmaster in 1706 and held this office for twenty-four years. He took vigorous charge of college affairs, representing the members in the many lawsuits in which it was involved, putting the library in order, and keeping a commonplace book in which he recorded matters of interest. He also recommended—since the finances of the Estate were now in a much healthier condition—that the surplus monies should be shared among the members of the corporation. His suggestion was adopted, and this dividend continued to be paid until the reconstitution of the Foundation in 1857. Another reform which he instituted was the curbing of the overlavish hospitality traditionally accorded to every visitor who set foot within the college gates. He is the author of the Latin inscription (commemorating the Foundation) over the entrance to the chapel, and he presented the font bearing the Greek palindrome 'Wash away sin, not the visage only'. Two centuries later the copper-gilt lid, green with verdigris, was found in the attic of the chaplain's apartments in the old college. Cleaned and shining, it has now been restored to its proper place.

Another outstanding exception was James Allen, first Warden and then Master from 1712 to 1746, who brought to his task a rare degree of probity and good sense. Much rebuilding was carried out, the estates were carefully administered, and the welfare of the pensioners benefited from the well-ordered régime. He was very conscious of the duty of the Foundation, stressed by Edward Alleyn in the statutes, to provide education for the boys of Dulwich, and, since

Hume and succeeding fellows were reluctant to do anything about this, in 1741 he made over to the college six houses near Kensington gravel pits, the rents to be used to establish two little schools in Dulwich where boys from the village would be taught to read and girls to read and sew. This was the genesis of James Allen's School for Girls. It was James Allen who dropped the 'y' from his name, an example which, with one exception, successive Masters and Wardens copied.

Then there was Thomas Allen, Warden and Master between 1752 and 1805. Although his profession had been the humble one of malt-factor, the college prospered during his rule, and there were fewer quarrels than usual among the fellows. He was very small, and in the neighbourhood was affectionately called 'the little old master'.

Another noted Master was John Allen (Warden 1811–20, Master 1820–43), but he was remarkable for his eminence in other fields, rather than because of his contribution to the welfare of the college. He trained as a doctor, and though he never practised medicine he was appointed medical attendant to the famous Lady Holland. He became indispensable to her, spending almost all his time at Holland House, and because of this becoming known as Holland House Allen. Noted for his brilliance and learning—Byron described him as 'the best informed and one of the ablest men I know'—he was also much liked and respected for his kindness and integrity. One contemporary described him as 'a stout strong man with a very large head, a broad face, enormous round silver spectacles before a pair of peculiarly bright and intelligent eyes, and with the thickest lip I ever remember.' When he was elected Warden in 1811 he wrote, 'On the whole, it is a very pleasant situation, and to a literary man gives perfect independence of the world,' and nine years later, on his appointment as Master, 'I have this summer more to do than formerly at Dulwich, but so far as I can judge I have been very fortunate in my new warden, and hope to have little to do there in future, except to superintend and see that other people do their business.' Recent Masters, with the well-being of somewhere in the region of two thousand souls in their care, must find a certain irony in this pleasant detachment.

*   *   *

In the college library there is still to be found the diary and account book which Alleyn kept between 1617 and 1622. (He may have kept these records at other periods too, but if so they have long since disappeared.) In it he minutely noted all the details of his expenditure; and from these entries much can be learnt about his life and his dedicated work for the college. On the day following his death, 26 November 1626, the book was taken up again by the Warden, and, with a two-and-a-half-year break in the middle of the seventeenth century, faithfully kept until 1857.

The entries give a delightfully intimate picture of life within the college. One of them reveals that Jacob, the cook, had to have lessons in making raised pastry, 'at a cost to the college of ten shillings'. The boys, in the meagre amount of time the fellows could spare from their comfortably undemanding life, were taught Homer, Cicero, Virgil, Phaedrus, Terence, and Ovid, the way being paved by a study of Lily's grammar, Farmaby's Epigrams, Cordier's Colloquies, and Ray's Nomenclature.[1] These, at any rate, were the textbooks they were supposed to study, but that they actually did so seems largely open to doubt. They were also instructed in mathematics, religion, and singing. Brass buttons adorned their coats, and they wore flat caps with bands.

Alleyn had expressly laid down in his statutes that 'none of the fellows, poor brethren or sisters shall keep any dogs, poultry, or other noisome cattle, besides a cat'. This restriction cannot have applied to the Foundation as a whole, since there are several references to dogs, who were no doubt selected for their skill in keeping intruders at bay, for they seem to have been mostly 'mastive dogs', with such names as Lion, Venture, and Thunder. A quarter of a horse, costing 6d, was bought for one of them, and another was given into the

---

[1] John Ray (1628–1705), sometimes called the father of English natural history, published the first edition of his *Dictionariolum Trilingue* (subsequently called *Nomenclator Classicus*) in 1675. It included not only place names and expressions not found in written Latin or in dictionaries of the day, but also, for the first time, a number of natural history terms. So it is conceivable that the poor scholars learnt a little natural history as part of their studies.

charge of a man to be trained, together with the sum of 2s, but all to no avail 'for he learnt nothing'. On one occasion the son of Thomas Hammond was unlucky enough to incur a 'large wound in his thigh bit by the college dog', though fortunately it was 'made well by the Warden'.

During Charles II's reign the countryside surrounding Dulwich was invaded by Londoners fleeing from the plague, who set up tents there; the register for this period burgeons with the names of unfortunates who died of the disease and were buried in the cemetery. From the beginning of the eighteenth century there are many more entries for weddings, christenings, and burials in the chapel, showing how the village was beginning to grow.

There are frequent records of sums paid for plants and flowers to adorn the college gardens: sweetbriars, apples, red roses and damask roses, $1\frac{1}{2}$ bushels of camomile, gooseberries and currants, 'plumbs', cherries, and artichokes. And there is a vivid account of one distressing incident in 1661, the breathless punctuation lending an extra touch of drama:

> On Monday the 20th day of May last Barrett the college servant helping the plumber's men when they soddened the leaden gutters on the forefront of the college the stone rails broke and he fell from thence down into the court upon the hard stony ground the length of way from the said gutter to the ground he fell on was 30 foot and bruised his body very much as may be imagined by the length of the way he fell. He was taken up supposed to be dead and carried into his chamber and put into his bed.

Among the notable visitors to the college during this period was John Evelyn, who wrote in 1675, 'I went to see Dulwich College, being the pious foundation of one "Allen" . . . The chapel is pretty, the rest of the hospital very ill contrived, it yet maintains divers poor of both sexes. 'Tis in a melancholy part of Camberwell parish.' Horace Walpole, visiting over a century later, commented that his party was 'received by a smart Divine (*très bien poudré*) and with black satin breeches, but they were giving new wings and *red satin breeches* to the good old hostel too, and destroying a gallery with a very rich ceiling; and nothing will remain of ancient, but the font, and an hundred mouldy portraits among apostles, sybils and Kings of England.'

In 1808 William James, a surveyor, was asked to inspect the college property and advise on what improvements could be made. He painted an idyllic picture:

> The estate for its entirety, the beauty and variety of its views, occasioned by the gentle slopes and undulations of its surface, is scarcely in those respects to be equalled, and certainly not exceeded by any property in the neighbourhood of London . . . It is embosomed in a rich and fertile vale, whose surface is varied by detached eminences and is thus secluded by its situation from the pageantry of the gay Metropolis, from the bustle and activity of trade and commerce, from the noisome air of manufactories and the 'busy hum of many men'.

His report on the college buildings was less satisfactory, however, for he declared them to be in a state of decay, and in parts only fit to be pulled down.

Another account is interesting for a different reason, since it gives a faithful picture of how the poor scholars lived in the 1830s. It is written by H. J. Hartley, who was later apprenticed to a printer, and was published in the *Alleynian* in 1905. It describes first how the boys were chosen: 'A sort of matriculation examination by one of the fellows' was followed by morning service in chapel and then by the election in the college hall:

> . . . conducted with due form and ceremony before the members of the College and any of the inhabitants of the village who chose to be present. The Master first read the Founder's statute detailing the manner of drawing the lots. Two equal small rolls of paper, 'indifferently made and rolled up', one containing the words 'God's gift', and the other a blank, were put into a small cylindrically shaped tin box, which box was 'thrice shaken up and down'. The rolls were then placed in the lid and set before the two selected candidates. My companion, being the elder, took his choice. It proved to be a blank, and I was elected a 'poor scholar' of Dulwich College, and came into residence forthwith, the unsuccessful boy receiving as a solatium the sum of fourpence a day from the time that the vacancy occurred, which was usually about a month.

From the point of view of the average boy, Dulwich College in

1836 was the ideal school. Lessons were easy and holidays numerous; there was much liberty with little supervision; the diet was good and ample, and we were comfortably lodged and well clothed.

The boys were taught writing, reading, grammar, music, and good manners. In 1836 elementary geography and arithmetic were added to the curriculum, followed by:

> . . . vocal music (Hullah's system) . . . but in arithmetic no one in my time went beyond the rule of three, and neither fractions nor decimals were ever touched. Particular prominence was given to Latin, a portion of the Eton Grammar being set for repetition every day except Saturday, which was devoted to the Church Catechism and Ostervald's *Abridgement of the Bible*. Aesop's Fables were used for Latin translation, and at one time a little Caesar was done, but there was no turning English into Latin . . .
>
> My earliest recollection of schooling at Dulwich is of our assembling at seven o'clock on a frosty winter morning, and with cold fingers practising writing for an hour by candle-light, flint and steel, timber, and brimstone matches being used in the lighting of the said candles. This was exceedingly unpleasant, and as the ruling principle at the College seems to have been that everything was to be made as easy and comfortable as possible for everybody, the practice was soon discontinued, and after 1836 the school was from 9 a.m. till 1.30, with an interval from 10.30 till 11.00 for daily service in the chapel. Dinner was over by 2.30, and the remainder of the day was at our own disposal.

The boys' diet included a pint of beer with every meal. 'During the last year of my stay in Dulwich we were offered tea for breakfast, but it was regarded as an effeminacy and "declined with thanks".' (How William Cobbett, who in his *Cottage Economy* had directed such a passionate attack on the terrible, debilitating evils of drinking tea in preference to beer, would have applauded this decision.)[1]

Each boy had a daily ration of half-a-pound of meat. On Shrove Tuesday dinner consisted solely of pancakes, and on

---

[1] The last mention of beer as part of the college diet seems to date from 1885, when the Science Society held an impromptu debate on 'the College beer and ginger beer'.

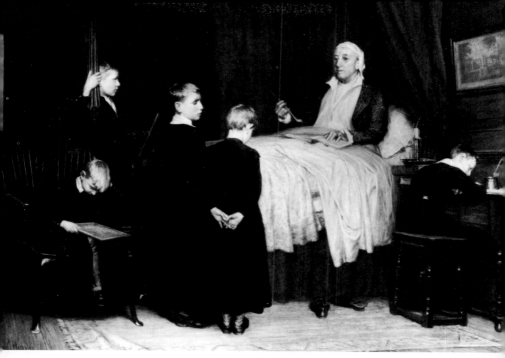

Fig. 1.3   Old Time Tuition by W. C. Horsley (1828): the gentleman in bed
must be the formidable John Vane

Ash Wednesday and Good Friday of salt fish and parsnips,
while on Michaelmas Day roast goose was served.

Whenever there was a funeral, the whole college took part.
'A procession was formed, headed by the Sexton, with the
Founder's staff, or walking stick, about 5 ft. 6 in. in length.
The Poor Scholars in their surplices came next, followed by
the poor Brethren and Sisters. The Fellows, the Warden, and
the Master, in their surplices and robes, immediately preceded the coffin, the relatives following.'

No one, he goes on, was allowed to walk on the grass in
front of the school buildings, on payment of a fine of sixpence.
One day the Prince Consort and Sir Edward Bowater came to
visit the schoolmaster, John Vane, who was one of the Deputy
Clerks of the Closet to Queen Victoria, and committed the
crime of treading on this sacred turf. The intrepid Master
Hartley stepped forward, undaunted by the Royal Presence
(it is not quite clear whether in fact he knew who the

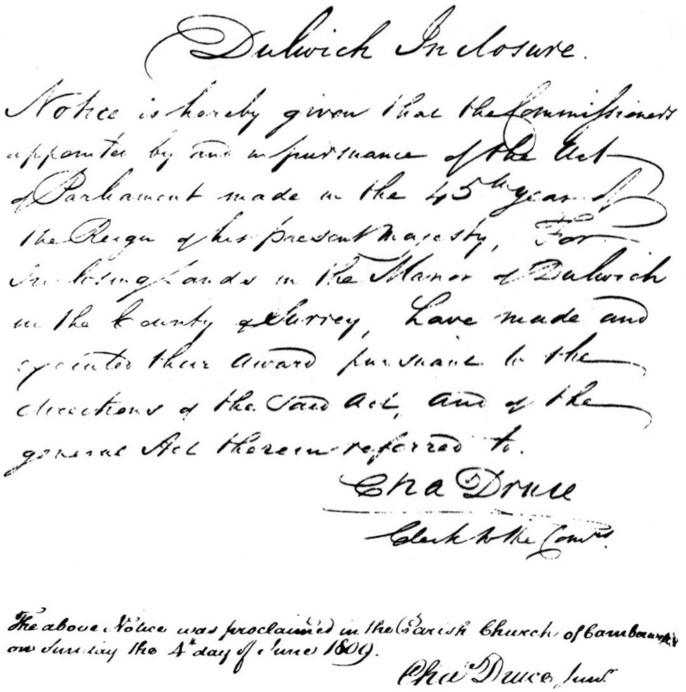

Dulwich Inclosure.

Notice is hereby given that the Commissioners appointed by and in pursuance of the Act of Parliament made in the 45th year of the Reign of his present Majesty, For Inclosing Lands in the Manor of Dulwich in the County of Surrey, have made and executed their Award pursuant to the directions of the said Act, and of the general Act therein referred to.

Chas Druce

Clerk to the Commrs.

The above Notice was proclaimed in the Parish Church of Camberwell on Sunday the 4th day of June 1809.

Chas Druce Junr.

Fig. 1.4 The Enclosure of Dulwich Common

gentlemen were), and demanded the prescribed fine: the sixpences were meekly handed over.

Hartley's account continues:

> From the circumstances here detailed, it may be gathered that a boy's life at Dulwich College seventy years ago, provided he was not timid and nervous, and under the ban of Mr Vane,[1] must have been a happy one. His bodily training was all that could be desired, if his mental training was unsatisfactory. He had little real work and a considerable amount of liberty . . . Education was the weak point. The boys entered the College as 'Poor Scholars', and when they left their Scholarship was poor indeed.

[1] By all accounts a most fearsome man.

In Trollope's novel *The Warden*, published in 1855, the college is referred to by name as 'a hotbed of peculation'. At the same time, perhaps it was not so bad as some of these charitable foundations, for, if the boys were abominably educated, at least their material needs were cared for, and they were not ill-treated. Nevertheless, in no way were Alleyn's wishes for their proper education and training being carried out, or his endowment being used in the way he had intended. As one historian put it:

> Alleyn's grammar school was a grand and noble scheme, but its realisation was a miserable and lamented failure. 'Foreigners' were but partially admitted to its cloisters, the 'men-children of the inhabitants of Dulwich' were not 'freely taught' as ordered; boys were not sent to the university as Alleyn had ordained, for in 250 years only eighteen had been so treated.

He had laid down that every poor scholar who was sufficiently apt should be sent to Oxford or Cambridge and should then, if this were possible, be offered a position as fellow in the college; but in the whole history of the Foundation, prior to its reconstitution, this happened only twice, and on the first occasion the scholar concerned, one Benjamin Bynes, was expelled a year after his election, because he refused to sign what he considered to be falsified accounts. The preparation for 'good and sweet trades and occupations' was hardly any better, for the trades chosen were generally of the most menial kind. Moreover, by the early nineteenth century 'the monkish restrictions' to celibacy of the whole corporation were now deemed *contra bonos mores*.

Part of the trouble was that Alleyn's provisions for the education of the boys turned out to be quite inadequate; perhaps he dotted his i's and crossed his t's too conscientiously, thus proving once again that a written constitution is much more difficult to administer than an unwritten one. Probably the situation would have been less disastrous if the six chanters specified in the statutes had actually been appointed, for at least they would have been able to pass on their skills in a variety of useful occupations, as well as in music; but in the event they never were. However, the main reason why the college had never, in the intervening years, grown into the kind of school which Alleyn had visualized probably sprang from the fact that it had neither a disinterested body of governors to which it was answerable nor any connection with Oxford or Cambridge.

The situation was aggravated by the increase in the value of the endowment. At Alleyn's death the income from the estate had been £800; by 1738 it was £1,368. In 1805 the corporation obtained an act allowing it to enclose and develop the 130 acres of common and wasteland within the manor, which was judged to be in a condition incapable of improvement for the grazing of livestock. This enabled them to divide the land into allotments and enclosures, with penalties for cattle feeding and straying, and gave them powers to stop and divert ancient bridleways, footways, and paths. In consequence it became possible to encourage building and the construction of roads, which led to a considerable increase in the revenue.

In 1808 came the Dulwich College Building Act, allowing the corporation to extend the period during which leases ran from twenty-one to eighty-four years. The sale of these longer leases brought in a great deal of money. Dulwich, still 'the prettiest of all the village entrances in the environs of London', had become a popular place to live in, easy of access since John McAdam had revolutionized the art of roadmaking; and by 1835 the revenue had reached the considerable sum of £7,881. Small wonder that there were endless disputes between all the parties involved—Master, Warden, fellows, poor brothers and sisters, churchwardens, out-pensioners—about the division of what they one and all looked upon as their inheritance.

They were not, however, to enjoy their spoils much longer. Reform was in the air in almost every area of life—public spending, parliamentary representation, local government, the abolition of slavery, the protection of factory and child workers, law and order, the legalization of trade unions, and many more. It was unlikely that education would escape the vigilant eye of the reformers. For the College of God's Gift, as for many other charitable foundations which had slumbered through the centuries, the years of delightful indolence were coming to an end.

Fig. 1.5 The Old College in 1846

2 A New Identity

A. J. Carver (1858–83)

'His object was to encourage all learning.'
(*Obituary*, The Alleynian)

IN 1818, as a result of the vigorous campaigning of Henry
Brougham, a commission was set up to enquire into the
education of the poor in the metropolis. Gradually the
commission cast its net wider to encompass a much wider
range of schools, despite the protests of some of them. This
and subsequent investigations revealed the inadequacy of
most schools of the day, including many of the ancient
foundations. Few of the public schools escaped open revolt
during this period, while the numbers of pupils declined in
many cases to an almost unbelievable level. In 1798
Shrewsbury had under twenty pupils; a few years earlier Oundle
had had one. When Thring went to Uppingham in 1853
he found twenty-five boys there, while thirty-eight endowed
schools in Yorkshire and Durham which claimed to be
providing a classical education had not a single child between
them. As for the lucky head of Whitgift, in the second quarter
of the nineteenth century he enjoyed his tenure for over
thirty years without one boyish face to disturb his calm.[1]

---

[1] He would surely have regarded as eminently reasonable the comment of
one assistant master of Dulwich College a century-and-a-half later, who,
when the 1,400 boys had dispersed for Easter, heaved a sigh of relief and
said how pleasant the school was in the holidays. 'Yes,' a colleague replied
drily, 'the boys *are* a bit of a drawback!'

Nor was the curriculum in many of these schools changing to meet the needs of a world where scientific knowledge and physical boundaries were expanding with such speed. The narrow classical education, comprising little more than Greek and Latin grammar and divinity, which had once sufficed for the well-educated man, no longer automatically opened the door to a successful career. Foreign trade was growing apace, calling for new qualities of military and civil leadership and of business acumen in the far-flung corners of the Empire; and a powerful, wealthy middle class was coming into being which demanded for its sons a first-class education that would enable them to take advantage of opportunities they had never enjoyed before. With a rapidly expanding population there was an ever-increasing need of doctors, lawyers, churchmen, teachers, engineers, civil servants, and administrators; and professions such as these, once regarded as unsuitable for gentlemen, were acquiring an aura of respectability. Many of them required specialist training in science, mathematics, and modern languages, and this the great majority of schools were woefully unable to provide—not least because there were few teachers equipped to instruct in these 'new' subjects.

The beneficiaries of Alleyn's bequest were caught up in the general movement of reform. The outer parishes, as always convinced that they weren't getting a large enough slice of the cake, took their claims for more to the Charity Commission which had been established as a result of Brougham's work; and the Commissioners decided that there was a good enough case to set up an enquiry into the advisability of widening the application of the funds. In 1841 the matter came before the Master of the Rolls, Lord Langdale. He rejected the appeal, on the grounds that Alleyn had had no right to alter his original statutes by increasing the number of beneficiaries, and that legally the college was not, therefore, abusing its application of the funds: privately, however, he expressed to the Master in sharp terms his dissatisfaction with the 'education' which the college was providing.

There was much to find fault with. Although the income of the Foundation had increased enormously since the early part of the century, the only people to profit from this were the

Fig. 2.1   The Old College today

eighteen members of the corporation, who enjoyed lives of cushioned idleness at the expense of the poor scholars. True enough, since no attempt was made to assess their intellectual capacity when they were elected, they were slender material to work with; but once accepted, as H. J. Hartley's testimony showed, they were taught virtually nothing. Now and then a village child might be taken in, but otherwise Alleyn's wishes with regard to the education of boys outside the twelve foundation scholars were totally ignored.

With a rare access of conscience (or was it perhaps panic?) the college decided to meet Lord Langdale's criticisms by establishing a grammar school for the education of about sixty poor boys from the parishes of Dulwich and Camberwell. It was designed by Charles (later Sir Charles) Barry, the college surveyor and architect, who was responsible for many famous London buildings, his best-known monument being the present Houses of Parliament. This school—which can be seen today at the corner of Gallery Road and Burbage Road, and is still in use, even if not for its original purpose—was opened in 1842. Here were transferred the boys of the James Allen Foundation, which now became responsible for girls only.

Alleyn's foundationers continued to receive a sketchy education in the college buildings. Their meagre preparation for life greatly concerned some of their predecessors, who in 1841 had formed themselves into the Dulwich College School Association, with the object of finding suitable apprenticeships for the boys when they left the college. At first the Master and his colleagues were in sympathy, but relations deteriorated as the Association began to criticize the abysmal standard of education provided. Most of the boys went out into the world so illiterate that they had no chance of following anything except the meanest apprenticeships: within a short space of time, for instance, seven of them were apprenticed to tailors, which the Association described as 'a beggarly calling'. Many reached manhood in abject poverty. The quarrel escalated, and once more the Archbishop was appealed to. In 1851 he issued various injunctions which in theory should have led to a considerable degree of improvement: that, for instance, the most promising boys should stay on at the college until they were fifteen or sixteen, instead of leaving at fourteen, and should receive training in skills such as surveying, chemistry, civil engineering or applied science. As usual, nothing came of this attempt at reform.

And so matters remained until 1853, when the Charitable Trusts Act set up a new Commission with considerable powers to examine and control charities. Among the many schools which the Commissioners investigated was Dulwich College, and for four days in June 1854 a searching examination was held *in situ*. During the enquiry some remarkable facts emerged; above all it was found that, though the annual income had risen to £9,000, the running expenses amounted to little more than half this sum, the surplus—in accordance with the ingenious scheme which James Hume had introduced a century earlier—being divided among the members of the corporation, who were thus able to live in great style. The Rev. Charles Howe, preacher and senior fellow, testified that in addition to his salary he was provided with two good sitting-rooms, two good bedrooms, 'kept in good order and repair by the College (and, I may add, well situated in every particular)', all his food and wine, the services of a butler, footman, housemaid, cook and undercook, coals and candles, rates and taxes, and 'the enjoyment of large common rooms, such as dining-room, etc., use of a good library, and a large and even beautiful garden'. His duties consisted solely of the obligation to preach one sermon each Sunday.

'The benefits of the college are so considerable,' the Commissioners reported, 'that few of the poor men and women who have been sent from any of the parishes for a considerable number of years back have exactly answered the description given in this statute; most of them have been decayed housekeepers of respectable character.'

They produced a scheme for the complete reconstruction of the Foundation, and it was from this that the new college emerged. On 25 August 1857 the Dulwich College Act dissolved the existing corporation, and the charity was reconstituted under the name of 'Alleyn's College of God's Gift, at Dulwich'. It was divided into two separate parts with a common Board of Governors—the educational, which was to receive three-quarters of the endowment, and the eleemosynary, which was entitled to the remaining quarter. The Master and Warden, the four fellows, and the college servants were pensioned off, the first two with remarkably big annuities which in the early years effectively crippled the college finances. The needs of the poor brothers and sisters and of their successors were also provided for; and today sixteen pensioners still live in comfortable flats in the old college, looked after by a warden.

The college itself was split into an upper and a lower school, the terms defining not age levels, as we should understand them today, but the type of education provided.

The upper school was to cater for boys between the ages of eight and eighteen, preference being given to the children of Dulwich residents, and after them to boys from the four parishes. The syllabus, which was laid down in meticulous detail, was immensely wide—far too ambitious, in fact, to be possible of practical application. The lower school was for boys of eight to sixteen, with smaller fees and a syllabus considered to be suitable for children of 'the industrial and poorer classes'.

The new Governors met for the first time on 1 January 1858, coming together, as it were, to create a school; meanwhile the Foundation scholars continued to be taught as usual. An entertaining glimpse of their life during the next few months can be caught from the 'Black Book' (nowadays it would be called a mark book) in which the teachers recorded their progress. The entries tell a familiar tale of classroom warfare: 'This mg I found out that Flin had done Potter and Powell's Arnold exams on a slate from which Powell was copying it when discovered. *Powell told the most gross and barefaced falsehoods* but Potter was not guilty of such low and degrading conduct'; 'Brice does practically *nothing* from day to day'; 'Tatlock simply bungled through the Arnold' . . . The biggest culprit was a boy called Outram (in a variety of spellings): 'Outram *all but found out in copying his sums: his truthfulness questionable ! ! !*', 'Outram dirty!', 'Outram *again filthy*', 'OUTREM WHIPPED'.

The Black Book also records the many holidays, which included saints' days and, as befitted a good royalist foundation, the day of Charles II's restoration two centuries earlier.

On Wednesday 21 July 1858 the entry reads: 'The work was finished today as the clock struck 12 and the old system passed away with it.' 'Good thing too,' comments another hand. The following day the last words were recorded: 'Cupboard emptied: boys books packed up etc. Holidays commenced and boys went home to their dinner.' And William Fellows, the second fellow, completed the entry with his signature. The only unfinished business was an outstanding bill for washing.

An era had come to an end. While rebuilding took place to

house the larger number of pupils who were now to be educated, the Foundation scholars were packed off to the seaside. They returned, not to the college, but to the grammar school across the road, where they were later joined by the children who were to attend the lower school.

The first Master of the new school, the Reverend Alfred Carver, had been appointed the previous April. Under the 1857 Act he had overall control of both schools, and in conjunction with the headmaster of the lower school took a very considerable part in its early organization and development, and in helping to rescue it when it was threatened with extinction.

He said forty years later:

> I well remember my first visit to the college. At that time it included amongst its administrators and the recipients of its benefits a master, a warden, and four fellows, courteous polished gentlemen who led, as it seemed to me, their gentle, and easy, and somnolent lives. As I gathered, their one sole duty, after dividing, as we are told they did most fairly and legally, their share of the proceeds of the Alleyn Estate, was to clothe, feed, and educate twelve foundation scholars.

Although primarily a classicist (and an exceptionally brilliant one), he was a man of wide interests and talents, for he was a senior optime in mathematics, and had carried away from Cambridge first prizes for English declamations, Latin declamations, Latin elegiac verse, and the best reading in chapel. In his letter of application for the mastership of Dulwich he wrote, 'From my early boyhood till almost the close of my university career, drawing, mechanics, and natural science in several of its branches, occupied nearly the whole of that leisure time which I was able to reserve from severer studies.'

He came to Dulwich from St Paul's School, where he had been Surmaster, or Second Master. It was said of him there that the boys always took care to post someone to keep *cave*, for 'Carver is no sooner at the bottom of the stairs than he is at the top'. Slight and nimble, to the end of his days, his sister declared, he ran up steps two at a time, his silvery hair, which he wore rather long, floating away from his shoulders. He loved entertaining, and a charming picture of this side of his life emerges from a diary kept by his oldest daughter Constance, who often acted as his hostess.

> Our home to the end of [my parents'] lives was called 'The Free Hotel', so great was their hospitality . . . The Master's House at the old College was a delightful one, with its quaint corners and unexpected steps. The rooms were very large and numerous and there were many of them. Opening out of the drawing room which was up a spacious and fine staircase and entering by a large anteroom, was a small oak-panelled room with massive doors and some very fine oak chests. This was the Treasury room of the College and Estates, and in it were kept the many valuable pieces of ancient plate and old manuscripts.

In these beautiful surroundings there were dinner-parties where the staff and Dulwich residents met and talked, and dances and receptions to which the boys were also invited, resplendent in tails, pumps, and white kid gloves.

When the sixty-eight boys assembled on 10 November 1858—no longer dressed in the traditional uniform of long gown and flat cap, for this had been abolished when the original Foundation came to an end, sooner than most public schools modernized their antiquated garb—the oldest of them was fifteen. The first words uttered came in the form of a command from the Master: 'All boys who know any Greek step forward!' Eight or ten did so, and they constituted the fifth form, since as yet there was no idea of a sixth. The number of pupils gradually increased to 130, and there it stopped for want of room to expand further. To teach them there were in the early days five masters: Dr Carver and the Rev. A. Povah, both classicists, a master for writing and arithmetic, another for drawing, and a part-time French teacher. Most of the pupils were day-boys, but three boarding-houses, known as dames' houses and kept by respectable ladies in the village, were at first licensed by the Governors, with a fourth following soon afterwards.

In many ways Dr Carver's views on education were greatly in advance of his time. R. J. Mackenzie wrote:

> His conception of intellectual education was liberal in the best sense of the word. It rejected the narrow specialisation to which modern school organisation tends, and aimed at producing a wide culture as the result of a sufficient variety of studies. Fine scholar as he was, he was no blind devotee of classical training. Under his system the modern subjects had an equal chance. For art study, so generally neglected in public schools, he had a marked sympathy.[1] Unlike most Headmasters of the day he disapproved of the division of a School into a Classical and a Modern side. His own object was to avoid the disintegration which such a system involves, while at the same time providing a sufficient variety of studies. For these purposes he combined the boys in classes for English, Divinity, Latin, Mathematics, and French, and offered in the higher forms an option between Greek and the higher Classics, on the one hand, and German and Physical Science on the other. In the Sixth Form there was a wide choice of special subjects. Thus German might be learned without abandoning the study of Greek, while a boy who declared his intention of studying art professionally might devote half his whole school time to that subject. Another striking feature of the system was the provision in the Senior Section of special classes during four hours in the week. At these times a choice was offered between Drawing, Greek, French, German, Physical Science, and Mathematics. It was an ingenious and original method of School organization, looking less to the winning of special prizes than to the production of a wide and varied culture.

The anonymous obituarist in the *Alleynian* said of him:

> His object was to encourage all learning, and he would have a boy's faculties developed on those lines most congenial to his natural aptitude. He believed in giving to the senior boys in the school a greater degree of independence than many educationists have believed in, and insisted on the management of all the school institutions, such as the field sports, the debating and science societies, and kindred institutions, being left to the boys themselves.

'He taught all the senior pupils,' Mackenzie records:

---

[1] This aspect of his work is discussed in Chapter 10.

With the idle members of the class he did not much concern himself: shortsighted, buried in his author, declaiming ever and anon in that sonorous voice of his some passage that took his fancy, he might not observe that some youths on the back benches were reading novels or writing letters. It was to the earnest student that his lessons were addressed, and of these there were always enough to reward his care.

Outside school hours the boys had much more freedom than they have today. In most schools organized games barely existed, for there was a strong, indeed a moral, conviction that when lessons were over children should enjoy themselves as they pleased. Many of the boys had ponies, and careered wildly over the surrounding hills and commons. Birds' nesting was popular, as was the trapping of grass-snakes, which, one boy wrote, 'introduced into another boy's desk during the French class would make quite an agreeable diversion to the afternoon's monotony'—though he himself preferred a young thrush for the purpose. One of the boarders made friends with the blacksmith and forged crude, sharp-edged saucepans which he sold to other boys in his house at sixpence apiece— they were excellent for boiling chestnuts in. Hoops and marbles were other popular forms of amusement.

For Carver his years as Master of the college were to be a period of constant struggle. At the time of his appointment no one knew what type of school would emerge under the new constitution. He himself had the clearest conception of what he wanted it to be: a 'public school' (something of a catchphrase at the time) where the highest standard of education would be available, equipping boys for Oxford and Cambridge. But there was by no means total agreement about this. One of his supporters referred at the time to 'the opposition of the Governors, the wretched salaries and ex-hibitions, the constant Board meetings, the inciting of sedition amongst assistant masters and the persecution of those who were loyal'. Carver himself was well aware that a strenuous fight lay before him. 'I feel,' he wrote in 1858, 'like a man swimming for his *life*, having both hands and *feet* tied.' Eleven years later he wrote to the Archbishop of Canterbury that he was warned from the first that he was 'coming into a wasp's nest . . . Our life here has been one of ceaseless agony.'

When he took up his post he met with a good deal of hostility from the inhabitants of Dulwich, who, as the *Christian Globe* commented, resented 'the introduction of two schools into their quiet hamlet,[1] whilst they did not hesitate to declare that the College never had prospered and never would'. But his most formidable opponent was the Rev. William Rogers, who was first the incumbent of St Thomas Charterhouse and then the rector of St Botolph's, Bishopsgate. He was made a Governor at the behest of the Prince Consort, who took a great interest in the school: he was, indeed, invited to become first Chairman of the Board, but declined 'after fourteen days' consideration'. Rogers was appointed the third Chairman in 1862, a position which he held for thirty years. His predecessor was the second Duke of Wellington, who was Chairman for a brief period but who rarely attended Board meetings. He was not an enthusiastic educationist, perhaps, to judge from his dislike of the founding of Wellington College as a memorial to his father: he would, he said, have preferred a bronze statue of the great man to have been erected in every sizeable town in England. One of his colleagues on the Board went so far as to say that 'he acted wisely in withdrawing from the chair, his ineptitude for its duties being painfully apparent'.

But Carver's path might have been smoother if the Duke had remained on the Board, for there must have been mutual liking between the two men. Wellington was godfather to the Carvers' second son, the first child to be born within the Foundation, and the whole village was *en fête* for the christening. The Duke himself named the baby Arthur Wellington, and guests and villagers alike, as Constance Carver recorded, were 'most charmed with him as he went amongst them very freely; the Nurse who held his Godson received a £10 note, and gold was distributed among the Almspeople.'

Rogers was a remarkable man, a liberal with a profound

---

[1] Mackenzie comments that their fears were justified, for the boys got up to all kinds of pranks.

belief in the right of every child to be educated. Finding not a single school in the parish of St Thomas Charterhouse, he had rented a derelict blacksmith's shed and opened it as a school for boys; within a few years many thousand children were being educated in this and other schools which he established who would otherwise have had no chance of schooling. Rogers paid for much of this out of his own salary, and was crippled by the subsequent debts.

Filled as he was with a desire to help underprivileged children, he believed that Alleyn's legacy should be used to establish 'middle-class schools' of a rather lower grade than Carver was aiming at. He wanted the college to become such an establishment, and felt that the endowment should be spread among the outer parishes in order to provide them with schools of a like nature. Carver, on the other hand, was as inflexible in his belief that the college must provide a first-class education. The two men were, indeed, a contrast in every respect: Rogers was big, jolly, outspoken, an autocrat who liked to get his own way, while Carver was a sensitive, genial person, acutely uncomfortable in an atmosphere of strife and discord, yet prepared to make any sacrifice for the good of his school. Beneath the benign exterior, too, there beat a fiery heart: before meeting the Governors he would often kneel with prayers, which were not always granted, that he would not anger them or lose his temper. There was bound to be antagonism between the Master and his Chairman, holding, as they did, such divergent views on the future of the school, both views so honourable yet so incompatible.

While the outer parishes went on pressing their claims for more money, the various commissions which were set up in this period of reforming ferment continued to probe into the state of education in England. In the 1860s two Commissions were appointed to investigate schools: the Clarendon Commission, which was concerned with nine major public schools; and the Taunton Commission, which carried out an immensely wide examination into every kind of educational establishment—girls' as well as boys', private, proprietary, and endowed. Few schools escaped withering condemnation. Dulwich, as one of eight with an endowment of over £2,000 a year, received special attention, and a long and comprehensive report was issued in 1868 by one of the assistant commissioners, Mr D. R. Fearon.

He was severely critical of many aspects of the school, and of the failure to bring into operation the reforms which had been spelled out at the time of the reconstitution ten years earlier. The site, the buildings, and the playgrounds were all inadequate; there should be more teachers; and the emphasis on the classics was still far too great for a school where 'the bulk of the boys' were about fifteen years old and the normal leaving age sixteen. It was, he commented:

> ... like Marlborough or Winchester, with its two highest forms lopped off ... Most of the masters are zealous and efficient ... But I believe that they are engaged in a task which, from the nature of the case, is hopeless ... The Act, by putting the Latin and Greek languages in the foremost ground, and the Governors, by electing ... high classical scholars to the head and second masterships, appear to give sanction to the line which the school is taking ... If the Governors thought it desirable for the sons of these warehousemen, warfingers, solicitors, and leather merchants to be principally educated on classics, the Head Master and his assistants ... must do their best to carry out these wishes.

The syllabus which had been laid down by the Act was in fact ludicrous, embracing—if it was to be interpreted literally—almost the entire field of human knowledge, from every ancient and modern language and the literature thereof, through mathematics, simple and applied, to the whole of natural science, as well as anything else which the Governors might have a fancy to decree. 'No school system ever devised,' the inspector commented drily, 'could go much further than that.'

It was quite true that, as in every secondary school of the day, the curriculum at Dulwich at this time still leaned heavily on the classics. Apart from anything else, Carver knew that if he was to establish the school in the front rank he must build up its academic reputation with the utmost speed. But in any case, within the cramped quarters of the old college, and with a small, badly paid staff, a very much wider syllabus was out of the question. During the 1860s he was constantly making proposals for the improvement of the school and the creation of exhibitions, but these were almost invariably rejected by the Governors.

Nevertheless, within the limitations imposed on him he managed to put into effect many reforms. Writing in 1865, Howard Staunton says in his survey of *The Great Schools of England,* 'The scheme of instruction [at Dulwich] is an unusually comprehensive one, including, in addition to the ordinary curriculum of the Great Public Schools, a systematic course of teaching in English,[1] Modern Languages, Drawing and Natural Science.' The school's growing reputation is shown by the fact that by the mid-1860s there were already competitive entrance examinations because of the pressure for places.

Fearon's strictures, unfair as they were in many respects, heralded yet another era of struggle and contention which attracted a vast amount of publicity. It was intensely distressing and discouraging to Carver. 'When he discussed the matter with me a few years ago,' Mackenzie wrote a long time afterwards, 'he was far from having forgotten his resentment. The lapse of half a century had barely dulled his anger.'

His position was immensely difficult. Not only were finances at a very low ebb in the early years of his mastership—mainly owing to the huge pensions which had to be paid to the former Master (who unfortunately lingered on until 1883) and to the Warden and fellows; when funds did begin to flow in they were used to develop the estate, and to create a fund for a grandiose building project, since everyone agreed that, whatever the nature of the school that was eventually to emerge from all the strife and battle, it must provide for a large number of pupils.

Dulwich village was growing fast, attracting professional families and men of moderate income who wanted the best possible education for their sons but many of whom disliked conventional public schools, and preferred day to boarding. Here was a ready-made clientele. And a new prosperity had

---

[1] Then not taught at any of the following: Eton, Winchester, Westminster, Charterhouse, Harrow, Rugby or Shrewsbury.

been brought to the neighbourhood by the Crystal Palace, when it was removed from Hyde Park in 1854. It had become fashionable to drive down from town to enjoy the concerts, pantomimes, fireworks, flower-shows, and other amusements; and this led to profitable contracts between the college and the Crystal Palace Co. regarding roads, land, and buildings. Most important of all, however, was the advent of the railways. An astonishing number of companies applied for permission to build lines over the estate; and the money for the new building programme came mainly from the sale of land to three of these—the London, Chatham and Dover Company, the Crystal Palace and South London Junction, and the London, Brighton and South Coast Railway. Their contracts obliged them to provide above-average stations and bridges, and 'to submit to the addition of some grace and comeliness in passing through the College property'.

Charles Barry, the oldest son of Sir Charles who had designed the grammar school in 1842, was commissioned as the architect for the new building, which was to be situated a little way away from the old college, on the Common. Among Barry's other works were the Piccadilly frontage and the courtyard of the Royal Academy, but apart from these most of the buildings which he designed are to be found in Dulwich.

The foundation stone was laid in 1866, and even this happy occasion was not free from acrimony. The ceremony should have been performed by Gladstone; but Palmerston's government fell and he was summoned to Windsor. Rogers took his place, which was much resented by many of the company, including some of the boys, who made their disappointment felt—and were afterwards ticked off. No silver trowel had been provided; and not until many years later was Rogers' name carved on the stone (below which had been buried a copy of *The Times*).

The architecture, in a style described as 'thirteenth-century North Italian Renaissance', broke decisively from the popular Gothic of the day, and was at first much criticized. 'There is a great outcry at Dulwich,' *Building News* wrote early in 1869. 'The people are complaining that Mr Barry has been expending on bricks and terracota what was intended for education—

Fig. 2.2 The New College, 1869

and that instead of brains Dulwich has been cultivating drains.' Some months later it returned to the attack:

> A glance at the building shows that while the general aim has been to attain the quiet and refined effect of the palatial structures of Italy, with their unbroken rectangular masses and low roofs, this has all been marred by the intrusion of the . . . high pitched roof in the centre, and a crowd of fussy erections which break the sky-line, and the nature of which it is difficult to describe. Chinese pagodas are temperate in comparison with the little pear-shaped roofed temples set round with queer terminals, like bottles in a cruet stand, which do service for pinnacles upon the several angles of the central building, and the chimney shafts, which Classic men delight to hide, are here rendered unusually obtrusive by being cut up into little piles of red and white layers, sandwich-wise. The dormers also, and almost everything above the eaves, are alike objectionable excepting the principal campanile itself, which is very elegant.

But tastes change, and a modern writer describes it as 'the most striking [school] rebuilding of the 1860s . . . If the colleges at Clifton and Malvern represent the highest point of development in the planning of the privately-financed secondary schools of the period before 1870, we may certainly say that the new college at Dulwich was the climax of the movement to reorganize the older endowed schools.'

Moreover, it represented an extremely interesting experiment, for no other building on so large a scale had been built entirely of terracotta, which was chosen for reasons of economy. The materials used came from the Stamford Brick Works, which had been established in 1858 by J. M. Blashfield, whose bricks were used in the decoration of Buckingham Palace, Marlborough House and the royal mausoleums at Windsor. '[Dulwich College] is the most complete specimen of terracotta building in England . . . As an early example of architectural ornamentation of the period, [it] stands alone in its class of ceramic art applied to buildings [and] exists as a purpose building decorated in the finest manner and taste of the day.'

The work was not completed until 1870, but by the end of the summer term of 1869 it was sufficiently far advanced for

Carver to take possession of his new school. On 5 July he led a triumphal procession of Governors, guests, masters, and boys from the old college to the new.[1] From this moment the numbers increased rapidly, doubling within the next year and reaching 550 by 1876, where they remained—give or take fifty or so—until the late 1890s.

It was in the following spring that Camille Pissarro painted his lovely picture of the college, now in a private collection in America.[2] Pissarro had fled from France at the time of the Franco-Prussian war and the siege of Paris, finding lodgings in Upper Norwood. He was entranced by the London landscapes, and years later wrote, 'Living at Norwood, at that time a charming suburb, I studied the effects of fog, snow and springtime.'

In the summer of 1870, on Founder's Day, the new school was officially opened by the Prince and Princess of Wales, the latter dressed, as Constance recorded, 'in her favourite colour at that time, of Primrose'; in the Great Hall they listened to the recitation of speeches from Shakespeare and Racine, and in Latin and Greek. 'The Prince looked bored,' one boy commented, 'but brightened up, I remember, when he spoke' (though another witness said that he did not utter a single word, but merely handed over the prizes). 'Princess Alexandra looked charming, if rather sad. Perhaps she was bored too.'

Lunch was provided for the occasion by the college caterer, Mr Mole, formerly of the refreshment department of the British Museum, who had contracted to supply the boys with a good dinner daily of hot and cold meat and vegetables at 6d per head. Later he got into trouble with the Governors, as he fell behind with his payments to the butcher and other suppliers, and 'tumblers and other plant' mysteriously vanished. He was declared to be in debt to the college to the tune

[1] Constance Carver was not very happy with the family's quarters in the south block. 'Here we had again a very large house and nice gardens,' she writes, 'but oh we did miss the old place, it was all so terribly modern.'

[2] Some additional information about this painting is included in the references, p. 296.

of £25, but pleaded destitution. Cooks and waiters were thereafter employed, but, 'inasmuch as women could not be so efficient as trained men waiters'—though they would have cost less—it was decided not to employ them.

The provision for teaching in the new building was far in advance of that in most schools of the period. The boys were not taught in groups in one big hall, as was still generally the custom, but in classrooms, where $12\frac{1}{2}$ square feet per pupil was allowed, as against the normal allowance in elementary schools of 8 square feet. The teaching staff was increased to keep pace with the growing number of boys, and by 1877 there were twenty-six masters, with degrees not only in classics but also in mathematics, modern languages, science, natural science, economics, and other subjects in tune with the developing world—there was even an expert in navigation and nautical astronomy. In these conditions Carver could put into practice his advanced ideas about education.

In reply to a questionnaire from the Devonshire Commission, which was appointed in 1870 to enquire into scientific education and which reported five years later, he said:

> I am convinced that the introduction into our great schools of a wider range of optional studies is productive of incalculable advantage, not to the few alone (as is sometimes supposed) but to the many also. It gives the opportunity of searching out and developing tastes and talents, where the very existence of any taste or any talent at all was before scarcely suspected.

One boy remembered that 'we were allowed to choose, to a limited extent, what we would like to learn'; and Carver himself said that anyone who looked at the list of distinctions obtained by the boys 'would find it difficult to discover a subject in which instruction had not been given or distinction obtained'.

It was in the provisions for science teaching that the new building was most in advance of its time: there were three laboratories, a classroom for geology or botany, and a lecture theatre (by the late 1870s, out of 128 public schools only 13 had laboratories of any kind). Carver, who had worked closely with Barry in the design of the building, must have played a considerable part in this visionary concept, for he was a firm believer in the importance of a scientific education.

It is not known just when science first made its appearance in the public schools: it did so against fierce opposition from the strongholds of educational conservatism and the vested interests of the classics,[1] and not until the mid-1860s did Oxford and Cambridge offer scholarships in science. In 1861 the Clarendon Commission had reported that 'natural science, with a few slight exceptions, is practically excluded from the education of the higher classes in England'. Even when it was taught the norm was one or two hours' teaching a week, with rarely any practical work. Dulwich seems to have been quite unusual, in the early 1870s, in the time which was devoted to such subjects as chemistry, electricity and magnetism, heat, geology and physical geography; and later in the decade still other subjects were taught—designing, practical geometry and mensuration, the principles of civil engineering, physics, mechanics and the natural sciences, especially in their application to the industrial and practical arts—none of them normally appearing in the curricula of 'first grade' secondary schools of the day. All the senior boys could take science if they wished; there were evening lectures which the boys were encouraged to attend; and comparative anatomy was taught to a few of the more advanced pupils, including some who intended to go on to the medical schools of the London hospitals (as a considerable number did).

Not the least obstacle to the teaching of science in schools was the lack of qualified masters, the demand greatly exceeding the meagre supply. In 1870 science at Dulwich was in the charge of Dr Heinrich Debus, though I can find no record of his name in the college archives, the only clue being a reference to his position at the school in the report of the Devonshire Commission. He had studied at Kassel under R. W. Bunsen, of Bunsen Burner fame, before coming to

---

[1] Darwin records that while he was at Shrewsbury Dr Samuel Butler once publicly rebuked him 'for wasting his time on such a useless subject as chemistry'.

England, where he first taught at Clifton (also notable at this time for its pioneering work in science) and then became Lecturer in Chemistry at Guy's Hospital and Professor of Chemistry at the Royal Naval College, Greenwich. It is not known how long he taught at Dulwich, but in 1874 Carver engaged Dr Alfred Tribe, an extremely distinguished chemist who had also studied in Germany under Bunsen (though at Heidelberg, and at a later epoch than Debus), so there must have been some connection between the two men. In any event, their work paved the way for the immense strides which were made at Dulwich in the teaching of science during the last quarter of the nineteenth century. Tribe, whose official position was lecturer in chemistry and director of practical chemistry, was an excellent teacher who communicated his own enthusiasm to his laboratory classes. According to the *Journal of the Chemical Society* his practical classes were well attended even though they were on Wednesday half-holidays, and many of his students distinguished themselves at university later on.

In 1855 entrance to the Civil Service, formerly a matter of patronage and nomination, had become possible through examination, and fifteen years later open competition became the general rule. This greatly widened career prospects for boys from schools like Dulwich, and before long, if you wanted your son to get into the Indian Civil Service, Dulwich was where you sent him. If, on the other hand, you were the Maharajah of Kashmir, this was where you sent him too. 1858 had seen another innovation, the beginning of the Oxford and Cambridge local examinations; nineteen years later Dulwich came fourth out of all the schools which entered, and the following year it was third. In 1881 the examiner in history wrote, 'There was scarcely a school in the country, the work of which was more honest and thorough than that of the Dulwich boys. They have been well taught and have learnt well.'

Despite his approval of these external tests, Carver felt that the strain on the boys was sometimes too heavy—and modern parents and teachers would be of the same mind. He said one speech day:

There are many boys here who have been nearly three weeks under examination, during which they have taken between thirty and forty papers. Besides that, several of the head boys have had to go in for other competitive examinations. The fact remains that during a term of some twelve or thirteen weeks a boy may be kept five or six weeks under actual examinations.

Dulwich was establishing its identity in other directions besides the academic, for, like every new public school in the mid-nineteenth century—and, despite its ancient beginnings, in its reconstituted form it was, of course, a new school—it was struggling to create the kind of *esprit de corps* which gave the older foundations their flavour and individuality. 1873 saw the first issue of the school magazine, the *Alleynian*,[1] after an abortive start nine years earlier with the *Dulwich College Magazine for School News and General Reading*, which came to an abrupt halt after fourteen issues with the departure to Cambridge of the editor, C. H. Lane, who had been captain of the school, captain of games, and one of the first boys to go to university. He was the founder, too, with thirty-two other Old Alleynians, of the Alleyn Club, which also came into existence in 1873. Not till about 1880, incidentally, was the term Alleynians in general use; before that the boys had called themselves Dulwichians.

The first editor of the *Alleynian* was (Sir) Herbert Thirkell White, who was also the first Alleynian to enter the Indian Civil Service and was later to be Lieutenant-Governor of Burma. (Mr Fearon, who had reported so scathingly on the quality of the intake to the school, would have been interested to know that he was the offspring of a warehouseman.) The pages of the *Alleynian* reflect poignantly, in frequent obituary notices, how early the flame of life was often extinguished in those days. Teenage boys are described as having died 'after a short illness', of consumption, rheumatic fever and pneumonia, 'of fungus poisoning', drowning or malarial fever. F. W. Anstie, an outstanding captain of the school after whom

[1] 6d when it began publication, and still 6d in 1950.

a reading prize was named, died 'after a long and painful illness', and another boy, 'returning home one evening after examination, sickened, and died before school hours next morning'.

The school colours came into being quite early on. According to tradition they were copied from the Marlborough colours, but it is difficult to square this theory with the facts: it seems more likely that Haileybury was the model. Whatever the truth of the matter, caps were introduced in 1864 for the senior school with cross-ribbons of purple, soon altered to blue. The school arms were added about eleven years later. In 1878 a chiding note appeared in the *Alleynian*: 'We remark, with disgust, that the habit amongst Day Boys of swaggering in hats is on the increase. Surely it is the mark of a very small mind to be above wearing the school cap in the field on half holidays.' Quite early on it became the fashion to wear caps back to front.

As staff and boys grew in number, so the school expanded upwards. 'By degrees we became a fairly strong Sixth,' one boy wrote. 'It is true that we had no formal Sixth meetings, no power of the cane, no right even to set lines; but somehow or other we had the unquestioning obedience of the school. We improved the organisation of the games, we stopped some attempts at smoking, we crushed disorder in the streets.' History does not reveal who was responsible for the petition which 'Alleyn's God's Gift College, Dulwich' presented to the House of Commons in 1880, begging that the school might be permitted to return a Member to the Mother of Parliaments.

Canon Carver encouraged drama, and from 1875 plays were performed every other year—first *The Rivals*, next *She Stoops to Conquer*, and then a succession of Shakespeare. Carver, with his love of the spoken word, took a great interest in these productions, and used to ask the actors to come to his study and repeat their lines to him, to ensure clearness of diction and proper enunciation.

Constance records that Irving heard of the plays:

and . . . expressed a wish to see my Father, and go over the College with many other leading artistes. One morning about 11

Fig. 2.3   *The Merchant of Venice*, 1881: what on earth is the anachronistic waste-paper basket doing?

o'clock a telegram came to my Father saying Sir Henry Irving was bringing down a large party of actors. At once orders were given for lunch for the whole party, not an easy thing in a country village, but somehow all went well, and our visitors were much charmed with all they saw and heard.

Music was encouraged too. There was singing on speech days, and a 'college male quartette'. The earliest regular concert of which there is any record took place in the summer of 1871, when Sims Reeves, a famous tenor of the day, who had a boy at the school, added his contribution with some popular ballads.

The Debating Society held its first meeting in 1874, discussing the proposition 'That the English people are essentially unsociable'. The motion was thrown out by eight votes, and the society itself sank into a decline, as it was to do several times in the years to come, despite efforts to revive it. On the other hand the Natural Science Society, which came into being in the same year, flourished, and before long incorporated the Photographic Club. By 1885, two years after Carver's retirement, it had about sixty ordinary members, forty corresponding and thirty honorary. Amongst the last were several Fellows of the Royal Society, including T. H. Huxley, one of the foremost advocates of the introduction of science into schools. The annual report which it produced was regarded as of sufficient calibre to be sent to the Linnean Society, the Geological Survey Office, the Royal Society, and the British Museum. Alfred Tribe was the President, and he did much to encourage it.

One of Carver's earliest pupils who was later to attain fame was in fact a scientist. 'Few men can have influenced modern civilisation to a greater extent than Sidney Gilchrist Thomas,' a science master of a later era wrote in the *Alleynian* in 1950. He devised a process which has made it possible to use for steel manufacture hundreds of millions of tons of iron ore which otherwise would not have been available, by removing the phosphorus that had formerly rendered so many iron ores useless as a source of steel. One by-product of his process was basic slag, an extremely important agricultural manure. Never strong, he died when he was only thirty-four, worn out by his unceasing work. He bequeathed his fortune to his sister for the purpose of 'doing good indiscriminately', a task which she carried out most efficiently with the help of Margaret Bondfield and others. Gladstone spoke of him as 'having an enthusiasm for humanity'.

Another eminent Alleynian of Carver's day, though in quite a different line of country, was A. E. W. Mason, novelist, actor, dramatist, politician, mountaineer, and yachtsman, whom *The Times* described in its obituary notice as 'one of the most successful of popular authors during the greater part of the last half-century, a craftsman of superlative skill, economy and finish'. He took a very active part in school life: he was President of the Swimming Club, Secretary of the Rifle Corps and the Debating Society, and one of the star performers in the school plays.

In 1875 Dr Carver acted as host to the Headmasters' Conference. (He had been included in the list of invitations to the first H.M.C. in 1869, and was among the fourteen who accepted, but for some reason now lost to history he failed to turn up.) Constance Carver writes:

Some of the guests on this occasion were the future Archbishops Benson and Temple, the present Master of Trinity, Cambridge, Dr Butler, and many other notable headmasters. Everyone in the house, nearly, had to give up their rooms, for their benefit, and myself and sister had beds made up, in the then small museum, in one of the wings of the College. Fortunately we were not nervous children, for opposite to us, mounted in full, was a large skeleton ... All these leading Masters, over one hundred, met in conference, in our large College Hall, and two evenings were given up to social entertainments to the neighbouring gentry.

Meanwhile Carver was still carrying on a vigorous battle with the Charity Commissioners, the outlying parishes, his Board of Governors, and even some of his assistant staff, in his determination to establish Dulwich as a great public school. One scheme after another was put forward to the Commissioners by the various interested parties for the further reorganization of the college, all of them to its detriment. The most drastic would have divided the upper school into a modern and a classical side, each with its own headmaster; done away entirely with the lower school by engulfing it in a new school to be built in Camberwell; and established a college department. (At one stage, in an article on the various projects being considered by the Charity Commissioners, the *Evening Standard* referred scathingly to 'the destructive zeal which animates this select committee of educational reformers'.) The conflict became so bitter that many of the Governors would gladly have rid themselves of their determined Master, and on one occasion even suggested that a specific charge should be brought against him, 'so as to enable them to decide authoritatively whether Dr Carver is worthy of their confidence, or merits dismissal from his office'.

Carver had one weapon, which he wielded consistently and skilfully. In accordance with the custom of the day, in addition to a small salary he was entitled to further remuneration based on the size of the school, in his case £3 for each boy above the number of fifty pupils, plus a sum amounting to half the capitation—or, as we should call them nowadays, tuition—fees. As the number of pupils shot up, so did his salary, until eventually, if he had claimed it all, it would have risen to £6,000 a year. However, he was not totally dependent on the college for his income, since he had private means, which he used with the utmost generosity for the good of the school. He provided exhibitions for the first Alleynians to go to university; paid the salary of the Sergeant Instructor of the Corps; headed with a bumper sum every good cause for which money was raised at the school; and augmented the miserably low salaries of the assistant masters. Quite early on he had offered to forego part of his capitation fees if the money thus saved could be put towards scholarships and salary increases; and in 1868, when the Governors announced a massive increase in the fees, an agreement on these lines came into effect. The intention was that it should last for five years, but later the period was extended to seven. Carver calculated that as a result he forfeited £15,000.

Under the particularly draconian scheme which brought to a head the dispute about the future of the school he would have lost all financial security as Master, for it was proposed that a large proportion of the endowment should be diverted to founding new schools in the outer parishes—that is to say, to purposes foreign to the interests of the college. This could quite well have led to its insolvency, leaving no funds to pay Carver's salary; and it was this threat to his income which gave him the one weapon he could use in opposing the scheme. His motives in doing so were much misunderstood: the accusation was made that he was seeking to feather his own nest, whereas the truth was the exact opposite. Confronted by the combined might of the Charity Commissioners[1] and the Governors, with William Rogers at their head, his one hope was to stand on his legal rights, and refuse to agree to a scheme which so gravely damaged his financial security; there was no other way in which he could save from dismemberment the school he had created and in whose future he had such inextinguishable faith.

[1] Who on one occasion, Mackenzie reports, after the Endowed Schools Act of 1869 gave startling evidence of their authority. 'Our powers are such,' they said, 'that we can change what is a boys' school in Northumberland into a girls' school in Cornwall.'

As usual, the outer parishes were quick to leap into the fray, hoping to gain what they regarded as their share of the endowment, and anxious not to lose any part of what they already had. Echoes of the struggle were heard far beyond the confines of the school. A Dulwich Committee was formed and public meetings were held, at least one of which, according to the press, broke up in scenes 'of indescribable uproar and confusion'. Letters and articles appeared in the national and local papers, one of them dramatically headed 'A Diabolical Plot at Dulwich College'. 'The inhabitants of Dulwich are to a man opposed to the proposed changes in the College,' said the *South London Courier*; and one correspondent wrote, 'We have at Dulwich the only first grade school in South London ... It has proved successful beyond parallel ... It is well known that the college has made Dulwich and the neighbour- hood what they are, and that hundreds of families have taken up residence there solely because of the great educational advantages.'

At last, in 1876, Carver took his case to the highest point of appeal, the Privy Council, where Lord Selborne gave judge- ment in his favour, quashing the scheme on the grounds that it would deprive the Master of his financial rights. Great were the rejoicings among his supporters, not least the boys, who were stoutly on his side.

But the pressure was too great for matters to remain as they were, and two years later the Charity Commissioners issued yet another scheme, under which Carver could rest assured that the educational aims of the college would not suffer. This scheme, with some modifications, was the one which in 1882 passed into law. The upper school became Dulwich College, the lower (which since 1870 had operated in the Old College) Alleyn's School. Two Boards of Governors were set up, one to administer the estate and the eleemosynary side and the other the two schools, the chapel, and the picture gallery. Sites were to be found for new buildings for Alleyn's School and for James Allen's Girls' School,[1] both of which moved to new premises in 1887; and sums of money were allocated for

---

[1] The latter had its own Board of Governors.

educational purposes in the parishes of St Saviour's, St Botolph's and St Luke's.

One clause of the scheme laid down that 'no person shall be disqualified from being a Head Master or Assistant Master or Teacher ... by reason only of his not being, or not intending to be, in Holy Orders.' This was in line with an important provision of the Endowed Schools Act of 1869, which stipulated that ancient trusts should be free from denominational restraints unless there had been instructions to the contrary by the founder. It was to prove of particular value to Dulwich. Without it, the man who was to bring Carver's work to fruition might not have been appointed, since until the 1890s it was quite unusual for public schools to appoint a non-cleric as headmaster.

So in 1882 the future of the college, which Edward Alleyn had brought into being with such faith and vision two hundred and sixty-three years earlier, was finally assured.

It gave Carver another victory too, for he had always been opposed to the idea, which had been part of the original plan for the new buildings, that the upper school should occupy the south block and the lower school the north block, and that they should share the middle block. Luckily the college had grown so rapidly that there had never been an opportunity to put this highly impractical scheme into effect.

But he had triumphed at great personal cost. Long before the scheme was passed he had become *persona non grata* with the Governors, and there was only the most brief and formal intercourse with them. The few cold, impersonal letters from Rogers which still exist must have given him great pain. And in 1878 there was an extremely unpleasant legal battle when the Undermaster brought a libel action against one of the assistant masters who was particularly close to Carver. There was a great deal of publicity which did the college much harm by bringing into the light of day the dissensions that were tearing it apart.

As soon as Canon Carver[1] knew that the terms of the

---

[1] In 1882 he was appointed an Honorary Canon of Rochester Cathedral. It is said that he had earlier been offered a bishopric, but refused it because of his devotion to education.

scheme would safeguard the future of the college he sent in his resignation, to take effect when the new regime came into operation. In April 1883 he ceased to be Master, though he lived on, in the best of health, for another twenty-six years. He continued to take a lively interest in the school, and attended almost every one of the annual Alleyn Club dinners up to the day of his death.

In an article on his achievements, *The Times* commented that in the course of a generation the school had attained to a position of remarkable influence and importance.

> The list of school honours seems to show that the distinctive character of the course of instruction at Dulwich has been breadth and variety. While holding its own at the universities, Dulwich has won a large number of places of honour in the Indian and home Civil Services, at Woolwich (taking on several occasions the first place in these examinations) and in various other public competitions, including some in which the older schools have suffered themselves to be left behind, especially the public schools medals of the Royal Geographical Society and the prizes of the Art Schools of the Royal Academy.

And in an early issue of a new journal, *The Public School Magazine*, (Sir) William Beach Thomas wrote in 1898, 'There is on record no single instance of an establishment expanding with the rapidity with which Dulwich expanded during the Mastership of Dr Carver.'

Canon Carver's greatest memorial, of course, can be found in the continuing success and achievements of the school which he did so much to create. In more concrete terms, he is remembered by an organ erected in his honour (later replaced), the reredos in the chapel, which was dedicated in 1911, and a wing of the old school library, opened in the same year. The last would have been a particular pleasure, for he had vigorously supported the building of a library. At first, he once said, when the school moved to its new home 'the books were stowed away in a kind of cupboard lying between the dissecting room and the laboratory claimed by one of the masters for the manufacture of sulphuretted hydrogen'. Gradually a reading and lending library was established: the first book to be taken out was *Alice in Wonderland*, borrowed by the school captain.

3 The Golden Age

J. E. C. Welldon (1883–5)
A. H. Gilkes (1885–1914)

> *'I think we are now far enough away from those days to see clearly that Canon Carver in his time fought a great fight to save the body of Dulwich: Gilkes gave it a soul.'* (W. D. Gibbon)

LIKE his predecessor, the new Master of Dulwich was a clergyman. When he came to Dulwich in the spring term of 1883 J. E. C. Welldon was twenty-nine, and a Fellow of King's College, Cambridge. The boys dubbed him 'the Butcher', though it is said that his looks belied his nature. Nevertheless, he had a reputation for being too strict for their liking, and it is certain that he was a stickler for discipline, which he believed to be crucial to good teaching, while a failure to achieve it could ruin a child's chances in life. The role of the headmaster he saw as essentially a lonely, somewhat autocratic one, since ultimately decisions affecting the school as a whole must be taken upon his judgement: he should be admired for his courage, respected for justice, but only afterwards should the boys think of him as having been a friend. 'I used to say,' he wrote many years later, 'I wished to be unpopular and successful.'

He was just the kind of live wire Dulwich needed at this juncture. When he was appointed the college cannot have been a happy place: for years it had been rent by the controversy between Carver and the combined forces of the Governors and the Charity Commissioners, as well as by uncertainty about the future. And there is no doubt that, though Carver's selfless and unremitting work achieved so much, during the latter years of his mastership he had been too preoccupied with the struggle to give enough attention to the day-by-day running of the school.

As a young man Welldon had an extraordinary reputation: he possessed unflagging vigour and an outstanding personality, and, like most masterful men, got things done with great despatch. He spent only two-and-a-half years at Dulwich, but during this period he persuaded the Governors to allocate money for more exhibitions, including one for natural science and another for carpentry; established a science side as well as a modern form for boys preparing for the army; appointed the first music-master who was at the school on a full-time basis; initiated a scheme for raising money for the badly-needed swimming-bath; put the commissariat on a sound footing; set up better facilities for a library and reading-room; put in train the building of a new science wing and music-room; instituted workshops and facilities for teaching practical mechanics; and (since the age of admittance had been raised under the 1882 scheme from eight to ten) helped to bring into being a flourishing preparatory school for the college. By preaching all over the country he created a great deal of excellent publicity for Dulwich. He was also responsible for making Founder's Day, 21 June, the chief festival of the year, although the distribution of prizes still took place at the end of the summer term.

From the moment Welldon entered the college it was clear that he attached great importance to practical science; so perhaps it is not surprising that one of his most inspired appointments should have been that of F. W. Sanderson as senior physics master. Sanderson was then coaching and lecturing at Girton, and he was to spend seven years at Dulwich before moving on to become headmaster of Oundle. H. G. Wells describes him as 'beyond question the greatest man I have ever known with any degree of intimacy', and his influence on education was seminal. He electrified the science department at Dulwich, though his most important work there was done under Welldon's successor, A. H. Gilkes. Gilkes is reputed to have had little interest in science and rarely to have put his nose into the science block, but he supported Sanderson in every way—though according to the historian G. C. Coulton, who taught at Dulwich between 1892 and 1895, there was a certain personality clash between the two men, Sanderson being of too independent a mind for Gilkes, who preferred greater malleability in his assistant masters.

Sanderson had little belief in the usefulness of classroom work, and, though later he became an excellent teacher, in his early days at Dulwich he had difficulty in keeping order. Fundamentally a social reformer rather than a scientist, he felt passionately that education is important only in so far as it relates to life and the betterment of humanity; competition should be replaced by corporate service and interest in the work for its own sake; and every boy should participate as much as possible in all collective functions of his school.

One Alleynian of this era wrote later:

> While [Sanderson] was to Gilkes, I think, merely the man who could teach workshops and somewhat surprisingly get boys to win major scholarships at Trinity, he was himself developing his ideas of a broad curriculum of education based on scientific method. He taught us by means of the simplest experimental apparatus, made by the boys themselves to a large extent in the workshops, to rely on experimental evidence for scientific facts. What we learnt from him, apart from a valuable acquaintanceship with scientific apparatus, was a kind of fundamental belief in the scientific method as a means of solving all problems in life.

He instilled into the boys, that is to say, the most vital of all educational skills—the art of learning to acquire knowledge for themselves.

The first reference to his work at Dulwich seems to have been at a meeting of the Science Society in 1886, when he 'worked the magic lantern' for a lecture on the somewhat umpromising subject of Tiryns, 'this most interesting specimen of the so-called Cyclopean architecture'. Under his influence, and that of H. B. Baker, who succeeded Alfred

Tribe and eventually became head of the science side, the society lectures soon began to have greater practical relevance, on topics likely to interest a schoolboy audience; the museum had a badly-needed face-lift; the boys were encouraged to make natural history collections; photographic and astronomical societies were established; and a meteorological observer was appointed whose findings were posted on the school board.

One of Sanderson's most successful ventures was the establishment in 1887 of an engineering side, with workshops and forge, with the aim of encouraging boys who wanted to become engineers, and who had formerly tended to leave at fifteen or sixteen because Dulwich offered no opportunity for specialist training, to stay on for a further two or three years. The experiments were carried out on a more ambitious scale than was usual in public schools at this time, with actual working engines, dynamos, and testing machines rather than models.

One interesting development was the purchase in 1888 of an experimental steam engine, described as a 'Horizontal Fixed Engine of 6 Nominal Horsepower with separate Jet Condenser and Boiler for 80 lbs pressure of steam'. It lived in

Fig. 3.1 One of the workshops in A. H. Gilkes' day

the engineering workshop, and was one of only six or seven in Great Britain at this time.

H. G. Wells wrote:

> The most valuable result of Sanderson's Dulwich period was the demonstration of the interestingness of practical work in physical science for boys who remained apathetic under the infliction of the stereotyped classical curriculum. He was not getting the pick of the boys there but the residue, but he was getting an alertness and interest out of this second-grade material that surprised even himself.

So, just as was later to happen at Oundle, boys who were regarded, and who regarded themselves, as failures in school-work found that they were good at practical engineering; and the discovery gave them self-confidence and the realization that, though they might be duffers in academic subjects, they had a solid contribution to make in other directions.

Gilkes' annual reports to the Governors show how profound Sanderson's influence must have been. Several times the report included (as it had never done before and was not to do again) a detailed account of what was happening on the science side and of what was needed to develop this work adequately. The Governors grumbled at the expense, but, with Gilkes backing Sanderson, they paid up.

In 1886 four Dulwich boys won honours in the national competition for scholarships at the Royal School of Science, the only students from any London school who obtained awards. Seven years later an article on the college in the *Ludgate Monthly* (one of a series of eighteen on 'Young England at School') commented 'the engineering side is indeed unique', and praised 'the four good lathes', the drilling machine, forge, and 'every appliance for casting and mould-ing . . . Instruction is given to those mechanically inclined by a thoroughly practical engineer.' The floor above, the article went on, was fitted out as the physical laboratories, and for lectures the rooms could be lit with electricity from a dynamo made by the boys.

In 1909 the answers to a questionnaire sent out by the recently formed Association of Public Schools Science Masters showed that Dulwich was one of only ten schools with biology

laboratories, and one of only two with engineering laboratories (the other, predictably enough, was Oundle); that it
was fifth in the table for the number of boys learning science;
and that a great deal more space was given to rooms for
practical and theoretical scientific work than at any other
school, including Eton and Oundle.

Welldon came and went like a gust of fresh air, remembered
amongst other things for his witty after-dinner speeches at
Alleyn Club dinners. He said at one of them—and though he
wasn't talking about Alleyn's Foundation he might well have
been—

> They say that when the Commissioners were enquiring into the
> different public educational institutions of England, they came
> upon one school which had a large endowment, fine buildings and
> a good situation, and yet so dwindled in numbers that there was
> only a handful of boys—not so many, I think, as there were
> Governors of the school. And when the Commissioners asked the
> Governors how it was that a school of so much promise had
> proved such a failure, the only answer which the Governors made
> to the Commissioners was to return by post a photograph of the
> head master.

At the last prize-giving before Welldon became headmaster of
Harrow, in the summer of 1885, the guest of honour was
Matthew Arnold, who spent thirty-five years of his life as an
inspector of schools, and who played a large part in the work
of the Taunton Commission. Welldon, he remarked, had been
the strong man when the strong man was most needed, and
had done more for the school in his two years than many
might have done in ten. Dulwich College, he went on,

> ... is a signal and splendid type of just that description of school
> which I have long desired, and vainly desired, to see put at the
> disposal of the professional and trading classes throughout this
> country. How very seldom the English middle classes elsewhere
> find themselves with advantages of this kind, and how very little
> they in general seem to care whether they possess them or not! I
> am filled with admiration for the school.

So on this high note Welldon departed; and his place was taken by the greatest Master of them all—Arthur Herman Gilkes.

Gilkes came from Shrewsbury, where he had been an assistant master, teaching, at his own desire, the lower classical forms. With a tawny mane of hair and beard (did he sleep with it outside or inside the bedclothes, the boys used to wonder?), he was a giant of a man, 6 feet 5 inches tall and weighing about 18 stone; he used to say that his great height was a terrible handicap. Time and time again old Alleynians who were at the school during his mastership said to me, while I was doing the research for this book, 'He was the nearest thing to God', or 'He was the small boy's idea of God'; and there is no doubt that his majestic figure, almost invariably clad either in cap and gown or in tail-coat and tall hat, struck terror into the hearts of many of the younger ones.

To some extent this impression was created deliberately, for he had a deep, some would say exaggerated, sense of the dignity of his position. With the staff he tended to be as austere and distant as he was with the boys, which some of them found hard to take. 'It is your own fault,' he might say to a master beset by troubles. 'Your nerves are out of order. Have you not been smoking too much?' One of his staff wrote:

> To a man who had not been educated under him, service must have been hard. He seldom showed outward appreciation of your efforts; he seemed to care little what, or how, his staff taught; he was apparently indifferent to their poverty or wealth (though I suspect that his private charity was generous and widespread); he frequently took a boy's word against a master's. He gave an onlooker the impression that, though he accepted the staff as a necessary part of the machinery of the School, the boys were his only interest. Those of us who had been boys under him knew how mistaken was this impression. His own view that service to the School brought its own reward of happiness to the individual, made praise of the members of the staff in public, or in private, unnecessary.

'Rightly or wrongly,' writes Coulton, 'there was a fairly

Fig. 3.2 A study in headgear: nine of the seventeen school caps

widespread feeling that he was more loyal to the school than to his colleagues.' He placed much faith in his prefects, on whom he depended a great deal in the running of the school, and was bitterly grieved if they failed to live up to his high expectations of them. He did a great deal to strengthen the prefect body. It appears, from the diary which he kept between 1899 and 1910, that there were no prefects when he arrived, but 'a sixth form considered to exercise certain prefectorial functions of a very vague character. They wore round caps, shaped like a pork pie, with a tassel.'

His attitude to his pupils can be assessed from a letter which he wrote in 1901 to one of his assistant masters to whom he was offering the housemastership of The Orchard. 'Boys,' he said, 'always should be treated with the utmost politeness and with everyone's best manners. Respectful kindness is more or less the secret of the whole matter, combined with a patience and a watchfulness and a charity and a trustfulness that never dies. As to discipline, prefects should keep it—when they are there, a master should work through them.' Diffident in manner, with a tendency to stammer, he is said by one boy to have pursued his purpose quietly and with apparently unruffled serenity, and never to have shown impatience or anger—though this is not entirely true, for on occasion he certainly showed the latter when any of the boys failed to live up to his terrifyingly high moral principles.

One man, who had been his pupil at Shrewsbury and who later taught under him at Dulwich, wrote, 'He once said to me, when he was defending his attitude of reserve: "You know, I have to be very careful: I was meant by nature for a buffoon." Anyone who ever saw him in moments of relaxation will easily understand what he meant. He had a power of merciless chaff which I have never seen equalled in any other man.' He was impatient alike with exigent parents, complaining staff, and tiresome boys, withering them with a very chilling irony.

On the other hand, to those who came into close contact with him he was revealed as a different man. For much of the time he took the sixth form in Latin and Greek, and he would set the prefects a weekly essay which, one by one, they would read to him in the evening. Relaxed in his study after the day's work, his tail-coat exchanged for a comfortable jacket, he often sat and chatted to them with, apparently, all the time in the world. To many of them these encounters transformed him from a figure of awe into a wise and understanding friend—though P. G. Wodehouse, one of the school's most eminent alumni, brought away a different impression, describing these sessions as 'an unpopular and nerve-destroying practice akin to suicide'. Gilkes was a good teacher because he obviously loved classics, and had the gift of imparting this love. He once said that his own style in English was very poor—and certainly his spelling was far from infallible—but that without Latin and Greek it would have been considerably poorer.

His work-load was unbelievable. Besides sixth-form teaching and occasional visits to each form in turn, he taught English and Divinity at intervals to the non-classical sides, so that he had an opportunity to meet all the senior boys. He also took the boarders' prep for two hours twice a week. His classroom visits were unannounced and dreaded, for he would come armed with the form-placings of the boys. 'Pettigrew,' he might remark, 'I see that you are seventeenth for the second time in succession. Now if you worked a little harder, you know, you might go up to sixteenth or even fifteenth.' With luck that would end the inspection, and Nos 18 and 19 would sigh with relief at being let off so lightly. His own teaching made few concessions to examinations. 'The boys take their history paper to-morrow,' he remarked to a master on one occasion. 'Can you tell me what is the period?' He used to take an essay lesson once a week with the non-classical boys, and invariably, so I was told, marked all their essays '20'. But there was a subtle distinction: if he thought the essay was good the 20 would be large and bold, but as the standard tailed off he would write the figure smaller and smaller.

Whereas Carver had been a great time-table man, under Gilkes there seemed to be no time-table; he appeared to keep it all in his head. Another idiosyncracy was his intense dislike of clock-watching. 'Now do you not look at the clock,' he would say in that curious Quaker idiom of his. 'I think I shall hate you all the holidays.' Yet he himself was an inveterate clock-watcher, punctual to the minute in beginning and ending his classes. This could be disconcerting, as on the occasion when he asked his form what one should pray for. Success? No. Wealth? Still less. Virtue? Not even that. The bell rang, and the answer was lost for ever. He was reputed to have a photographic memory, and he always seemed to know everything that was going on in the school, no one quite understood how.

Throughout his mastership the school suffered badly from lack of money, making it impossible for capital to be set aside for any extensive building programme, though in 1906 a new science block—in 'North Italian style' like the rest of the school—was built. The foundation stone was laid by Lord Rayleigh, Nobel prizewinner and President of the Royal Society, and 'we slid peacefully into these buildings in the autumn,' Gilkes recorded in his diary, 'occupying first one room and then another, until by mid-term the workmen were all out.' The £8,000 needed for this project had, however, to be borrowed from the Estates Governors.

Nor were there funds enough to pay the staff adequate salaries. Though to his assistant masters Gilkes may often have seemed cold and impersonal, his reports to the Governors, like those of Carver a few years earlier, are full of pleas for better salaries for his staff, who earned less than their colleagues at comparable London schools, and especially for the establishment of a pension fund, since in those days no contribution was made by the school towards staff pensions. This parsimony was harmful in many ways: excellent masters left for better-paid posts; others (perhaps the less talented), because they could not afford to retire, stayed on long past the age when they could be effective teachers; and too many of them had nothing but a poverty-striken old age to look forward to. 'There was throughout the staff,' Gilkes said, 'a constant feeling of deadness and depression produced by the knowledge that they were underpaid. It was impossible to keep a good man, and all the Assistants were constantly on the lookout for fresh appointments.' He even offered to give up part of his share of the capitation fees, if this could be used as the nucleus of a pension fund.

The system in operation at the time was for a lump sum to be handed over to the headmaster, based on his estimate of the expenses for the coming year; out of this he found the running costs of the school. In 1894, for instance, Gilkes, with around six hundred boys, was given £10,828; from this—having drawn up the kind of careful budget which would be laughably impossible in these days of inflation—he paid the assistant masters' salaries and was responsible for all expenditure on scientific apparatus, masters' and porters' luncheons, furniture, paper, pens, ink and other equipment, printing, the library, gas, water, coal, the matron's wages, prizes and prize day expenses, and a proportion of the engineer's wages—while leaving aside enough to provide for contingencies. Not surprisingly, this arrangement was a fruitful source of contention between Master and Governors. And, though many of the latter took a great interest in the school, their general attitude towards headmasters was considerably different from what it is today: some years later Gilkes told the Board of Education that though he was invited to attend the Governors' meetings he was 'sometimes dangling his heels in the hall or the street for a long time—and then perhaps not called for'. Not till 1935 did the Board pass a resolution asking that the Master of the college and the Headmaster of Alleyn's should in future attend every Board meeting in an *ex officio* capacity.

By the early 1890s the college was a busy, flourishing place, with several sides now successfully established—classical, modern, science, engineering, mathematical, and army—and with the boys winning more and more awards at Oxford and Cambridge and places at Sandhurst and Woolwich and in the Indian Civil Service. Their reputation at Sandhurst was particularly high. With the 'public school phenomenon' still very much to the fore, newspapers enjoyed analysing the record of Oxbridge scholarships, and it was calculated that in the seven years 1885–92 twenty-two schools each won between twenty and a hundred awards. Dulwich was one of these, coming eighth in the table. And whereas falling numbers were worrying some of the famous London schools, such as St Paul's and Merchant Taylors'—partly because, as the *Daily Mail* expressed it, 'the school that has not placed itself in the healthy, open country is doomed'—Dulwich could point to a satisfactory enrolment. Twenty-five years later H. A. L. Fisher, then President of the Board of Education, was to remark on its astonishing emergence as a public school at this time, 'Alleynians carrying off scholarship after scholarship at the universities'.

As has so often been the case throughout its history, at this period Dulwich was in the forefront of a movement of educational reform. Until now elementary and secondary education had been regarded as two parallel streams, with no point of meeting: the potential leaders of state, industry, the armed services, and so on, attended public or grammar schools, often going on to university or some other form of further education, while the 'working classes' spent their much briefer period of instruction at elementary schools, in order that they might be prepared for careers on the lower rungs of the occupational ladder. Many of these children came from homes which were deprived to a degree it is almost impossible to imagine nowadays: they were under-nourished, ill-clad, dirty, verminous, and suffering from a variety of diseases that were largely the result of the conditions in which they lived. Without help from outside they had little chance of overcoming the disadvantages of their birth.

Gradually it became apparent that not only was this system inherently evil, but that to allow children to be so badly educated and so riddled with physical ills was a national disaster in an age when there was a crying need for skilled and educated citizens; so from the mid-nineteenth century onwards successive legislation, and especially the Education Acts of 1902, 1903, and 1907, made it possible for children from poor homes to win scholarships to public and secondary schools.

Since most of the college records for the period have disappeared, and since there seems to be some confusion between the college and Alleyn's in the London County Council records—themselves incomplete—it is difficult to establish just when Dulwich began to accept L.C.C. scholars. Of course, it was far from unique among London public schools in this, since many others—St Paul's, University College School, and Merchant Taylors' among them—were doing so as well. That Dulwich was, however, either taking more of them, or began to do so earlier than most comparable schools, seems to be shown by the minutes of a conference that took place on 15 February 1928 between representative Dulwich Governors and members of the Board of Education and the L.C.C. At this meeting Sir Arthur Hirtzel, chairman of the Governors, said that Junior County Scholars had first been accepted by the college in 1903, and that 'Dulwich had been the first Public School to admit such scholars voluntarily, and no other Public School had been, or was at the present time, prepared to admit them in the same way'.

However, it appears as if these boys were attending the school even earlier than this, since in 1903 three of them won scholarships to Oxford and Cambridge; presumably they came into the category of intermediate scholars, who were admitted when they were under sixteen, as opposed to the junior scholars, who came at under thirteen. By 1904 there appear to have been ten of these intermediate scholars at the college, and in 1906, in his annual report to the Governors,

Gilkes wrote, 'An increase in numbers, however small, is unusual at this time. It is owing in some measure to the County Council scholars, whom we have admitted to the number of, I think, 17. I am very glad to have these boys, and to help them. They work well and do well.' There is, too, the comment of a Board of Education official in 1905 that Dulwich was 'of a higher type than the schools usually aided by the L.C.C.' The college continued to take a small number of intermediate scholars up to the end of the First World War.

The second reform in which Dulwich took part was in the general broadening of the curriculum through the scheme of grants for the teaching of technical and scientific subjects— which fitted in, of course, with the school's own aspirations on the science side. There was throughout the country a widely felt uneasiness about the low standards of education in this field, and the Department of Science and Art, which had come into being in 1853, was empowered to give *per capita* grants to schools for instruction in science, art, and literature, and in commercial and practical subjects. Here again the records are incomplete and there is confusion between the college and Alleyn's; but there appears to be no doubt that in the years 1901–5 between 150 and 250 boys were taking the special course which entitled the school to an annual grant. The additional revenue was particularly welcome, for in 1902 the school's finances were so bad that special arrangements had to be made with the Estates Governors for a grant which should have come to the school in the form of an annual pay-ment to be given as a lump sum instead.

The acceptance of L.C.C. scholars, with the life-giving fees which they brought, and of the grant from the Department of Science and Art, carried obligations also: L.C.C. representa-tives had to be admitted on the Board of Governors, and the school was obliged to submit to regular inspection by the Board of Education, which came into existence in 1899 and gradually took over the educational responsibilities of the Charity Commissioners. The first of these inspections took place in the summer term of 1908.

'Eight inspectors came and spent from Tuesday to Friday here inclusive,' Gilkes wrote in his diary.

They visited every class and form room and heard masters teach. The Inspection was proposed to us and to St Paul's Endowed Schools. St Paul's I believe refused to accept the right of the Inspectors into the Class Room, and the Board did not press the matter, having a doubt as to their powers. We did not know that we had power to object; and accepted the inspection freely but with distaste: I mean that we made no objection, but did not like the plan. The inspectors were kind courteous and able men; and I am not sorry to have had the experience, trying though it was: but I am of opinion that the method is wrongly conceived. It is good for a school that visits should be paid from the outside by competent men. The chief good is that thus we are led to examine methods, and, by thinking how they will appear to others, mend

Fig. 3.3   The Assistant Masters, 1908
(*standing*) Atkinson, Leake, A. R. Taylor, Oldham, Adams, F. A. W. Taylor, Beesley, Beachcroft, Edwards, Hutchings, Kittermaster, Bauer, Ellis, Chapman, Hose, J. A. Joerg, Boon, Wilkins, Rev. Cocq, Nightingale, Rumsey
(*sitting*) Russell, Ulrich, Stretton, Doughty, A. H. Gilkes (The Master), Mellor, Robinson, Rev. Escott, Doulton, J. B. Joerg

them. But it seems to me that real teaching is hardly possible with another in the room, thus coming there. Lecturing, maybe, but teaching is what is wanted. I think that the old plan is best, by which examiners took forms, and examined paper work and exercises, done ordinarily.

The Inspectors had a number of criticisms, notably that the total income from fees and the endowment from the Estate was inadequate for the needs of the school, and that the strength of the staff, which then consisted of thirty-eight full-time masters and five visiting ones, was insufficient for a school of seven hundred boys. But their approval was considerably more generous than their blame, and in particular they praised Gilkes' own contribution, not least his habit of delegating authority (as he had always made a point of doing), so that 'the varied abilities of the staff are used to the great advantage of the School'. They found the whole college to be in a state of high efficiency, with every department showing a vigorous and healthy life, a very high standard of intellectual activity and a remarkable record of success alike at the universities and on the playing fields. 'It is to be hoped that the School may long have the benefit of the Master's long experience, his deep insight into character, his kindly severity, and, above all, of the personal influence which he is so well able to exert over boys and masters alike.'

One of Welldon's most priceless legacies to the college, during his brief span as master, was the real genesis of the remarkable tradition of music which continues to this day. Recitals of madrigals and part-songs had been given from quite early on; but not until Welldon appointed E. D. Rendall in 1884, with the dual duties of teaching mathematics and directing the music, did the musical activities begin to flower. It was Rendall who formed the orchestra. He also appointed the first two of a long line of distinguished music masters—Arnold Dolmetsch and A. H. Fox Strangways, later to be director of music at Wellington, who founded *Music and Letters* and became one of the most respected music critics of the day.

As for Dolmetsch, though he is not mentioned as being on the music staff until 1885, he was in fact closely connected with music-making at the school from at least two years earlier. It was through the influence of Sir George Grove that Rendall appointed him as a part-time violin teacher. Just as Sanderson was at this time introducing revolutionary methods of teaching science, so Dolmetsch instituted the equally unconventional ways of teaching violin-playing that were to mark his later work. As Margaret Campbell writes:

> The school permitted the boys only half-an-hour's music practice each day and he soon found that it was useless to burden them with technique . . . So he taught the boys to hear first and thereby develop their musical sensitivity. He would allow them to play tunes right away on the open strings and once they had accepted the violin as an instrument related to their own efforts, not merely as a means of conveying sound, he could safely introduce technique.

He encouraged the boys to play music which was quite unfamiliar in that era, and under his influence the number of violin pupils increased from a mere handful to over forty.

Together Welldon and Rendall wrote the school song, Rendall the music and Welldon the words (changing the original motto, in the interests of rhyme and scansion, from *Detur Gloria Soli Deo* to *Detur Soli Deo Gloria*). It was sung for the first time at the Founder's Day celebrations in 1884. However, Rendall wrote many others—in fact, it became something of a convention that he should produce a new school song for every concert—before '*Pueri Alleynienses*', so melodious and unpretentious, was finally adopted. Rendall also wrote the music in 1899 for what Gilkes described in his diary as 'a new song of fairwell [*sic*] which was sung at the end of the summer term by E. C. Walter. The song was very pretty and touching: and has been sung at this time ever since, always with excellent effect.' At the concerts the boys, even the small ones, wore evening dress and white ties, and this custom continued for many years.

From the beginning the boys had always performed 'Speeches' on Founder's Day—that is to say, extracts from

Shakespeare and from Greek, French, and German plays. From 1895, Gilkes wrote:

> The Greek play has always been done in costume, and has been the most prominent of the speeches. This is due partly to the costumes which are always interesting, but also to the singing of the choruses. For these Mr Rendall has continually written excellent music and the boys have sung it excellently and with great effect. The great window at the west of the Hall has been blocked with red baize, and thus the stage and the performers have been visible. Before this their faces were all in shadow.

In 1887 the biennial play was replaced by an annual concert—an unpopular move, for the boys were proud of the dramatic tradition of the college and its connection with their founder. The change was made partly because Gilkes felt that the play took up too much time which should be devoted to work, but also because he deeply disapproved of boys acting female parts, believing that this introduced an unwholesome element into school life (a point of view which many modern educationists would echo). He had equally strong ideas about boy trebles, who were banned for the same reason. Some music he regarded as virile and good, other kinds as enervating and decadent (Chopin belonged to the latter category). He used to bowdlerize Shakespeare when the boys studied the plays in class, as well as the passages from the Bible which they read at Assembly; but no one could make head or tail of what he regarded as corrupting in some of the offending passages.

In 1901 Rendall was lured away to become head of music at Charterhouse, and his place was taken by H. V. Doulton (known as Spud because of his shape), who had been a pupil at Dulwich from 1872–82.[1] He was a man of immense zest and a brilliant all-rounder—one colleague describes him as 'towering over everybody'. Somehow or other he managed to combine the functions of form-master, housemaster, principal

---

[1] In his last year the *Alleynian* reported that several morning papers had carried the warning, 'Clergymen and Registrars are cautioned not to marry a young gentleman whose initials are H.V.D. as he is under age.'

music master, conductor of the orchestra, choir, and band, and teacher of classics, football, and cricket.

As a cricketer he must have been formidable. While he was at Oxford (where he captained his college eleven) he once, at a Visitors v. Residents match at Herne Bay, took 5 wickets in one over and all 10 wickets in one innings for 19 runs. He brought his bowling prowess, as well as a somewhat choleric temper, into the form room: when the boys read or construed they had to stand on a kind of rostrum in front of the class, and if they made a mistake he would catch them neatly on the jaw with the blackboard duster. He kept a pile of books on his desk, which he would hurl one by one at offending boys, who became adept at fielding with the lids of their desks. Sir Melford Stevenson, who later achieved great eminence in the law, still bears on his forehead the scar from one of these missiles. Doulton was also a versatile composer, and wrote good incidental music for the Greek plays, continuing to do so even after he had retired in 1929.

Before his day, music was not regarded with much esteem by the boys; but as he was both musical and good at cricket and rugby, under his regime it became respectable and popular. The orchestra expanded—at one time there were five French horns and a full set of trombones—with so many masters and boys playing that there was rarely any need to import professionals for concerts.

One pupil in the early part of the present century was Gordon Jacob, later to become one of our most renowned composers. He had started to learn the piano when he was eight, and soon afterwards, triggered by two musical brothers, began to write music himself. At Dulwich he was encouraged to compose by another first-rate musician on the staff, H. W. Russell ('Stalky'), and his work was played by the school orchestra.

Then as later, close links were formed with India and the Far East, for many of the boys entered the Indian Civil Service or served in the Indian Army, which attracted young men who were seeking an interesting and adventurous career but who could not have lived on their pay in a good regiment in this country. (The link remained: one speaker at the Alleyn

Club dinner in 1946 remarked that 'if you go East, it seems that you fall over Dulwich boys at every turn'.) Maharajas and other Eastern potentates continued to send their offspring to Dulwich, and from time to time descended on the college in person and even distributed largesse in the shape of prizes. This happened in 1893, when the Rajah of Bhavnagar visited the school and donated the vast sum of ten guineas for some worthy object. The entire school was divided into seven divisions and commanded to write a poem on Dulwich, the boys who produced the best offerings sharing the Rajah's gift. Predictably, the results were mediocre, with one stunningly apposite exception:

> Well I know how thou hast brought me
> Up: thou art my nurse.
> But thou hast not, Dulwich, taught me
> How I ought to write a verse.

A charming and much-cherished custom of the college dates from Gilkes' time, though tradition puts it considerably earlier—the wearing of a cornflower on Founder's Day. Legend has it that the cornflower was Edward Alleyn's favourite flower, but there seems to be no evidence for this; in the early days of the Foundation roses were often worn, perhaps because of the heraldic rose-like flower in Alleyn's coat of arms. The cornflower tradition seems to date from around the turn of the century, thirty years or so after black and blue were adopted as the school colours. In 1900 a correspondent wrote to the *Alleynian*:

> It is some years since I left the college, but every time I see a bunch of cornflowers adorning a black coat in this none too sentimental city I think again of the old school. Founder's Day is coming round again, and I wonder whether it would be possible to adopt by unwritten law and gradually build up into a school tradition the wearing of cornflowers by present and past members of the college on Founder's Day? By the middle of June the flower itself is very plentiful, and 'black and blue' are so becoming.

It seems that this idea was taken up, while the custom of placing a wreath of cornflowers on Alleyn's grave on Founder's Day was introduced a few years later. The money for the wreath was raised by a penny subscription among the boys; and by 1911 the cornflower tradition had become firmly enough established for the flower to be introduced as a motif in the window above the Carver Memorial Reredos which was consecrated in the chapel in that year.

Like the rest of the country, in 1900 the school celebrated the relief of Mafeking. 'We came out of school at 10 o'clock,' Gilkes' diary entry runs:

> At prayers in the morning I spoke to the boys about it: and we sang God Save the Queen: and cheered Colonel Baden Powell, and the defender of the town. Then at 10 o'clock the Corps paraded, I should think about 200 strong, with the band: they fired a *feu de joie*; and then marched past two or three times. The whole sight was very pretty: and very well done. The Corps and the band give wonderful help to anything of this kind. Indeed I do not know what we should do without them. The band playing was not quite so good as it usually is: but it helped much. After that the Corps and band had a local march out. Then there was cricket until the evening. The extra lesson was excused; and we made arrangements for having a collection for the Indian famine on Monday morning in Hall. In the evening between the first and 2nd football grounds there was a bonfire; which the boys built, to a height of about 20 feet. Mr Street and other masters helped them. After fireworks, it was fired by E. J. Hall the Captain of the school at about 8.30 o'clock; and burned beautifully to the great delight and pleasure of us all. At about 9.30 the boys went away: before they went away they pleased me very much by coming to my door: where they cheered: I said a few words to them. I think it is not possible to speak too highly of the pleasure everyone felt throughout the day, and too highly of the demeanour of the school, loyal, sound and enthusiastic, without the least trace of anything disagreeable.

In an era of such intense social reform many public schools, both boys' and girls', were concerned that their pupils should be made aware of the misery and deprivation in which less privileged people lived, and encouraged to play their part in helping to right social injustice. During the last thirty years of the nineteenth century all the major schools established missions in slum areas, the pioneer of the movement being Thring of Uppingham. While Gilkes was at Shrewsbury he had already begun to combine social work with his other commitments, and one of his first acts at Dulwich was to form a committee, under the presidency of the captain of the school, to consider the possibility of setting up a mission. Money was raised, premises were found in Walworth Road, Camberwell, and in the Christmas holidays of 1886/7 the Dulwich College Mission was formally opened.

Here about twenty destitute 'London-born orphans' between fourteen and eighteen found a home, as far as possible living like a family, with the minimum of rules. They paid a small sum for their keep, and were helped to find jobs or apprenticeships. The Mission also established a club where boys could come who would otherwise be roaming the streets. In the early days the cost of running the club was estimated at about £140 a year (this sum included rents, rates and taxes, furniture, and the manager's salary!), and half of it came from school subscriptions. Theoretically these were voluntary, but at the end of every term the donation of each form was read out aloud by Gilkes, and it was something of a disgrace to be low on the table, while boys who refused to contribute anything at all ran the risk of being thrown out of the window.

Wodehouse, as usual, has his gently sardonic comment: 'The school[1] by (more or less) voluntary contributions supported a species of home somewhere in the wilds of Kennington. No one knew exactly what or where this home was, but all paid their subscriptions as soon as possible in the term, and tried to forget about it.' Another comment comes from an anonymous contribution to an illustrated weekly dating from 1910:

> If, when a coin falls noisily to the ground, one of the company murmurs, more or less audibly, the word 'Mission', you have infallible indication that he is an old Dulwich boy. The origin of the exclamation lies in the custom of confiscating to the School mission any money dropped during school hours. On such

[1] Dulwich, of course, though veiled under the familiar pseudonymous cloak of Wrykyn.

occasions the form, according to its discipline, more or less loudly reminds the offender of the penalty for his unlucky display of wealth. In a certain mathematics class, not unknown for the hilarity of its proceedings, it was for years remarkable how many coins, mostly farthings, were dropped in the course of every lesson!

Alleynians were encouraged to help by regularly visiting the club, and football, cricket, gymnastics, boxing, swimming, and summer corps were part of the fare offered to the boys. Many of the staff gave devoted service—indeed, without their help the Mission's existence would have been impossible.

It was very dear to Gilkes' heart, and every Sunday afternoon he would walk over to Camberwell, where he held the boys spellbound with the stories he was so skilled at telling. Or his butler would bring round to the front door the bicycle which he had had specially constructed to bear his great weight, and off he would slowly pedal—'Perhaps no one ever rode so slowly on a bicycle as he did,' one master commented.

The last ten years of the nineteenth century were Dulwich's 'Golden Decade', not least in terms of the boys who were later to be famous. The best known of all was Ernest Shackleton, who was there from 1887 to 1890. He was a reluctant schoolboy, coming well down in the form and totally uninterested in lessons. The story is told that years later someone said to him, 'We never found you at school,' to which he replied, 'No, I hadn't found myself then.' 'Some boys,' he said on another occasion, 'take to school like ducks to water; for some boys, whether they take to it or not, the discipline is good; but for a few rough spirits the system is chafing, not good, and the sooner they are pitched into the world the better. I was one of those.' So when he was sixteen his parents decided that after one more term he should be allowed to do what he had set his heart on, and go to sea. (This hadn't always been his ambition: as a small boy he had loved digging holes, and had decided that when he grew up he would be a gravedigger.) From the moment the decision was taken he did excellently at his work, especially mathematics, the basis of navigation. And perhaps he gained more at school than he realized, for on one of his expeditions he argued the merits of practical rather than pure scientific research—so entirely the philosophy of Sanderson, who was teaching science at Dulwich during the whole of Shackleton's time there.

In 1890 he set out on his first voyage, under a captain who described him as the most obstinate and pig-headed boy he had ever come across. He took with him many books, for he had not only a restless mind, craving adventure, but a romantic mind as well: he loved poetry, especially the poets—Browning, Shelley, Keats—who epitomized for him the spirit of greatness, wildness, freedom.

Eleven years later he went with Scott in the *Discovery* to the Antarctic. And in 1908 he led his own party on an expedition which made him world-famous, for he reached the furthermost point south yet attained by man, coming within 97 miles of the South Pole. Soon after he arrived back in England, fêted and honoured in country after country to a degree it is almost impossible to imagine nowadays, he came to Dulwich on prize day and 'spoke nicely to the boys', as Gilkes records. He remarked that never before had he been so close to the prizes, and was presented with a rosebowl. The same year he was guest of honour at the Alleyn Club dinner, when 'pêches glacée Shackleton' were served, and the next year he lectured to the school on his famous expedition, speaking, Gilkes wrote, 'with perfect simplicity and absolute modesty'. One boy who was there remembers that he put on a slide showing a wilderness of ice and snow, with small men and tiny sledges, and was perfectly silent. The boys thought he had dried up, and started fidgeting. Shackleton said, 'You stuck it for forty-four seconds: we stuck it for five weeks.'

In 1914 he set off once more, this time on the Imperial Trans-Antarctic Expedition, his goal being to cross the South Polar continent from the Weddell Sea to the Ross Sea—the greatest Polar journey on record, 1,700 miles in all, with 800 of those miles over unexplored land. A small, fragile boat at the National Maritime Museum in Greenwich is a permanent record of this ill-fated expedition. It is the *James Caird*, named after the Scottish jute manufacturer who partly financed the venture; in it Shackleton and five companions crossed 800 miles of ocean to fetch help for the rest of the party, stranded on Elephant Island when the expedition had had to abandon ship. After Shackleton's death in 1922 the *James Caird* was presented to Dulwich College by an Old Alleynian, Dr J. Q. Rowett, a philanthropist and man of many parts who had put up the £70,000 needed for Shackleton's last expedition, the voyage of discovery of the *Quest*. Originally the *James Caird* had a purpose-built enclosure between the old science and bath blocks, but this was destroyed during the Second World War; and many years later, when Charles Lloyd was Master, he found it lying forlorn and derelict, a repository for old toffee-papers, in the college grounds, with the sledges, mast, and oars split beyond restoration. He offered it on permanent loan to the Maritime Museum, and there, restored by the museum staff, it rests today on a bed of stones and shingle specially collected in 1973 by members of the British Antarctic Survey. The stones came from South Georgia, where the *James Caird* made her first landing; there, too, Shackleton was buried when he died from angina pectoris on his final expedition.

Shackleton was built in such a heroic mould that I hope I may be forgiven for ending this brief account with a very human comment by P. G. Wodehouse. 'Under certain conditions,' Wodehouse wrote while he was a German prisoner-of-war in the 1940s, 'the mind is bound to dwell on food. Shackleton once told me that when he was in the Polar seas, he used to dream every night that he was running about a field chasing those three-cornered jam tarts which were such a feature of life at our mutual school. And if that was how Shackleton felt, I am not ashamed of having felt that way myself.'

Wodehouse himself (later to become Sir Pelham, but known to his friends as Plum) was at the school from 1894 to 1900, and remained devoted to it until the day of his death. His life there was full and many-sided. In his last year he edited the *Alleynian*, contributing many verses and articles, as well as a famous column, headed *Contemporaries*, in which he aired his views on the magazines of other schools. He played in the 1st XV and the 1st XI, though the *Alleynian* had some disparaging comments to make about his cricket: 'Bowled well against Tonbridge, but did nothing else. Does not use his head at all. A poor bat and very slack field.'

His schoolwork seems to have been hardly more distinguished, if his report for the summer term of 1899 is anything to go by. He was third from the bottom in a class of twenty-five, and the comments on his work vary from 'Bad' (for 'Critical Paper') to 'Not very strong' (for English essay). 'He is a most impractical boy,' the report went on:

> Continually he does badly in examinations from lack of the proper books; he is often forgetful; he finds difficulties in the most simple things and asks absurd questions, whereas he can understand the more difficult things.
>
> He has the most distorted ideas about wit and humour; he draws over his books and examination papers in the most distressing way and writes foolish rhymes in other people's books. Notwithstanding, he has a genuine interest in literature and can often talk with much enthusiasm and good sense about it. He does some things at times astonishingly well, and writes good Latin verses.
>
> He is a very useful boy in the school and in the VI Form, and one is obliged to like him in spite of his vagaries ... If he perseveres he will certainly succeed.

Paradoxically enough, it was not until after Wodehouse had left Dulwich that his closest association with the school seemed to start. (Not that he would at that time have used the word 'school'. In his first novel, *The Pothunters*, his hero gives 'a convulsive shudder' when a detective, come to investigate the disappearance of the school cups, refers to 'St Austin's School'. 'The most deadly error mortal man can make,' the hero tells him chillingly, 'with the exception of calling a school a college, is to call a college a school.') In his early novels there are endless oblique references to Dulwich, and the life which he describes there is bathed in a perpetual rosy, nostalgic glow. 'Six years of unbroken bliss,' is how he paints his schooldays.

Until the mid-thirties he came down regularly for matches, running at top speed (though by this time he was a pretty portly gentleman) along the touchline and behind the goal-posts, clad in grey plus-fours, grey overcoat, and grey felt cap. Or he would go off with the teams on tour, writing witty, perceptive, refreshingly literate reports for the *Alleynian*. Some of these were blue-pencilled, as being too exuberant, by one of the editors, who with the wisdom of hindsight offers, as 'the only possible plea in mitigation, the fact that Wodehouse was then just a popular comic writer'. 'Isn't it amazing that you and I, old buffers of 55,' P.G. wrote in 1936 to William Townend, a one-time fellow boarder at Elm Lawn and a close friend, 'with Civilization shortly about to crash, can worry about school football? It is really almost the only thing I do worry about.' And ten years later, 'I often wonder if you and I were unusually fortunate in our schooldays. To me the years between 1896 [sic] and 1900 seem like Heaven. Was the average man really unhappy at school? Or was Dulwich in our time an exceptionally good school?' By now he was living in America, but he would think nothing of coming back to England to see a rugger match at Dulwich.

Later there was to be the grief and alienation caused by the broadcasts which he gave as a prisoner-of-war, and which were so greatly misunderstood. Naïve he certainly was in giving them, as he himself subsequently realized, but a traitor he was not. At Dulwich most people regarded the broadcasts as just a bit of characteristic Wodehouse: no one seriously thought they 'gave encouragement to the enemy', and there is no truth in the rumour later spread about that he was struck off some unspecified roll of honour.

To the day of his death he kept his affection for his old school. Writing to a friend in 1945 he said, 'I believe a boy has a much better time at Dulwich than anywhere else. I don't know why it is, but we seem to turn out such an awfully nice type.' One visitor in 1972 to his Long Island home wrote that 'The old man talked of nothing but his days at Dulwich.' He zealously read the *Alleynian* ('They have ruined it,' he commented, 'with all this art photography and bad poetry'), and took a lively interest in match results. 'If I do come to

England,' he wrote not long before his death, 'the only place I really want to see is Dulwich.'

When he died Lady Wodehouse gave to the college his desk, typewriter, books, photos, and similar mementoes. In a corner of the boys' library these articles are displayed, a replica in miniature of his study, as a memorial to one of Dulwich's most loyal, famous and above all deeply human and lovable sons.

At this point a short digression is necessary to bring into the story Treadgold *père* and *fils*, whose combined connection with Dulwich must come near to breaking all records, for it spans seventy-eight years. T. G. Treadgold joined the staff in 1876, remaining on it for fifty-two years. For exactly half this time he was housemaster of Elm Lawn, which he occupied with thirty or so boys, six children of his own, and a full staff. He was extremely angry when Gilkes, who retired in 1914, refused to recommend him for the mastership: he was then getting on for sixty-five (he died at the age of ninety-six). Wodehouse boarded at Elm Lawn, and in after years Mrs Treadgold used to say how annoyed she was to think that he had sat at her table day after day without opening his mouth or giving any hint of wit or eloquence.

However, she had her own moment of glory in a charming incident which Gilkes relates in his diary. In the summer of 1887 the Crown Prince of Germany and his wife, who was the oldest daughter of Queen Victoria, visited the school unannounced. 'I was told that a company in which it was suspected was the Crown Prince and Princess were in the hall,' Gilkes wrote. He went to round up some boys to provide a suitable welcome, and when he returned to the hall 'found some of them talking to the Crown Princess, under the impression that she was Mrs Treadgold ... The Crown Princess told me that she was anxious to come to see Dulwich College, because her father had been the first Chairman of the Governors of it,[1] and when it was being built she had been

---

[1] This was, of course, a mistake on the princess's part, for the Prince Consort had declined the offer.

accustomed to come with him to see the building, and run about on the scaffolding, when she was a girl.'

In 1922 T.G.'s son, G. W. R. Treadgold, who had been a boy at the school, came back on the staff, by all accounts one of the sternest disciplinarians Dulwich has ever known, for he firmly believed that children are miserable in a disorderly class. 'They're immensely conservative,' he said to me with a wintery smile. 'They'd rather be told the same story ten times over than a new one. And they hate their teacher to be wrong—they got very angry with me if I worked out a sum incorrectly.' He couldn't abide stupid boys, and some of the less able used to find his strictness difficult to take. 'I don't know how he did it,' one colleague remarks. 'He never raised his voice, and he never had any disciplinary trouble. Geoffrey fixed them with his snakelike eye, and that was *it* . . .' His weekly 'tea-parties' were famous: you would see a dispirited line of boys making its way across the cloisters for an undiluted hour of Latin verbs. But he was an excellent teacher because no one would dare not to listen intently—even today Old Alleynians, faced with some particularly appalling crisis, will say to one another, 'You've got to be a Tready Jnr trained chap to cope with that!' Many of his pupils remember him with affection, not least, perhaps, because he brought them on so fast, which sometimes got him into hot water with the powers that be; and sometimes boys actually asked for a course of Tready, as a kind of discipline, like cold baths or jogging. For many years he and his father played flute and oboe in the school orchestra, Treadgold Snr's performance being of the hit and miss variety.

Another of the considerable number of writers whom Dulwich has produced was Raymond Chandler. He took little part in school life, but even as a boy of fifteen he developed one habit which must have been of priceless value later on, noting down in a little book anything he heard which seemed to him of interest, and then transferring it to a card index. Dennis Wheatley was briefly a pupil before being expelled (as he was from many other schools). He loathed his two-and-a-half-term sojourn—'God, how I hated that rotten school!' he writes in his autobiography (the copy in the library falls open at this page, well thumbed by successive generations of Alleynians). However, he has the grace to admit that any other public school would probably have been no less depressing. He obviously disliked Gilkes as much as he did the school, describing him as tall, grim and unapproachable, 'a living symbol in our minds of harshness and punishment', whose one idea was to force the senior classical boys to win scholarships, thereby bringing kudos to the college.

Other Alleynians of Gilkes' day who afterwards won fame in a wide variety of occupations include Sir Arthur Hirtzel, one of the most brilliant pupils of his era, later to be Permanent Secretary of State for India, and the first Old Alleynian to be elected Chairman of the Governors of his old school; Sir Cecil Wakeley, who was to become President of the Royal College of Surgeons; Sir Edward Harding, Permanent Under-Secretary of State for the Dominions and High Commissioner in South Africa; G. F. Stainforth, the first man to fly at over 400 miles an hour, thereby both confounding scientific prophecy (for no one had expected him to reach such a speed) and making an important contribution to technical progress; the versatile Arthur Wimperis, who started the 'Follies' with H. G. Pelissier and worked closely with Alexander Korda on many famous films; Maung Tin Tut, the first Burmese to enter the Indian Civil Service and the first High Commissioner for Burma in London; the Rt. Rev. R. H. Owen, successively headmaster of Uppingham, Bishop of Wellington and Archbishop of New Zealand; Kenneth Carpmael, listed in Ormiston's *Register* as one of twenty-three Carpmaels who attended the school, a well known K.C. who did much sterling work for the Dulwich College picture gallery and for the restoration of the Middle Temple after the Second World War; G. Wilson Knight, the Shakespearean scholar; and Professor C. D. Broad, philosopher and Fellow of Trinity College, Cambridge, who was a great benefactor of the school, his legacy making possible the establishment of scholarships for all-round character and academic ability.

The most brilliant trio of all, however, were academics, and men of a strongly individual genius. The first was G. E. Moore, who was at Dulwich from 1882–92. One of the greatest philosophers of his era, his thinking influenced, among others, Bertrand Russell, G. Lowes Dickinson, Keynes, and Lytton Strachey; his papers, sold in 1979 for £52,800, are a valuable source for historians and philosophers. It is reputed that though he was mild-mannered even Russell and Keynes were frightened of him. His older brother, Thomas Sturge Moore, who preceded him at Dulwich by three years, was one of the finest poets and artists of his generation, and a friend of Yeats.

Then there was Sir John Sheppard, classical scholar and lecturer, whom Sir Roy Harrod described as 'a young man of cherubic countenance'. He was the first non-Etonian to become Provost of King's, and the first Old Alleynian to be head of an Oxbridge college. For many years he produced the triennial Greek plays at Cambridge, and students flocked to his open lectures on Greek and English poetry.

The third was Alic H. Smith, later to be Warden of New College and the first Old Alleynian to hold the position of Vice-Chancellor at either Oxford or Cambridge. In a collection of essays published in 1963 he wrote in exquisitely stylish English in praise of some of the masters at Dulwich who had influenced him and nurtured in him a love of the classics.

At an Alleyn Club dinner in 1950 he pinpointed what has always seemed, to its most perceptive sons, the fundamental strength and most enduring characteristic of the school: 'As I think of it in my time the distinctive feature . . . was the great variety of the boys who were there, their differences of character, and their differences of upbringing, and somehow it seemed to be almost a kind of microcosm of England.' At the dinner in the following year Christopher Gilkes took up this theme in a fascinating survey of the changing 'clientele' of the school over the years. The golden age of Dulwich, he said, had lasted up to 1914:

> The backbone of Dulwich in that period was all those large families who inhabited the big houses which run up College Road to the top of Sydenham Hill. Those large houses provided large Victorian families all of whom had a number of sons, and all those sons came to the College . . . When I was a boy at school,

practically everyone in the School came from the neighbourhood of the College, with a few train boys, upon whom we rather looked down.

These families sent their sons to the college in droves: you have only to look at Ormiston's *Register* to see the numbers of siblings and cousins and uncles and fathers who went there, with perhaps as many as ten brothers from one family. But it was not only the traditionally middle-class families who found that it offered the kind of education they were seeking: fathers who had recently made their money in humbler spheres of life were equally attracted. The point is well made by one man who was there from 1902–8:

> I remember when I first went to the college that there were traces of a snobbish prejudice against people who were 'in trade': it was silly and quite unreasonable, because our prosperity depended on our world-wide trade. I don't think we boys ever took this view at all—on the contrary, I think we found it rather intriguing to be rubbing shoulders with sons of well-known manufacturers such as Epps (cocoa), Johnston ('Bovril'), and above all Brock (fireworks).

It is no exaggeration to say that Dulwich village developed as it did almost entirely as a result of the reputation of the college, a fact that the Board of Education stressed when a new scheme was discussed in 1913 which would make better provision for the allocation of the undistributed income of the estate. 'It is the case,' a Board minute commented, 'that the majority of the people who live on the College estate do so or did so originally simply to give their sons the educational advantages provided by the College.' (Among them were G. E. Moore's parents, who moved from Hastings to Norwood because they had heard such good reports of the school under Carver's mastership.) Stressing that it was both a great public school and a local school, the minutes pointed out that the prosperity of the college and of the estate were interdependent, in that the attractiveness of the former affected the prosperity of the latter, on which depended the prosperity of the Foundation as a whole.

However high the reputation of the school at this time,[1] prosperous it was not (in 1914 the total credit balance was £10). The number of day-boys, though not of boarders, had fallen; and the Governors had allowed to slip through their fingers one way of increasing the income which had been urged by Gilkes—the purchase of the preparatory school by the college when the headmaster died in 1909. This would, he felt, have put the finances on a sound basis, 'besides doing away with a kind of competition between the preparatory school and the College which is disagreeable'. This competition behind the scenes was not, however, apparent to outsiders or to the boys, many of whom came on to the college from the preparatory school. One of these pupils comments today that the latter 'through many years educated children in the widest context, and was conceived and directed as an enlightened preparation for the college and its ideals.'

Matters came to a head when another Board of Education inspection was made in 1914. Six years earlier, when the first one had taken place, Gilkes had already been doubtful of the wisdom of staying on as Master. He wrote to the Governors in 1909:

> At my age and in my condition, I ought to retire in a year's time . . . I have never known of anyone who stayed for more than 25 years in such a position as mine without harming the school, and I cannot persuade myself that I am different from other people in such a matter. I have written this because if the Governors asked me to stay on I should do so, and I should like them to know exactly what I feel. Of all things I should dislike that the school should suffer any harm in the slightest degree from me.

---

[1] Though there was no personality clash between Rogers and Gilkes, as there had been in the case of Carver, Gilkes had had his own difficulties in persuading his Chairman of the need to establish Dulwich as a school which gave a first-rate education. William Rogers handed in his resignation in 1895, shortly before his death, saying to Gilkes, 'You wish to make Dulwich a public school, and I have no wish to enter into conflict with you; and therefore I shall resign my office.' 'He was a man,' Gilkes noted in his diary, 'who in his relations with the College earnestly desired to do it good, and was without stint in his exertions for it. But it is the case that he took too low a view of its mission and its position.'

His diary entry runs, 'I did not resign because I was tired of my work but because I felt sure that a younger man should take it up. The School has assumed the shape and position which when I came I desired it should assume. I expect that I shall be, as I am, always disinclined to make any changes in its condition; and thus I think it is good for me to go. But I stay willingly for a few years longer.'

All thirty-eight masters signed a petition expressing the hope that he would remain Master for many years to come, and presented it to the Governors. As for the latter, they seem to have been chiefly concerned by the fear that, whenever Gilkes did go, 'there is sure to be an exodus of his older assistant masters. In our present financial condition it will be difficult to deal with them.' So they asked him to continue, and for a few more years he did so, though by now he was not at all well, and in 1912 underwent a serious operation which kept him away from the school for most of the summer term.

The 1914 inspection was extremely critical of many aspects of the school, commenting that the sums allocated to scholarships and exhibitions had always been too low, as were the funds available for the masters' salaries and equipment. Once again the inspectors criticized the ratio of staff to boys (1 to 21 or 22). They went on:

> Broadly speaking the School shows little traces of the improvements in methods of teaching which have come or are coming about in the country generally. This shows itself specially in the Junior School, in most of the work in English and much of that in Modern Languages, and in nearly all but the highest work in Mathematics ... English is largely a new subject in schools ... and there seems to be no one on the staff who has made a thorough study either of the proper content of the subject from the school point of view, or of the proper methods of dealing with it.

The report also commented unfavourably on the isolation in which the teachers worked, each having complete autonomy within his classroom—a particularly important point, since it was then customary for the form master to take his class in every subject that he was capable of teaching, which might mean English, history, geography, mathematics, religious instruction, and Latin. This system was much favoured by Gilkes, who regarded it as the best way of organizing a day school, with the form-master taking the place that a housemaster does in a boarding-school. Since the beginning of the century, however, there had been a growing movement in the direction of specialist teachers, largely because of the widening of the curriculum, the need for trained scientists for industry and the greater emphasis on 'modern' subjects. Though the earlier method enabled each form-master to get to know his class well, and perhaps integrate their studies in a way that was not possible with a different teacher for each subject, if he was inadequate the boys suffered, and doubly so if he enjoyed the great degree of autonomy of which the inspectors spoke.

'Boys are admitted with little or no regard to their previous education,' the report went on, which was true enough, for then as now Dulwich had its own entrance examination (though in 1980 Common Entrance was introduced as an alternative), which at the time consisted mainly of verbal questioning. Gilkes was in effect the arbiter of whether or not a boy should be accepted: if he thought you were the right kind of material for his school he took you; otherwise you hadn't a chance. The inspectors continued:

It is not contested that there may be good reasons for this, but it makes it unusually difficult to secure adequate diligence and it results in the presence of a large number of boys both in the Junior School and in the Lower Forms of the Modern and Engineering Sides whose preliminary education has been extremely poor . . .

The Inspectors have no doubt that there is a vigorous and healthy life in the School. The Master has a well-earned reputation for his strong personal influence over individual boys. In some directions the School is continuing to do thoroughly satisfactory work, and maintains its brilliant record of successes at the Universities. But . . . much improvement is needed, especially in the lower and middle parts of the School. Some reorganization and, still more, new ideas as to teaching, are required if full justice is to be done to the younger and less able boys.

After such a report it was inevitable that Gilkes should tender his resignation. When he had done so, but before it had been accepted, a meeting took place between the Governors and the Board of Education at which the standard of teaching

Fig. 3.4 The First Four Masters

Canon Carver.
1858 - 83.

Bishop Welldon
1883 - 85.

Mr. A. H. Gilkes.
1885 - 1914.

Mr. Geo. Smith.
1914.-

was criticized even more severely. The Chief Inspector praised the great and notable work which Gilkes had done; however, he went on, 'the Inspectors felt that the school requires drastic treatment. The Master had come thirty years ago from Shrewsbury with his mind made up on one point, that it would not do to interfere with a Master in the classroom. This still obtains in the School, and had a serious effect upon a young Master going to the School quite raw. The general result was a state of inefficiency in the matter of classroom teaching.'

Gilkes left at the end of the summer term of 1914. Perhaps he was relieved to lay down the burden of holding the balance between boys, parents, staff, and Governors (he would always have put the well-being of the boys first). Eighteen months later, at the age of sixty-five, he was ordained, and for a year he worked as a curate in a very poor parish in Bermondsey, before becoming vicar of St Mary Magdalene, Oxford. He died in 1922. His love for the school never weakened, and in an undated letter from Oxford he wrote, 'I dreamed last night that I was still at Dulwich, and I woke up sorrowful.'

And so ended the life of a remarkable, complex man, who for over a quarter of a century did such an infinite amount of good for the school that was his heartbeat.

So much has been written about him by colleagues and pupils that it is difficult to sum up in a paragraph or two his aims and achievements. Education, to Gilkes, was first and last a moral affair: his ambition for the school was that it should be a place where it was easier to do right than wrong, where work was generally valued and respected, where reverence for great things prevailed. He profoundly distrusted mere intellect, and regarded academic honours as worth very little if they were unaccompanied by strength of character, breadth of view, sympathy of disposition, and reverence for what is good. He wrote in 1907:

> Everyone who teaches properly must have always before him the knowledge that his object is to make his pupil into a real man, that is, to develop the qualities in him which are really manly. It is easy to say what these qualities are. They are health, truthful-

ness, self-restraint, kindness, patience, courage, judgment, quick-
ness and fulness of intellect, and the right attitude towards God.

In his diary, a few years earlier, he had written:

> The circumstances of each school have in them matters peculiar to
> each; and Dulwich probably has more of these than most others,
> since it is in the main a day school, and at the same time desires to be,
> in the fullest sense of the word, a public school: that is to say, it desires
> to bring to bear, upon all its members, every good influence that any
> school in the kingdom dispenses to those connected with it; to be
> governed by masters capable of spreading these influences, and to be
> filled with boys receiving them; and becoming, as fully as possible,
> good boys, loyal boys, boys doing their work well, associating freely
> one with the other out of school, subordinate to all proper authority,
> both of their masters and their own captains and prefects; co-
> operating earnestly in every way for the general good, and the
> renown of the school, and thus inheriting and maintaining good
> traditions, and becoming in every way that good product of English
> life, a body of good public schoolboys.

Sir John Sheppard remarked that in the classroom 'he said
simple things with grave sincerity and opened windows to our
soul. In all his teaching he seemed to be finding out, afresh for
himself as much as for us, the beauty and the interest of what
we were learning.' Though to his staff he must often have
seemed unappreciative, uncaring of what or how they taught,
taking a boy's word against that of a master, to the boys who
later in their lives understood what he was trying to achieve
he remained an unforgettable influence. 'We had for Master,'
one of them said, 'a man with a genius for friendship, and we
had him for a friend.'

4 From War to War

George Smith (1914–28)
W. R. Booth (1928–41)

'The fighting man shall from the sun
 Take warmth, and life from the glowing earth;
Speed with the light-foot winds to run,
 And with the trees to newer birth;
And find, when fighting shall be done,
 Great rest, and fullness after dearth.'
(*Julian Grenfell*, Into Battle)

THE two Masters who successively followed Gilkes spanned a little over a quarter of a century; and, since these years are marked by few major changes in the school, it is perhaps best to consider this period as a continuous whole.

George Smith came to Dulwich in 1914 from the head-mastership of Merchiston Castle School, Edinburgh. He was a fine classical scholar, a superb English stylist who communicated to the boys his own love of languages, opening the doors to new worlds of literature and writing. Spare, bespectacled, with a pawky Scottish humour lurking behind a somewhat dour appearance, he terrified many a small boy simply by the frostiness of his demeanour; and certainly he could be severe, for he was a firm believer in discipline. But besides being a man of high principles, with a strong sense of duty, he was possessed of much tact and kindness, which won him the respect and often the affection of masters and boys alike.

Eric Handscomb, who was a pupil at Dulwich from 1912–19, returning in 1927 to join the teaching staff, regards him as the ideal headmaster. 'I only once remember him giving me any advice, and it was, "Don't let teaching interfere with your work", by which I understood him to mean that a good schoolmaster is not to be judged by the amount of information he can force into boys' heads, or by examination results, and that there is far more to life than the mere accumulation of knowledge.'

Smith was as short as Gilkes had been tall, which caused him to remark some years later, 'When I came to Dulwich College there was only one reform which I found to be urgently needed, and that was that all the official chairs on which the Head Master sat had to be cut down three inches. I did not think it was consistent with the dignity of the Master that he should have to climb into a chair or sit with his legs dangling.'

He stayed for fourteen years, rejoicing throughout in the inappropriate name of Gunboat, after an American boxer and one-time sailor who had fought at the Albert Hall at the time of his appointment, and who was the possessor of exceptionally large feet. In 1928 he left Dulwich to become Director of the Department for the Training of Teachers at Oxford, dying at the age of eighty-nine. By some strange oversight the obituary notice in *The Times*, beyond the bare statement that he had been Master of the college from 1914–28, contained not a single word of all the services he had rendered it. But a charming obituary in the *Alleynian* helps to redress the balance: 'It was part of his modesty to be accessible; it was part of his wit always to have attentively two notebooks for masters' suggestions, one to remember and one to forget—none of us knew which was which, but we became respectfully convinced.'

Walter Reynolds Booth, who followed him in 1928 and remained until 1941, came from the headmastership of Wolverhampton Grammar School. Booth was a scientist. This was the first time the college had not had a classicist as Master, and some of his staff felt that the innovation was rather *infra dig*. His tenure was to be overshadowed by the depression, and later by the Second World War, but in the early days he tackled his job with all the missionary enthusiasm which every headmaster brings to a new appointment.

Booth was a striking figure, tall and well dressed, a likeable man who was interested in the staff and their families. He had a free, open manner, a large streak of Yorkshire hospitality, and a good deal of wit as an after-dinner speaker. His passion was riding, and he used to trot his horse round the playing fields (sometimes, it must be said, when he should have been teaching), the boys watching enthralled when a low branch knocked off his bowler. But as the years passed he showed an increasing reluctance to take decisions or to enter into the general organization of the school, which, after Smith's conscientious, military precision, was a change that many people found extremely disconcerting. More and more he was carried by the heads of sides, by other members of the staff and by the prefects, for he had a considerable gift for appointing good men, and the sense to let them get on with running the school.

When George Smith became Master in 1914, a particularly unflattering photograph accompanied some of the press announcements about the new post. In after years he enjoyed relating that next morning he had received a letter— 'Obviously,' he commented, 'from an old lady. She did not say much, but she enclosed a portrait of me which had appeared in the evening papers. She wrote underneath it: "Look at this face. What a cruel, cruel face! God pity the poor boys!"'

His correspondent would have been surprised to know how happily the school settled down under the wise guidance of its new Master, though for much of his time he was working under the great difficulties of war and its aftermath. At first life was little affected by the hostilities, for only one bombing attack took place in school hours, when fifteen German planes appeared over London, much to the excitement of the boys.

But as the years wore on the Zeppelin raids at night increased, which was bad for homework.

To conform with the requirements of the War Office the senior boys had to have at least ten hours' military training a week, including instruction in drill, signalling, operating field telephones, and bayonet fighting, as well as lectures on chemistry and explosives. (At Oundle, where Sanderson, once such a successful science teacher, was proving an equally brilliant and creative headmaster, the boys were busy making ammunition for the British army.) The time for this training had to be squeezed from lessons and games, and Smith commented that for these boys leisure had practically ceased to exist. Almost every boy over fourteen belonged to the Officers' Training Corps, and later in the war a Captain Johnson (quickly nicknamed Bum) was attached for the training of the special sections—that is, those nearing the age of call-up—though one boy on the receiving end remarked drily that what they learnt would have been more useful for fighting the Boer War than for the trenches in France.

Potatoes were grown on the school grounds, and during the holidays many of the boys worked on the land or felled timber for pit-props, barbed wire entanglements, and military camps. They worked in munition factories, made splints and other surgical appliances, volunteered for Red Cross and ambulance work or as hospital orderlies, and served in naval and military canteens. Money was raised by past and present Alleynians to buy an ambulance for Russia, then desperately in need of military equipment, and to support the public schools hospital in Rouen.

Smith's path was not made easy by a campaign in the press demanding the removal of two of his staff, J. A. and J. B. Joerg, who were of German origin. One was the head of the modern side and the other, paradoxically enough, took the army class, managing to push his not very bright boys through their examinations. His brother's delight was to prove that the English and German languages were indistinguishable. If a boy was translating he would stop him with the cry, 'Same vort, you poys!', and proceed to write the word on the blackboard, altering each letter to make the final result conform to his theory. With much searching of his conscience and considerable moral courage, Smith decided to keep the brothers on the staff, which cannot have been easy in the jingoist, white-feather atmosphere of the time.

As the war stretched on it began to affect the school more directly. Nut cutlets, tripe, and a particularly disgusting pie of swedes and potatoes appeared on the menu, and 'EAT LESS BREAD!' starkly urged one page of a 1917 issue of the *Alleynian*, the command inserted at the request of the Food Controller. There was a great sense of shock when three masters who had joined up were killed, all of them of a mild, unwarlike nature, dedicated teachers and scholars of great ability. Most mourned of them was A. N. C. Kittermaster, who was killed in action in 1916. He had run the Cadet Corps and worked at the Mission; he used to write songs which, set to popular tunes, the boys would sing on their marches; and a volume of his poetry was published as a memorial. The other two were F. L. Nightingale and G. W. Beachcroft.

Five of the boys who went from Dulwich were awarded V.C.s. The first of them, R. B. B. Jones, was only nineteen when he was killed. These boys were commissioned in the O.T.C., and, on the strength of a few hours' training on the school playing-fields or Epsom Downs, when they joined up were sent straight to France: it was calculated that their average expectation of life was twenty minutes in action. An unidentified, undated newpaper article vividly recalls the valour of some of these old Alleynians. There was C. H. Collet, one of the earliest air heroes of the war, who in September 1914 dropped three bombs from 400 feet on the Zeppelin shed at Düsseldorf, a feat then deemed impossible (he was also the first naval officer to loop the loop); Captain F. W. Townend, R.E., who, with both legs blown off by a bomb, said to his dressers that he thought he would 'give up football next year'; Major Stewart Loudon-Shand, propped up mortally wounded in the trench, cheering on his men until he fell dead; Major Alexander Lafone, who with two troops of a squadron held up a brigade of Turkish cavalry for seven hours, and when all his men were killed or wounded stepped into the open and continued the fight until he too was mortally wounded;[1] and Wing Commander Brock, one of the most famous sons of Dulwich, who earned his country's gratitude by his invention of the smoke-screen at Zeebrugge in 1918.

Of the two other V.C.s one, C. H. Sewell, was killed at the age of twenty-three in the second battle of the Somme, after repeatedly exposing himself to extreme danger to save the lives of his comrades. The fifth, and the only one to survive, was Gordon Campbell, one of eight brothers, all of whom had their schooling at Dulwich. Starting as Lt. Comdr. R.N. and ending as Captain R.N. with V.C. and three D.S.O.s, for nearly two years (twice as long as any of the other captains involved) he served in Q boats, those mysterious craft which, disguised to look like anything but what they really were (one carried a large haystack amidships, artfully concealing a healthy number of cannon), scoured the ocean for enemy submarines. Of the eleven which were thus despatched to the bottom of the ocean, Campbell accounted for three, leaving the remaining 179 Q ships to dispose of the other eight. 'He had a genius,' wrote Admiral Sir Lewis Bayly, 'for foretelling whereabouts a submarine was likely to be found and what its further movements were likely to be.'

One Old Alleynian writes of the war years:

> As more and more boys left for the front, and the casualty lists of Old Alleynians mounted, the continuous disappearance of well-known faces never to be seen again created a general atmosphere of depression. The terrible numbers of those killed were reflected in *The Times* at the time of the Battle of the Somme; the paper printed page after page of casualties under the heading 'All second lieutenants unless otherwise mentioned'.

There was scarcely a family which did not lose a son, a brother or a father. Perhaps the greatest impact of all was made by the death of L. W. Franklin, who died of wounds in 1918 at the age of twenty (he bled to death because a tourniquet had not been properly applied). He had been an

---

[1] Major Loudon-Shand and Major Lafone were both posthumously awarded the V.C.

outstanding athlete, an unstoppable wing three-quarter who would have been a great international if he had lived. To the school he had been a hero.

But at last the war came to an end. 'The signing of the Armistice in November is, perhaps, the most memorable event connected with this term,' the house book kept by the Ivyholme boys records. 'The disastrous epidemic of influenza,' the note goes on, 'which swept over the world during the autumn did not leave the School untouched; all school had to be stopped for a week, over 400 boys being absent.' And in the following summer term, 'Founder's Day had an unusual interest this term, since very few of us had ever experienced it under peace conditions.'

Over three thousand Old Alleynians served in the war, and of that number more than five hundred lost their lives. Of the ten masters who went to the front, four did not return.

Despite the sadness and strain of the war, the abiding memory of most of the boys who were at the school during these years is nevertheless one of happiness. One of them writes:

> When the time came for me to leave Dulwich in 1919, I did not want to go. I loved every minute of it, especially the rugger, athletics, shooting. Dulwich had got into my bones. I remember my last lesson the last day, in the science block with Mr Bauer (Mr 'Rhubarb', as he was always telling us how good rhubarb was for us), and I looked at the clock and impressed the time on my mind; I said to myself, 'Remember this moment', and I remember it as if it were yesterday.

Certain changes had been made in the financial arrangements at the time of Smith's appointment, the Master's former responsibility for receiving a lump sum annually, out of which he paid the salaries of the assistant masters and the general expenses, being taken over by the Governors. He was also authorized to appoint a typist–secretary to cope with his correspondence—for until now, it is amazing to recall, on top of the administration and a considerable teaching load, the Master had written all his letters by hand.

Like many public schools, after the war Dulwich had to grapple with an extremely serious financial situation. Although the number of boys was high (in 1919 it rose to just under eight hundred, at that time a record), there had been no rebuilding for years, and the masters' salaries, always low, became still more inadequate with the sharp post-war rise in the cost of living, which meant that it was almost impossible for many of them to make ends meet.

Neither an improvement in their salaries nor rebuilding was feasible without additional funds. The Governors decided that they must raise the boarding fees (the day fees were then £28 10s per annum), and applied to the Board of Education, as they were obliged to do, for the necessary permission. The Board refused: if the school wished to increase its income, the Governors were told, the remedy was to place itself on the list of secondary schools recognized for a grant, the *quid pro quo* being the admission of a fixed percentage of boys from primary schools and additional L.C.C. representation on the Board of Governors. The Board of Education was extremely keen that schools like Dulwich should take part in the scheme, as an internal memorandum dating from 28 April 1919 makes clear:

> I think it is quite inevitable that sooner or later Dulwich College should come into the grant system if it is to maintain its high standard; and if the Governing Body try to struggle along on their income from fees and endowments both the teachers and the pupils are bound to suffer, on the one hand from inadequate salaries, and on the other from inferior buildings . . . It is I think a matter of public policy to keep the fees of first-rate secondary schools as low as possible; and it is also desirable on grounds of public policy that a large number of first-rate public schools should come within the grant system.

The new arrangement came into effect in August 1920: the college received an annual grant of £7,000, and undertook to accept a yearly intake of 10% (increased in 1922 to $12\frac{1}{2}\%$, with a corresponding increase in the grant) of scholars from elementary schools. The normal percentage was 25%, but Dulwich was permitted to take a lower number since the

Board of Education considered that a higher percentage would jeopardize its character. A few other schools, among them Manchester Grammar School, Bedford and King Edward VI School, Birmingham, were similarly exempted. Later the regulations were amended so that not all the scholars had necessarily to come from elementary schools.

The boys entered in two stages: the junior scholars, who were admitted at eleven, and the senior scholars, who came at thirteen.

1921 had ended with a deficit of £967. By the next year the accounts had gone into the black, but even so the masters had to wait before their salaries could be increased to a reasonable level. After 1921 they 'followed approximately' (as the Board minutes delicately phrased it) the Burnham scale, which came into effect that year, but they still received less than the rate paid in state schools.

By the end of the first year as a direct grant school there were 44 L.C.C. scholars. Three years later they comprised nearly a sixth of the total number (138 out of 881).

No great feat of the imagination is needed to understand what an ordeal it must have been, in those considerably more class-conscious days, for some of these boys to begin life at Dulwich. A number of them came from homes where there was great poverty; they had the wrong accents and the wrong clothes, and often their parents had much difficulty in finding money for extras, over and above the clothing grants. There was a good deal of bullying the first year, though not afterwards; and at least one of the masters used to ridicule them because of their accents. Probably they were on occasion subtly discriminated against in sports awards; and to the more snobbish of their fee-paying peers they were generically known as 'Brickies', a term then in vogue at the school to describe the lower orders.[1] But of course the ability of these scholarship boys to adjust to their new life depended to a large degree on temperament: many found no difficulty in doing so.

---

[1] According to M. Marples (*Public School Slang*, Constable, 1940) Dulwich had a small vocabulary of its own (poon = disapproval, scram = shut up, tolly = cane, yard = hat), some of which was still extant in the thirties, but the words are quite unfamiliar to anyone with whom I have discussed them.

One of them writes:

At first, the black coat and long trousers of the school uniform seemed a bit like fancy dress, and I remember feeling very sheepish running the gauntlet of the local lads on the way home. Founder's Day was always rather an ordeal for me until I was older, as parents were expected to attend in garden party clothes, with pretty daughters, if any, and meet and chat socially. I was horribly snobbish in a defensive way, and it was a year or two before I 'allowed' my parents to attend!

Coming to scholastic matters, I don't remember having to struggle much to keep in the running. Looking back, I realise that the Dulwich curriculum by modern standards was far too academic and too specialised, although successful in its limited purpose of preparing for university entrance and scholarships. Overall I believe that I acquired some attachment to the traditional public school virtues during my life there, and some sense of values and of standards of friendship in the upper forms. I am glad to have had the privilege of going to Dulwich, and am grateful to the system that made it possible.

With his flair for picking the right man for the right place, Smith put the junior scholars into a special form under F. W. King, known as Gilbert (the Filbert, of contemporary music-hall fame) because he was a very sharp dresser. 'I recall copying his purple silk socks,' one of his former pupils remarks. King had a genius for easing his boys into school life, and for understanding their difficulties, which were increased by the fact that, since at this time the normal entry for the fee-payers was thirteen, the junior scholars tended to come in as an easily distinguishable bunch. Moreover, they arrived with only the most elementary knowledge of algebra and geometry, and with none at all of Latin and French.

'I was the best and brightest in my previous school,' another of these boys says:

No one told me IB would *all* be best and brightest. But as we were gradually sorted out and progressed up the school, it seems to me that we pretty soon became accepted—and acceptable. The young master in our second year, Mr Earle, was excellent, painstaking and full of fun, and I think we were properly settled by the time we left him for the third form. But for some the financial struggle was too hard. One scholar boy fell by the wayside early in the first term. His mother was a widow (and after the first world war there were, of course, lots of widows about). His clothing and mien were pitiful. Cost of clothing was a very serious matter, and I think it showed in the poor quality L.C.C. boys wore early on. And for some of them there was no question of staying on into the sixth form, for they had to get out into the world as soon as possible, and start to make a contribution to the family income.

Throughout the twenties the financial position of the Estate steadily improved, and the college Governors grew restive under the curb on their authority imposed by the agreement with the L.C.C. But without a larger grant from the endowment they could not regain their independence, and an increase was impossible without the sanction of the Board of Education. So in 1925 they applied for the necessary amending scheme.

For two and a half years a fierce battle was fought, and once more petitions were launched and public meetings held. Those who opposed the free place system argued that it endangered the traditions and character of the college; and indirectly they were supported by the 1922 Geddes Committee on Public Expenditure, which had severely criticized the system whereby independent, comparatively well-endowed schools such as Dulwich were being subsidized by rates and taxes. Those who felt that the scheme was beneficial accused their opponents of snobbishness, and of giving preference to the sons of professional and army men and retired Indian Civil Servants rather than to deserving children from the poorer sections of the community. Eminent politicians leapt into the fray, including Hugh (later Lord) Dalton, M.P. for Peckham, and C. G. (later Lord) Ammon, M.P. for Camberwell North, and impassioned letters appeared in the press, one *Times* correspondent claiming that the free-place boys had been more successful than the fee-paying ones.

In the end a compromise was reached under a scheme that came into force in 1928, whereby the Governors entered into a 'gentleman's agreement' with the Board of Education; the college ceased to be bound by a definite commitment to accept a fixed percentage of L.C.C. scholars, but undertook to

educate about a hundred of them at any one time, and that
undertaking was honourably observed in the years to come.
When the agreement came into force one L.C.C. councillor
remarked that 'the Council recognised with gratitude that
Dulwich had done voluntarily what no other public school
had done'. All in all, it was an experiment that seemed to
work remarkably well: the vast majority of boys who came
under the scheme benefited to an immense degree, and have
nothing but good to say of the opportunities which their years
at Dulwich gave them.

It was in the early 1920s that the whole school had the
experience of being photographed by a panoramic camera.
'Intending purchasers will be glad to hear,' wrote the *Alleynian*,
'that the symmetrical arrangement of the group was assured
by the thoughtful action of the Head Porter, who, after being
photographed at one end of the group, hurried round the
back in time to be taken at the other end also.'

As finances improved it became possible to start on the
much-needed building programme. When Smith became
Master the school covered a considerably smaller area, of
course, than it does today. The Master still lived in the south
block—and very inconvenient these quarters were as a family
residence—while the north block was occupied by the junior
school and by some of the bachelor masters. Most of the
communal activities took place in the Great Hall, then
painted a deep red and inscribed in gold with the Roll of
Honour of distinctions which the boys had gained (sometimes
very minor honours indeed). Long tables and benches, used
for dinner, filled the hall, and in the spaces between them the
boys stood for morning assembly and prayers. These incum-
brances removed, the hall was used for prize-givings, concerts,
Founder's Day Speeches, boxing matches, and the Corps
Shout, the occasion when the Corps returned hospitality to all
the 'outsiders' who had helped it during the year.

The Great Hall was also used for the entrance examination.
The boys sat at the long oak tables, set out rather as if for a
peace conference; in front of each of them was a large sheet of

paper on which he was instructed to write his name and address. The 'exam' consisted of one of the masters coming round with such questions as, 'Have you done any Latin?' or, 'Do you know what a quadratic equation is?'

Many of the rooms were still heated by coke stoves and illuminated by gas lamps which a porter would light on winter afternoons, and the inkwells (a perennial source of bitter complaint in the correspondence columns of the *Alleynian*) were filled by means of a species of watering-can by a boy deputed for the purpose.

So in 1927, as part of the programme of rebuilding and expansion, George Smith and his family moved to Bell House, a beautiful eighteenth-century dwelling nearly opposite the picture gallery, and the whole of the north and south blocks was turned into classrooms, with space also for art, a prefects' room, and other badly-needed amenities. The changing-rooms and the armoury were rebuilt and the music-rooms re-equipped, while fives and squash courts and a new pavilion were provided out of the profits of the Commissariat. What it never, however, became possible to build was an adequate assembly hall, though for years it had been recognized that this was necessary. In Booth's first report to the Governors, in 1929, he remarked how ludicrous it was that the headmaster should not be able to address all the boys at one time, for by now the school had become too big for this to be possible. During Smith's mastership—partly as a result of the L.C.C. scheme—the numbers had continued to rise, reaching a peak of 945 in 1928 (though during the next few years they fell drastically). Booth envisaged a hall holding 1,400 to 1,500—what a priceless asset that would be today!—provided with music-rooms, storerooms, and small workshops which the boarders could use at the weekend. Unfortunately nothing came of this project.

Academically Dulwich was not passing through one of its best patches in this between-wars period. Smith had found no central educational structure when he took over, and there is no doubt that the school was extremely easy-going during his era and that of Booth. The classical side was as strong as ever: set against that of most other schools it was, commented one

Old Alleynian, rather like the Brigade of Guards compared with the Army Catering Corps; but the disadvantage was that it tended to attract the cleverer boys, with the less able going, in descending order of preference, to the modern side, the science side or, as a last desperate resort, the engineering side. (However, it was by no means exclusively the duds who landed up in this nether region, for the parents of some of the bright boys were daring and sensible enough to insist that their sons should join this despised department, often with excellent results.)

Dulwich, like most public schools, still followed two practices which were soon to be swept into oblivion: termly removes (though by the early thirties this was changing to moves twice rather than three times a year), and the continuing custom whereby each form-master taught his form for a large number of subjects. In the early twenties, thirty of the forty-four masters were teaching English, twenty history, nineteen French, and twenty-five mathematics, and ten years later the situation was much the same. Obviously, only a small number of them could hope to be experts in all these subjects. (Even in the early fifties the form-master might be expected to take about four subjects in the lower school—that is, about half a time-table.) Nor was the matter helped by early division into sides with little movement between them; though mathematics was taught in sets, and under Booth a move in this direction began to be made in languages, Dulwich lagged behind in this respect, for in other schools the system had been either abandoned or greatly modified.

In 1934 the school was inspected by the Ministry of Education, and the report which followed not only pointed out these facts but criticized other aspects: the low ratio of staff to boys; the lack of time for private study; and the poor showing in public examinations (of all the boys who had left in the previous summer, for instance, only just over half had sat for the School Certificate). 'Satisfactory work is being done here and there in most subjects,' the Inspectors commented, 'but too often the performance in a given subject is not consistently good through the whole course of it . . . The whole organization, viewed as a working machine, is in need

of an overhaul.' They were unhappy, too, about one continuing weakness, the lack of scholarships; and in his comments on
their report Booth, who thoroughly agreed with them,
brought the facts starkly to light by comparison with two
other London public schools. St Paul's, he pointed out, then
had a total of 153 scholarships and Merchant Taylors' 83;
while Dulwich had only 30, worth about half the value. At his
urging it was decided, from 1935, to award twelve new
scholarships for day-boys and four for boarders.

One forward-looking innovation during Booth's reign was
the appointment of a careers master, then a fairly rare bird in
public schools. Visits were arranged to organizations and
firms likely to catch the boys' interest—the navy, army and
air force, *The Times* printing office, Peek Frean's biscuit
factory, Charing Cross hospital, and the laboratories of J.
Lyons—and visiting lecturers spoke on their particular fields
of work: they included one of the founders of Welwyn Garden
City, then a revolutionary concept of housing and community
life.

The careers master was H. E. Rubie, and an odd if highly
original offshoot of his work at Dulwich was a careers
laboratory, claimed as the first to be established at a public
school. Before starting it he took a course with the National
Institute of Industrial Psychology, and from this he developed
his own system of assessing the boys' aptitudes. This venture
caught—as well it might—the riveted attention of the press,
which excelled itself in describing what the boys called the
'black magic' room where experiments were carried out to
gauge their talents. 'The apparatus is simple but ingenious,'
one newspaper report ran:

> Boys are given lamp-holders, spring clothes pegs, cycle wheels and
> door locks in pieces which they have to put together. A steadiness-
> of-hand test is applied to boys wishing to become doctors and
> dentists. They have to pour water from one bottle to another
> without spilling a drop, and they have to put long steel stilettos
> through holes of varying sizes in a steelplate. A perseverance test
> is made with balls and hoops . . .

It is all amazingly reminiscent of Heath Robinson or
Emmett, and one suspects that these earnestly unscientific

experiments cannot have had much staying power. Certainly an expression of complete blankness comes over the faces of any masters or Old Alleynians of the period when they are asked about it nowadays. Rubie himself, however, apart from a wartime interlude, remained for many years as careers master, one of the most highly regarded in the country. Idiosyncratic to the last, his favourite punishment was to make transgressing boys lean out of the sash-windows, which he would then shut, giving, from outside the building, the effect of a bizarre frieze of imprisoned heads.

Music remained as strong as ever during this quarter of a century.[1] *The Times* wrote in 1926, 'It appears to be a tradition of the school that Alleynians should hide their light under a bushel, or it would certainly have been more generally known that they too, have demonstrated with Eton, Winchester, and Oundle that the bigger things of music are well within the grasp of schoolboys.' The flourishing state of the music owed much to A. W. P. Gayford, who came to the school in 1915 to teach the newly-created middle form. ('A kind of limbo,' a colleague wrote later in the *Alleynian*, 'into which were cast, together with Arthur Gayford, a clutch of youths who had reached the age of sixteen years or so without succeeding, on their scholastic merits, in passing out of the Junior School.') In 1924 he took over from Doulton as director of music, and also became head of English and history. He was a delightful and amazingly versatile man, one of the earliest broadcasters to schools—who, however, according to one of his pupils, ran the history department in a somewhat eccentric fashion, teaching mainly in free periods, and tending to give his class a book to read while he himself marked School Certificate papers from various quarters of the globe. He soon had a choir of about 160 boys, an orchestra of sixty, and a sizeable brass band; and the concerts which were

---

[1] On one occasion, however, an opportunity was missed. In 1917 application was made for the use of the Great Hall for a concert 'for the benefit of Solomon, the boy pianist'. The Governors returned a firm no. Solomon, then fifteen, had made his first public appearance in the Queen's Hall seven years earlier, and he had already given many concerts in London, so perhaps a point might have been stretched.

given in the summer term and at Christmas covered a wide spectrum of music, old and new. His excellent and enthusiastic work was reinforced by that of Sir Jack Westrup (as he later became), one of the finest music scholars of his day. Westrup, himself an Old Alleynian, taught classics at the school from 1928–34, later becoming Professor of Music at Oxford. As a Governor of the college for many years, he contributed a great deal to its well-being.

Gayford and Westrup were also responsible for a lively revival of drama. The first full-length play to be staged under their aegis was *Macbeth*, which Westrup produced in 1933 (a recent Attorney General, the Right Honourable Sam Silkin, playing the part of Second Witch), followed next year by *Twelfth Night*, with some of the music composed by Westrup himself. In 1939 Gayford produced *The Knight of the Burning Pestle*, but then the Second World War temporarily put an end to drama.

Gayford, for obvious reasons, was known as 'Guts'. Nicknames have gone out of fashion nowadays, at any rate in the higher forms, and boys tend to refer to the masters by their first names or an abbreviated version thereof ('If you talk about Dave or Pete, everyone knows who you mean'); but in those days few masters escaped one, sometimes self-evident, in other cases so obscure that the subject never quite understood why he had been so dubbed—Eric Handscomb, for instance, to this day hasn't the slightest idea why he was called Pip. 'Tew' Robinson was self-explanatory, for he used to say 'One—tew—three' (and was mercilessly ragged for it by generations of boys). His room sported an enormous globe, and new boys were instructed to ask him how he had got it through the door, which satisfactorily occupied the whole of the first period. The head of the engineering side, F. W. Russell, unkindly known as 'Spongy', was large and fat, and he used to pant up from the station, very late, hot, and steaming. He taught maths and was a senior wrangler, but most of the time hardly anyone had the vestige of an idea what he was talking about. His classroom contained at least three blackboards, and he would tear in, seize a piece of chalk, and dash off incomprehensible formulae in rapid

Fig. 4.1 The College, 1934

succession on all three, which he then swiftly wiped off before
anyone had time to copy them down. 'But he was a first-rate
teacher for those who could follow him,' one of his pupils says,
'and he certainly had the gift of making them see that maths
and its application to mechanics and physics is fascinating
and exciting.'

F. F. Edwards, dark and sinister in appearance but kind in
heart, was known as 'the Anarchist' because of his long
drooping moustachios, long black hair and stealthy, sliding
manner of walking. His most noted punishment was to say,
'Any more of this noise, and I shall scratch the blackboard'—
which he then proceeded to do, with hideous effect. F. J. Ellis
was called 'Bricky' because he wore a flat cap of the kind
which, it was supposed, workmen—and especially
bricklayers—would favour. His other clothes were equally
bizarre, and generally dishevelled as well, and the tale went

round that one parent, having asked him the way to the Master's study, tipped him sixpence. He was little regarded by many of the boys, but others remember him as the kindest of souls if one was in trouble; and after his death it was found that all his spare time had been devoted to dedicated, unselfish work at the Mission. He was often to be seen walking along with ten or twelve Mission boys, armed with boxes filled with hard-boiled eggs and other fortifiers, whom he was taking out on some excursion. Then there was Gilbert Stretton, a master of an earlier era, charmingly portrayed by Alic Smith, that brilliant scholar and Old Alleynian:

> He was slight and neat, with sandy hair and a waxed moustache. His dress suggested a Victorian dandy, but it had a certain careful negligence and his straw boater was worn with a modest tilt. His talk, like his dress, was precise, neat and slightly elaborated; and it was from him that I first had an inkling that words whether they were Greek or Latin or English could be attractive playthings. We read a good deal of Virgil in his form, and it is odd that now and again a passage of Virgil seems to be tinged with faint Victorian associations.

He bequeathed £15,000 to the college to be used for scholarships.

'Teddy' Hose, who spent most of his life at Dulwich as boy and master, used to be rather annoyed by his nickname, since his initials were H.F. Form-master of the classical remove for all his teaching years, and greatly revered, by 1933 he had taken the same form for one hundred terms. He was, one of his pupils comments, 'one of three great classics teachers in England, widening the minds of the boys he taught'. He was known publicly to scorn the works of Wodehouse as a disgrace to his teaching (of English!).

But it is perhaps invidious to pick out a few of these men, when the long procession over the years contained so many excellent, inspiring teachers. Most of them are remembered by their ex-pupils with affection, respect, gratitude and sometimes amusement—not as paragons, but as human beings with defects like the rest of us, as dedicated men who never seemed to lose their enthusiasm for teaching.

A number of them, then as now, came back as teachers to the school where they had spent their own schooldays. Eric Handscomb comments:

> This may have had its disadvantages, but though there were one or two who regarded any change as a change for the worse, on the whole it was a good thing to have some who knew 'the other side of the game', understood references made by the boys among themselves, and knew the places where they got together for mischief or to have a quiet smoke. On the whole the curriculum can benefit from the experience of old boys who are adaptable enough to accept change and see where there is something lacking.

C. G. Coulton, writing of the same phenomenon in his own school, remarked that though some of these homing masters 'had very little idea of what was done or might be done in other schools, but had passed by sheer weight of seniority into the lucrative house masterships, and remained little more than grown-up schoolboys to the end, they often possessed the one thing which might be most lacking in their busy and self-righteous colleagues; they had instinctive sympathy with boyhood.'

The masters who came to the school after 1918 brought a new spirit of liberation, with their wider experience of life, for many of them had served in the trenches—Eric Parsley, Charles Marriott, R. G. Evans, Geoffrey Earle, Hugh Morris, and others. It was they who took over the games; and instead of the three-piece suits in sombre hues affected by the older masters they tended to branch out into sports jackets and grey flannels, with even, now and then, a gorgeous waistcoat. But if the masters were allowed a certain licence in their clothes, this was not extended to the boys, and George Smith had his own, very effective, method of dealing with breaches of the rules regarding school uniform. At one point there was a fashion for violently coloured pullovers, which he quelled with the words, 'I have recently noticed an undue outbreak of sartorial efflorescence'. At the time when 'Oxford bags' were popular he remarked drily to one boy, 'Well, Talbot, what colour do your call your trousers? Would you say they are crushed strawberry?' On another occasion he was more directly

dismissive: 'I will not tolerate trousers tending to the volu-
minous and the oriental,' he said with finality.

The pupils these men taught included Hartley (later Lord)
Shawcross, who was to reach such eminence in the law and to
be Chief Prosecutor for the United Kingdom at the
Nuremberg trials after the Second World War (he was not
popular at school, one of his contemporaries remarks, 'because he was always so frightfully good at everything');
Melford Stevenson, later to be Mr Justice, 'just a nice
ordinary chap, but notable on account of his large head'; and
the six Brock brothers of the famous pyrotechnics firm, which
was closely linked with the fireworks displays held at the
Crystal Palace until it was burnt down in 1936. 'An entranc-
ing sight as it flamed away,' one boy comments. 'We didn't do
any work at all that day but just sat and watched.' In 1918 an
Old Alleynian became the college's second Lord Mayor,[1]
Lord Marshall of Chipstead, the first old Alleynian to be
created a peer. It was at his inaugural banquet that the Prime
Minister, Lloyd George, whose elder son had been briefly at
the school some years earlier, announced the abdication of the
Kaiser and the Crown Prince of Germany.

Other well-known sons of Dulwich at this time were W. L.
Reed, the musician; R. G. G. Price, the *Punch* writer whose
How to Become a Headmaster is required reading for all those
aspiring to reach these dizzy heights; and C. S. Forester, then
known as C. L. T. Smith. He spent only a year at the school,
of which he gives a vivid picture in his autobiography, an
account that is certainly coloured by his own extreme
individualism and refusal to be fitted into any pattern. Among
other things he describes the ferocious bullying which sup-
posedly took place. This has puzzled everyone, masters and
boys alike, with whom I have discussed the passage; they say
with one voice that, apart from some bullying in the
boarding-houses (but no more than is to be expected among
thirty or forty boys jumbled together all day long), an
occasional sadistic prefect, and some ill-treatment of the
L.C.C. boys, Dulwich has always been remarkably free from

[1] The first was Sir Horatio Davies, referred to in Chapter 8.

bullying. This is partly, no doubt, because it is primarily a day school, partly because it has always had a certain atmosphere of live and let live. R. G. G. Price makes the interesting comment, however, that in the climate of the First World War, when Forester was a pupil, there must inevitably have been some bullying in every school, among boys who knew that soon they would be going off to the trenches to kill or be killed.

In 1935 the college had to change its coat of arms and crest, since it was decreed by the College of Arms that the one they had used until now was the exclusive property of Edward Alleyn and his family (though they had never used the crest). The new arms granted were very similar to the old ones. The flames in the crest signify deism and learning, while the hand holding a heart probably symbolizes charity, thus alluding to Alleyn's charitable intentions in founding the college.

Another change was considerably more important. Under the 1857 Dulwich College Act it had been laid down that 'the Governors shall make suitable provision for the preservation and custody of the library belonging to the college'. Until recent years successive Boards of Governors have shown a marked reluctance to do anything about this, despite the fact that the library is among the finest of any possessed by a school in this country—a recent expert said that he could think only of Eton and Winchester with greater riches. It contains a unique collection of manuscripts relating to Elizabethan times, many of them from Alleyn's own library; the college accounts right from the beginning; the diaries kept by Alleyn and Henslowe and other fascinating documents relating to the college and the picture gallery; and twelve volumes of unpublished seventeenth-century music by John Reading, a musician of high repute in his time who was organist at Dulwich at the end of the seventeenth century. There are two first folio Shakespeares, albeit incomplete; a Mercator atlas; first editions of Donne, Spenser, and Dryden; a fifteenth-century illuminated Book of Hours; a book which once belonged to Cranmer's library; and a copy of the first book to be printed in London, in 1480. Not till 1880, as the result of pressure by Carver, were any of these treasures catalogued. In 1888 and 1894 more discoveries were made of books and pamphlets which had been concealed at the back of a shelf, and a second catalogue had to be compiled.

Years of neglect followed until 1935, when one of the teaching staff, W. S. Wright, was put in charge of the college archives and the Masters' Library.[1] For the first time, through his skilled and devoted work, not only the school but also scholars throughout the world were made aware of the treasures within the college walls, many of which he displayed in beautiful exhibitions on Founder's Day. Nevertheless, it was still to be many years before enough money was forthcoming for this astonishing library to receive the treatment and recognition it merited.

During the thirties, as part of the extensive building programme, the senior boarding houses, Blew[2] and Ivyholme, acquired new premises in College Road, on the site of what had formerly been the Master's garden, an oasis of peace and greenery stretching from the south block almost to the present junior school; here, in early years, it had been the custom to sing madrigals on Founder's Day.[3]

[1] The two wooden panels of *Pietas* and *Liberalitas* now in the Masters' Library were rescued by Canon Carver, who during the rebuilding of the old college before its reopening in 1858 arrived one day to find the workmen about to demolish them. Alleyn records that he acquired them in 1618 for £2 2s 6d: 'Bought off Matthewe all ye upper part off ye quene's barg'. They were reputed to have come originally from Drake's *Golden Hinde*. Carver had them fitted up as a chimney-piece in the old college, and in 1870 they were carried over to the new building and placed in their present position.

[2] The first Blew House, described as 'a tenement in Dulwich', was bequeathed by Edward Alleyn to the churchwardens of St Botolph's, Bishopsgate, for the benefit of the poor of their parish.

[3] Speaking at an Alleyn Club dinner in 1962 A. N. Gilkes, son of the 'Old Man' and High Master of St Paul's, told his audience, 'I am the only person in this room, and probably the only person now alive, who was born in one of the form rooms of Dulwich College. The other day I went to have a look at that former bedroom. It is now the form room of Science 5b.' He recalled how as a small boy 'I stood in our garden on a summer evening. There were lovely trees around me where the new science block is now, and the strange and astonishing cry of the peacocks came from the house of Sir Evan Spicer, "Belair".'

The whole pattern of boarding-house living was then quite different from what it became after the Second World War. There were house-prefects, who took their duties very seriously, and fagging (not too arduous), and in some houses there was a strict pecking order based on seniority and what each boy contributed to the house and the school, promotion bringing with it the privilege of a study earlier than would otherwise have been allowed, or exemption from fagging.

Fig. 4.2   Pietas and Liberalitas

All through the thirties the boarding-houses were a problem, the number of boys living in them steadily decreasing
with the worsening economic situation. The system—usual in
public schools at the time—was for each housemaster to look
after the finances of his own house, paying the Governors rent,
finding the furniture and equipment, and bearing the responsibility for the rates and repairs and the decorating. In return
he kept the boarding-fees and ran the house rather like a
hotel. His wife was very much part of the scene, in effect
carrying out the function of matron and in moments of crisis
of cook as well, and providing a sympathetic ear for tales of
woe. Since the economics of the houses were based on an
occupancy of thirty boys each, the master concerned could
not make ends meet if the number fell lower than this. So it
was decided that the Governors should assume the financial
responsibility for each house as the master in charge retired,
though in practice the coming of war delayed this change.

The pages of the *Alleynian*, filled in the early and mid-thirties
with the usual schoolboy preoccupations—school news,
matches, the activities of Old Alleynians, poems, essays, and
stories, and the meetings of the various societies (which had
proliferated over the past decade from virtually nil to more
than a dozen)—gradually changed. They began to reflect a
growing concern with the political situation, with articles on
Germany, debates on conscription and National Service, the
report of a lecture by Gilbert Murray on the League of
Nations and of a talk on pacifism. By the summer of 1938 it
seemed as if hostilities might break out at any moment, and
the Government drew up plans for the evacuation of children
from London. Booth decided to act independently, and a
project was swiftly prepared to take to the Forest of Dean any
boys whose parents wished to send them out of the probable
line of fire; here a disused fever hospital, depressingly fenced
round with corrugated tin, had hastily been requisitioned, as
well as a guest-house.

After many chops and changes of plan, an advance party
was despatched to get the two places ready; and on 29

September about four hundred boys, accompanied by forty masters and a handful of wives, set off by charabanc and car. (Ten boys made the trip there, and eventually back, by bicycle—a marathon 250 miles in all.) This, as it turned out, was the day before Neville Chamberlain flew back from Munich, after his meeting with Hitler, optimistically declaring that we were to have peace in our time, 'peace with honour'. There must have been a feeling of anticlimax in the fever hospital, compounded by a shortage of rations, which at first consisted mainly of tea, cocoa, bread, jam, and biscuits, until the heroic and hard-pressed wives were able to get going with great pans of sausages and other welcome fare.

It rained most of the time, and the hospital was bitterly cold. A sporadic programme of lessons, church, improvized games and a visit to a nearby coalmine was no adequate substitute for the efficient organization of work and leisure to which everyone was accustomed. 'It was absolutely awful,' and 'a rather miserable time was had by all,' were two of the heartfelt comments; and though morale was high no one can have been sorry when after less than a week, and with the shadow of war temporarily removed, it was decided to recall the evacuees. The lucky ones were the boys from The Orchard, who spent a pleasant few days in their own evacuation retreat at Looe.

But of course it immediately became clear that peace was not to be, as Germany successively occupied the Sudetenland, Bohemia, Moravia, Slovakia, parts of Lithuania, and eventually Poland, while Italy and Japan followed their own courses of aggression in Spain, North Africa, and China. Preparations for war became a way of life, and in the summer term of 1939 one of the rugger pitches was handed over as a barrage balloon station. Towards the end of the summer holidays boys and masters met daily at the college with emergency baggage to await orders from Whitehall, where once again plans were being made for the evacuation of schoolchildren from London.

It had already been decided that the Dulwich boys should go to Tonbridge School, and preliminary arrangements were made. On 1 September, one day after the general evacuation from London of women and children had begun, the college got its marching orders, and around six hundred boys set off for what was still, so far as they were concerned, an unknown destination.

The train took them from Denmark Hill to Eynsford, about halfway between Bromley and Sevenoaks. Here it stopped, and the boys were decanted. For several hours they sat by the roadside, until as dusk approached their leader, J. Scott Young, conjured up some coaches to take them forward on their journey. But when at last they reached Tonbridge they found they were not expected; there was no sign of the seven hundred billets which should have been ready for them, and they had to spend the night on the floor of the gymnasium. For a few days they lived in emergency accommodation in Sevenoaks, until, with superhuman efforts on the part of two of the masters, S. C. (Billy) Griffith and James Cobban, proper billets could be prepared, the boarders living in Tonbridge School houses under Dulwich housemasters and the day-boys scattered all over the town and its environs.

Despite good will on both sides, conditions were difficult. Tonbridge kept to their normal hours of work and play, while Dulwich fitted in with a Box-and-Cox arrangement, with games and prep in the morning and lessons in the afternoon and evening, when everyone was tired and disinclined to sit in stuffy, blacked-out classrooms. At the end of the day the boys had to find their own way back to their billets, through the pitch darkness and over strange territory. The Tonbridge landladies complained—with some justification, one feels, even taking into account the very different cost of living then—that the Government billeting allowance was inadequate (it was 6s 6d a week for small boys and 10s 6d for those over sixteen, respectively $32\frac{1}{2}$p and $52\frac{1}{2}$p in modern currency), and parents were asked to contribute an extra sum. Some of them could not afford to keep their boys as boarders, and took them away. The *Daily Express* had a caustic article, headed 'Muddle Magnified', describing the whole confused state of affairs.

So at the end of the term, to the inexpressible relief of everyone, the school returned to its own quarters, to find that during their absence, thanks to a loan from the Estates Governors, air raid shelters had been put up, classrooms provided for the junior school, the buttery rebuilt, and the heating system centralized. The barrage balloon unit, however, which had occupied the college for fifteen weeks, had disgraced itself (like the Puritan soldiers in the Civil War) by doing a great deal of damage, having spread—as the report of the Select Committee on National Expenditure put it—'into some 70 rooms, the fives courts and a gymnasium'. After a good deal of wrangling £2,200 was paid by way of compensation. There was also a certain amount of gentlemanly in-fighting to determine just how much should be paid to Tonbridge for the term's occupancy, and muttered jokes went round the college to the effect that their hosts were a Skinners' Livery Company school.

For a term the phoney war continued, and life proceeded more or less as usual; but in April and May Germany engulfed much of western Europe and everyone knew that war would soon overwhelm Britain as it had done our continental neighbours. In May, shortly before the British forces were evacuated from Dunkirk, the Home Guard came into existence and the college formed its own unit, composed of masters, senior boys, and some of the ground staff, to look after the defence of the grounds and buildings.

George Smith's son Christopher, himself an Old Alleynian, has a delightful story of these terrible days, when invasion by Germany seemed virtually inevitable. He was at the time head of Trinity College, Glenalmond, and, he recounted some years later, at an Alleyn Club dinner, he asked the highest local authorities what he should do in this ghastly eventuality. Back came a sealed document marked 'Very Private':

I opened it with excitement, and what I read was: 'In the event of there being fighting in the neighbourhood the boys should not be allowed to go out and watch the battle'. The document went on to say that it would be better if, during the fighting, the boys were kept in a sheltered room, and that, if possible, they should be amused, and it suggested by way of amusement that 'the piano might be played, tuck distributed, and harmless games of chance indulged in'.

In July the Blitz started in earnest, and the Battle of Britain was fought—often literally—over the heads of the boys. For ninety-one consecutive days and nights the raids continued, but, the *Alleynian* remarked, 'in spite of this there was a very successful cricket season'.

Four masters and six to eight boys were on duty every night, and during a period of two months at least nineteen incendiary bombs fell on the school. The main gate was destroyed, and windows were broken by a bomb that fell on the railway, scattering bits of an ornate iron bridge which spanned Alleyn Park Road as far away as the science block. Ceilings collapsed, the groundsmen's storehouse was demolished, part of the cricket pavilion (which had been taken over by Camberwell Borough Council as a first aid post) was damaged, and a bomb landed on the engineering block. One master who joined the staff at this time described the school as 'reeling from the effects of war. Like Samson in Gaza, it peered out through open windows, with not a pane of glass anywhere to be seen.' During the summer holidays about two hundred boys went off to farm in Buckinghamshire and Worcestershire, and for those who had to remain in war-racked London the school was kept open for a week in August as a recreation centre, and for two weeks in September for instruction in painting, sketching, carpentry, practical biology, modern languages and so on, under the supervision of masters who volunteered as part of their war work.

The autumn term came, and still the bombardment continued. By now several of the staff were sleeping in the basement of the north block and some of the college servants in the middle block—and they must all have been pretty cold, for it was an icy winter, and there was no form of heating. Some of the lessons took place underground too, and one article in the *Alleynian* commented that the benches must have been made by experts in the art of torture.

Booth reported to the Governors that:

> With up to seven or eight raid warnings each day, conditions are difficult. Football is impossible owing to shell splinters on the grounds; only 'minor' sports are being conducted. All away matches have been cancelled. Boys are given leave on any

occasions which are desired by parents; homework is set and done whenever possible. In general, each boy is placed on his honour to get here when he can, to leave when it is necessary for him to do so, and to do what he can in the way of preparation.

Towards the end of 1939, when the boys were still at Tonbridge, Booth had been told, as an urgent economy measure, to reduce the number of assistant masters, and to try to persuade them to accept a cut in salary. Though neither of these measures was put into effect, the whole climate of uncertainty about the future made the staff extremely uneasy, and deeply upset about some of the economies which had been enforced, especially in music, games, and the O.T.C. In the summer of 1940, as a result of the Blitz, the number of boys on the roll had plummeted in the course of a week or two from 675 to 450, with an average daily attendance of around 350 who struggled to school despite the dangers and difficulties. Finances became very critical indeed.

Alarmed by the whole situation, the masters begged the Governors to apply to the Board of Education for the renewal of a grant, as had been done after the First World War. The Board was approached and discussions took place, though the official view was that there was little chance of a grant being made; in the opinion of the Board of Education it was up to the Estates Governors to provide the additional finance needed, since by now the college was the only one of the schools under the endowment for which the Estate was wholly responsible, the others being grant-aided. The possibility of a second evacuation continued to be explored, and this too produced among the staff a feeling of great uncertainty.

Much of this atmosphere of tension was undoubtedly caused by Booth's inability to deal adequately with the situation, for by now he gave every indication of having lost his grip, advocating not only evacuation until the end of the war but even the permanent closure of the school. It has been suggested that his difficulty in dealing with the crisis was at any rate partly due to the very bad experience he had had in the First World War, when he had spent some time as a German prisoner-of-war in Ruhleben, a particularly brutal Oflag. Whatever the reason, immediately after a meeting between the Governors and the Board of Education in April 1941 he handed in his resignation, and the senior master of the college, the Rev. H. H. Dixon, was appointed acting Master for the duration of the summer term (and also, as it turned out, for the first part of the autumn).

Booth had arrived at Dulwich with an excellent reputation; he had been a first-rate head of Wolverhampton Grammar School, with personality and drive. But Dulwich was too big for him—though perhaps all would have been well if it had not been for the many problems that came with the depression, and above all with the war. He began to delegate far too much, leaving a great part of the organization in the hands of the prefects. 'We didn't see much of him,' one of his pupils comments. Billy Griffith, who taught under him during his latter years, feels that, though things turned out badly for him, he nevertheless had a genuine understanding of what Dulwich College represented, and was desperately anxious to retain this spirit, but that in his heart of hearts he was perhaps never convinced that he was capable of handling such a formidable assignment. He had other supporters too, both masters and boys, who, though they criticized certain aspects of his mastership, nevertheless felt for him admiration and affection. However this may be, the years that followed were to witness the greatest renaissance that the college had experienced since Canon Carver, nearly three-quarters of a century earlier, had fought to create, from the sad ruins of Alleyn's endowment, a great public school.

5 Renaissance

C. H. Gilkes (1941–53)

> '*The clouds dispell'd, the sky resumed her light ...*'
> (Dryden)

CHRISTOPHER GILKES was a man of courage, iron will, vision, and shrewdness, qualities which were to be of crucial importance in the difficult years to come. A son of the famous A. H. Gilkes, he had spent his own schooldays at Dulwich, becoming captain of the school and of boxing, a member of the 1st XV and editor of the *Alleynian*. It is said that he was popular among his friends because he never carried back to the 'Old Man' reports of what they had been up to. He won a classical scholarship to Trinity College, Oxford (where he came near to being a rugger blue), and afterwards taught at Uppingham under another Old Alleynian, R. H. Owen—later to be Archbishop of New Zealand—before becoming head of Stockport Grammar School.

When he came to Dulwich in November 1941 the Allies were about to enter the most perilous and agonizing phase of the war. But at home there was a lull in the heavy bombing, so that for a time it was possible to carry on with normal working hours, though sporadic raids still made life uncomfortable: matches and games tended to be interrupted by German planes, and often the grounds had to be cleared of shell splinters before they could be played on.

The period of relative quiet lasted until February 1944, when the Germans began their heaviest raids on London since 1941, leaving the college with most of its windows broken for the second time and the old Ivyholme and The Orchard badly damaged. Four months later the first flying bomb was dropped on the capital, and in July one landed fair and square on the college, flattening the armoury and the fives and squash courts, wrecking half the science block, severely damaging the roof of the gym and the baths, and removing the ceilings and all the windows of the south block. Half the north block was unusable and all the centre block more or less damaged, as were the engineering block, Ivyholme and Blew House. In Gilkes' words, every single room in the school was damaged in one way or another, so that when masters and boys turned up next morning there was not a single place where they could sit in safety. Fortunately the attack took place at 10 o'clock at night, a few minutes after the boarders had passed by *en route* for their nightly sojourn in the shelters under the centre block, so no one was hurt.

Fig. 5.1   Bomb damage, July 1944: the squash courts

This whole period is vividly remembered by George Way, who had come to Dulwich in 1937 as head of chemistry, becoming head of science eight years later:

> For the remainder of the summer term, practical science continued only by courtesy of James Allen's Girls' School, who placed their laboratories at our disposal. One of my classes was held there immediately after lunch. I couldn't understand why my pupils were always there so early, until I discovered that the girls could be seen through the windows of the gymnasium with their tunics tucked into their pants—a rare, if unintentional, display for those days!

'There was complete devastation in every hole and corner of the buildings,' Gilkes commented a year later. 'I really do not know what would have happened to the school if we had had another direct hit.' But, he went on:

> It was our duty, if we claimed to be a great school, to give a lead to London in resisting the attempts of the enemy to paralyse the normal life of the City, and I am proud to be able to say that we were the only school in London which continued its work above ground, in spite of the dangers and difficulties which beset us. At that time the coolness and courage of the masters and boys was beyond all praise. I remember many things happened at that time, and some of them stand out in my mind. I remember the prefects coming to me to protest that it was undignified and unmanly to retire into the passage when a flying bomb was going to fall close to us.

Gilkes' own bravery and moral leadership during this period were unfailing and unshakeable.

The masters who lived through those days have very clear memories of the problems which beset the school, and of the remarkable spirit of the boys, who seemed completely fearless, and co-operated cheerfully in all the makeshift arrangements that so often had to be made. When the railway was closed because the bridges had collapsed, a special bus was used to collect many of them and take then. to Beckenham; every day, as they passed through Forest Hill, it seemed as if there was an enemy plane overhead, but they were always lucky, and came through unscathed. A nightly guard was kept during term-time and holidays, composed of masters, boys, and non-teaching staff, and the boys became used to shovelling incendiaries off the roof, heedless of their own safety. Sometimes one of them would turn up with his prep written on a crumpled, grubby bit of paper, and when he was ticked off would say, 'Well, sir, I rescued it from the mess'—and it would turn out that during the night his house had been bombed, and he had salvaged what he could, and with immense spunk come to school next day.

As Professor R. V. Jones, himself an old boy of Alleyn's School, and until recently a Governor of the college, points out in his *Most Secret War*, the Dulwich area was especially vulnerable during the latter years of the war, being the mean point of impact of the VIs. It was known that enemy agents were sending back reports to Germany, and so misleading information was leaked out in order to connect the time of the bombs which fell short with the place of those which overshot. This was to give the impression that the range should be reduced, with the result that many bombs intended for Westminster and the City fell in south-east London.

The German press gave a highly-coloured picture of the attacks on Dulwich in an earnest piece of propaganda which came to light when an Old Alleynian picked up in a German trench a newspaper containing an article by the paper's Stockholm correspondent. According to this article, the claim that the college was still being used to educate boys was a lie.

> It is a well-known trick that when the English wish to deceive the world about the bombing of school buildings, they try to give the impression that it is still a school. We do not know what staff or department has taken over these buildings, but we have an idea that it is a high department because, among other things, the school buildings are near to a golf course on which high British and American officers must have played with zeal.

Not that this golf course could continue as it had been in peacetime, the article went on, for a balloon site was established on the edge, as well as an anti-aircraft battery in the neighbouring woods.

The prized College often presented quite a military spectacle on a peaceful summer evening. On the western edge of the playing fields is the important Dover–London railway, and this makes Dulwich College a further objective for V1 ... The cheap attempt of the English to call the attack on Dulwich College an attack on an 'innocent and peaceful school' is laughable to anyone who had any idea of the necessity for buildings and exercise grounds for military training in Southern England.

George Way comments:

Gilkes' over-riding principle was to carry on as normally as possible. During air raid alerts games usually continued, taking avoiding action when necessary; but classes, at least to start with, adjourned to the shelters in the basements of the three main blocks, which had been strengthened by steel girders. The most enduring memory of my whole time at the college is the wonderful spirit which prevailed there throughout the war, not least among the boys. One lunchtime during an air raid two juniors, munching whatever they could still get at the Butt, were taking refuge in the clump when a bomb dropped at the end of the 1st XI square. Before the last lumps of Dulwich clay had returned to earth, they were sprinting towards the crater to be first on the scene to collect the best mementoes (and were ticked off, not because they were risking their lives, but because they were running on sacred Dulwich turf). The site of the crater can still be seen to this day as a slight eminence where gully fields to a right-hander batting at the school end—they over-allowed for subsequent subsidence when refilling the hole.

The most difficult time was during the flying-bomb period, when perhaps we became over-confident and possibly somewhat callous. Alerts were so frequent that Gilkes instructed us to move to the shelters only when danger seemed really imminent. One games afternoon a V1 'cut out' over the school field. As it descended to explode in the Tulse Hill area, a small boy casually remarked, 'They've had it!'. On another occasion when I was teaching the science sixth in the last days before the science block was hit one boy—then a leading member of the 1st XV—put up his hand and asked with much diffidence, 'Please, sir, don't you think it's time we moved to the shelters?'. Perhaps the luckiest near-miss was the evening when the 1st XI were at the nets and a V1 came over. This time it cut out over the Crystal Palace and plunged straight for the nets, but at the last moment some miracle caused it to bank and fall on the old Alleyn's Head pub.

Strangely enough, on one Founder's Day during this period of constant raids, with the sun shining out of a cloudless sky, not a vestige of an enemy plane was to be seen all day long.

Fig. 5.2   Bomb damage, July 1944: the science block (the biology master, W. C. Crowther, surveys the scene)

The favourite explanation was that the German in charge of the V1 campaign on that particular day must have been an Old Alleynian—quite a number of Germans had been at the school in pre-war years—who had remembered the date, and whose affection for his old school had triumphed over patriotic zeal.

Dulwich clocked up two more V.C.s during the war. Philip Gardner was the first Londoner to be so awarded, 'for courage, determination and complete disregard for his own safety in saving the life of a fellow officer at Tobruk on 23rd November 1941'. He was captured in Libya in 1942 and imprisoned in Italy, but after the armistice he escaped and went into hiding in Rome, even attending the opera and sitting, in civilian clothes, among German officers. Brigadier Lorne Maclaine Campbell, nephew of the Gordon Campbell of Q-ships fame, won his V.C. in the Western desert in 1943. Though seriously wounded, he led a battalion of the Argyll and Sutherland Highlanders through an enemy minefield and captured six hundred German prisoners. Earlier, when he had won the D.S.O., one of his men had said, 'Dinna forget his name. You'll meet it again some day, for the Argylls will follow him anywhere. That's what I call a hero.' Prophetic words . . .[1] On 11 November 1952, Armistice Day, the two V.C.s unveiled portraits of themselves by another Old Alleynian, Peter Greenham, which today hang in the lower hall facing the five V.C.s from the First World War.

By early 1945 the tide on every front was running strongly in favour of the Allies, and in March the last of 1,050 V2s fell on Britain. In Shanghai an Old Alleynian, A. G. N. (later Sir Alwyne) Ogden, Counsellor at His Majesty's Embassy, Chungking, hoisted the Union Jack over the British Consulate for the first time since 1941. In May Germany surrendered, and four months later Japan followed suit. 'Not many are left,' ran an *Alleynian* editorial early in 1946, 'of that famous band who spent the Michaelmas term at Tonbridge; those few who do remain will agree that the spirit of the school has

---

[1] It was Lorne Campbell who had pruned Wodehouse's *Alleynian* contributions during the First World War.

remained unimpaired throughout evacuation, blitzkriegs, flying-bombs, rockets and all the other incidents of our wartime life; and can justly feel proud of the school's record during that critical period which has become a legend and a tradition.'

Windows and ceilings were repaired, and Camberwell Borough Council relinquished its hold on the pavilion; but it was to be a long time before the school ceased to feel the effects of the murderous bombing from which it had suffered—in common, it may be said, with the rest of the Dulwich estate: out of 2,400 houses, 2,060 had been either totally destroyed or severely or partially damaged.

At the time of Gilkes' appointment, with about four hundred boys 'on the books', the school was £15,000 in debt to the Estates Governors, with an overdraft of £8,000 and a running loss of around £7,000 a year. Indeed, at a meeting of the Governors early in 1942 one of them declared that it must be looked upon as a bankrupt concern. In choosing Gilkes the Governors were looking for someone who would have the necessary boldness and imagination to put the college back on a sound financial basis. As usual in times of distress, the possibility of reducing the salaries of the masters was considered, and Gilkes, who like his predecessors was always concerned that his staff earned less than teachers in comparable London schools, offered to forego 5% of his own salary also if this draconian plan had to be put into effect. Luckily, in the nick of time a life-saver appeared out of the blue.

When Japan entered the war in December 1941, and with the increase of tension in the Middle East, there was a great need for people in all three services who could speak eastern languages, and who would be able to act as interpreters and intelligence officers. The War Office decided to sponsor a scheme under which the School of Oriental and African Studies would provide a crash course in Turkish, Persian, Chinese, and Japanese for suitable men. It was next suggested that the scheme should be extended to include boys of school-leaving age, in the period before they were called up. The difficulty was to find somewhere for them to live while they were being taught, where they would receive the proper degree of discipline and yet have the freedom of university life. Gilkes was approached to see whether Dulwich would house them, and immediately agreed. Secondary and public schools all over the country were written to, and about seventy boys were accepted for the course, most of them, probably, with little idea of what was involved, but all eager to get into the war, and perhaps with a faint hope that the course might eventually open a path to the Foreign Service. In the morning they went to the School of Oriental Studies for tuition in whichever language they were taking, and in the afternoon they came back to Dulwich, the idea being that they would do more general work—though in practice they tended to concentrate on languages.

The Oriental scholars, or 'Course boys', as they came to be called, lodged in The Orchard (Turkish and Persian) and Ivyholme (Chinese and Japanese). At The Orchard the housemaster was Gayford, whose two pretty daughters were a great attraction (in fact, one of them later married a Course boy). Ivyholme was run by Gilkes, for, since it had not yet been possible to find anywhere for him to live, he volunteered for the time being to look after the boys there. They had little contact with the school and were left very much to their own devices, which they preferred, for they were jealous of their status as London University undergraduates. They were a fascinatingly diverse collection, from widely differing backgrounds—some from the most famous public schools of England, others from grammar schools in remote corners of Wales and Scotland. The common factor was that they were all extremely bright, and extremely anxious to cram as much as possible into their time at Dulwich. They ran a magazine, a highly successful rugger team, the London Orient—for which, since there were so few teams playing in the capital at that time, they had all kinds of remarkable fixtures, including Harlequins, the Public School Wanderers, and the London Fire Brigade—and a cricket XI of a rather lower calibre (no one was quite so interested in cricket, and it took up too much time).

One of the 'scholars' was (Sir) Peter Parker, later head of British Rail, who remembers it as an enormously exciting experience:

> We were all very eager to master our language and get out into the field. The course was extremely stiff, and we were working amongst seventy or so people of a pretty high voltage. It was almost test-tube stuff—nothing of the kind had ever been done before: it was the first time, for instance, that anyone had ever taught thirty boys Japanese in London—the teacher was a tiny Japanese who in the early stages taught entirely by phonetics. We were all away from home, quite a lot of us for the first time, and rather in limbo, neither schoolboys still nor genuine university students, working in an immensely concentrated atmosphere.

After the war a great many of the boys used the language they had mastered to follow careers which otherwise they might never have thought of, or might not have had the chance to pursue. Some went into the Foreign Office, such as Sir Edward Youde, from 1974 to 1978 our Ambassador in Peking, and Sir Michael Weir, Ambassador in Cairo. Others joined the Colonial Service and from there followed different paths, often very high up, in industry. A third group went into the academic world—Professor P. G. O'Neill, Professor of Japanese at London University, Laurence Breen, head of the Far Eastern Service of the B.B.C., Professor Cyril Birch of Berkeley University, Professor Michael Halliday of Sydney University, and Professor Ronald Dore of Sussex University among them. Sandy Wilson, famous for *The Boy Friend* and for a great number of other shows and songs, was also one of the scholars.

Writing in *The Times* after Gilkes' death Sir Ralph Turner, who had been Director of the School of Oriental and African Studies during the war, paid tribute to the notable contribution which Gilkes, through the course, had made to the war effort. '[The project] enabled the boys to finish their school life under a great headmaster, and made possible a scheme which proved of great value at a time when all three services were desperately in need of men with a knowledge of eastern languages.'

The scheme lasted for two years, from 1942 to 1944, and

provided a life-giving transfusion of money—amounting, in fact, to half the tuition fees for that period. By 1943 the school was once more in the black, and able to begin repaying its overdraft and its debt to the Estates Governors.

Blew House was the only boarding-house which remained in commission throughout the war for the Dulwich boys themselves, but with the War Office course at an end, and with a growing number of boys for whom boarding accommodation had to be found, it was decided to reopen Ivyholme as the second senior house, with The Orchard and Elm Lawn as the two junior ones. Eventually the demand for places became so great that for a time the cricket pavilion, renamed Carver House for the purpose, was pressed into use as a third junior house.

During and after the war the housemaster of Blew was Eric Parsley, whom his colleagues and the boys of his era remember with a very special affection. Not only was he the senior boarding housemaster and head of the modern side, but he was also president of the common room: 'Immaculate in dress, correct in all things, sympathetic but firm towards any shortcomings of his pupils or colleagues, and with a unique sense of humour, he was the ideal schoolmaster.' By two of the boys then at the school he is endearingly described as resembling a rather plump Noel Coward, a brilliant pianist, delightfully indiscreet, occasionally caustic of tongue, and with a richly cynical manner.

Good stories about him abound: the entire lesson which he spent discussing his colleagues' salaries and whether they were worth it; the extremely doubtful anecdotes which he told with such relish to the engineering form; the comment of one distinguished Old Alleynian, Professor W. K. C. Guthrie, at an Alleyn Club dinner that 'of all he taught me I can only now remember two things. One was a song called *The Old Bold Mate*, which was entirely in praise of rum. The other was the practical hint that before using a snuff box you must always tap the lid to dislodge snuff from it. We had to remember it for acting purposes.' A great bibliophile, he once heard that a first edition of *Phèdre* was going for a modest sum in the Dulwich village bookshop. He cycled madly down on his decrepit bike and bought it: it was inscribed by Louis XIV to Madame de Maintenon. He subsequently turned down some enormous offer from a parent who was keen to buy it, and gave it to Versailles, in return for which he was made *Officier de l'Academie des Arts*, an honour of which he was extremely proud.

During these years various changes took place in the boarding-house organization, for some of which Parsley was responsible. In 1942 the financial responsibility for running them at last passed to the Governors, and the boarders, instead of eating in the various houses, were fed separately in their own central dining-room. It was also decided to limit the tenure of office of the housemasters to ten years (later reduced to eight).

With Ivyholme once more a boarding-house, a new home had to be found for the Master, since it had been decided that Bell House, where Booth had lived, was now too large and expensive for the purpose. As Gilkes wrote to the Governors, he would himself have been perfectly happy in a small house which would be economical to run: 'But I know from experience that a school takes rank in the eyes of the world very much from the social position of the headmaster, and a certain degree of modest splendour is inevitable.' At first he and his family lived at The Chestnuts, but it was unsuitable and war-damaged. Eventually Bell House was adapted as a boarding-house for the Elm Lawn boys, which left Elm Lawn itself vacant. For a while it looked as if it might be sold, but fortunately an anonymous Old Alleynian philanthropist bought the lease and transferred it to the college for the use of the Master. Here Gilkes moved in 1949, and here the Master and his wife have lived ever since, in a beautiful house which is at once close to the school, comfortable, elegant, and eminently suitable for the hospitality which is such an integral part of their life. In 1954, together with Bell House and the picture gallery, it was included in a list of buildings of special architectural or historic interest in the borough of Camberwell.

The college was immensely blessed, in the war and post-war years, in having as its Chairman of the Board of Governors Lord Soulbury (formerly Sir Herwald Ramsbotham), who between 1931 and 1941 had been successively Parliamentary Secretary and President of the Board of Education. He was Chairman for eight crucial years, until his appointment in 1949 as Governor-General of Ceylon, and a great debt is owed to the influence and energy which he brought to the rebuilding, literally and figuratively, of the school.

The problem of rebuilding was acute—not only the restoration of the actual bricks and mortar, but also the recreation of a living, flourishing entity. When Gilkes became Master in 1941, with a mandate from the Governors to reorganize the school, there had been many aspects which gave cause for concern.

First, the steady decline in numbers which had taken place even before the war. Between 1928 and 1938 the total number of boys had sunk from 934 to 800, and while the intake of L.C.C. scholars had remained fairly stable there were over a hundred fewer fee-paying boys at the end of this period than there had been at the beginning. Moreover, the boys tended to leave earlier, with a consequent thinning of the ranks in the top forms. Where were the pupils to come from in the future? Dulwich has always been something of an anomaly in not having its own preparatory school. Although the Dulwich College Preparatory School had been established in 1885 during Welldon's mastership, it had never had any formal or financial tie-up with the college, and often relations had been strained. In one sense they were rivals, since for most of its life the college had accepted pupils from ten upwards, while the Preparatory School naturally wanted to keep its boys until they were thirteen. Though many of them did in fact then go on to the college, there was no absolute tradition or agreement that they should do so. Moreover, when Christopher Gilkes became Master he was reluctant to admit more than a handful of Preparatory School boys, since he considered (probably with justice in the difficult wartime conditions) that standards had sunk pretty low. Yet by 1944 there were only a fraction of the preparatory schools left within ten miles of the college of all those upon which it had been accustomed to draw.

As a corollary of this Gilkes was, as he told the Governors, worried about the level of education provided by the college itself, by 'the decline in its fortunes and reputation which has persisted for twenty-five years', and by the fact that many of the boys stayed such a short time in the school, for the average school life was now only about two-and-a-half years. There was an urgent need to raise the academic level necessary to enter the school. As part of the whole investigation into the matter, intelligence tests (then extremely fashionable, and much more revered than they are today) were carried out amongst the boys. The results certainly led Gilkes to attach far too much importance to the contribution to the school of the clever boys, and to underestimate that of the less bright ones: by this criterion neither Shackleton nor Wodehouse, both of whom were regarded as something of a dead loss in the classroom, would have had a chance of being accepted.

Then there was the question of finance, since, although the Oriental scholars had given a much-needed injection of money, this was only a temporary breathing-space; for some years after Gilkes' arrival it was touch and go whether survival was possible. Much discussion went on in the early forties as to the advisability of ceasing to be independent— and even whether there was any alternative. It was suggested that it might be best to hand the school over to the L.C.C. to be maintained as a state school, but the Governors felt overwhelmingly that everything should be done to retain the existing status. In 1944 the endowment from the Estate amounted to £11,152, slightly less than it had been ten years earlier, though expenses had escalated. St Paul's, at this time, was receiving £30,000 a year in addition to the fees: about one-third of this was spent on scholarships (of which Dulwich had always been short), and the remainder on augmenting the masters' salaries—which meant, as Gilkes told the Governors, that St Paul's attracted boys of a cleverer type and taught them better. The fees at Dulwich were still what they had been nearly a quarter of a century earlier, £45 a year, though in the following year they were raised by the princely sum of £9, where they remained until 1951, when they were increased to £75.

One difficulty was that the Estates Governors, however willing, were not empowered to increase the endowment to the college without permission from the Ministry of Education, as the Board of Education had become in 1944; and the Ministry, under existing legislation, was itself not free to give authority. So other sources of income would have to be found. With the lull in the bombing in the early forties people had tended to return to London, and since Dulwich was one of the few schools still functioning parents were thankful to be able to send their children there. The numbers rose accordingly: in the autumn term of 1943 there were nearly six hundred boys on the roll, and a year later nearly a hundred more. But this healthy increase could only continue in the post-war years if an extensive rebuilding programme could be put in hand. By the time peace was declared it was obvious that all the buildings lying between the south block and the sanatorium which had not been destroyed would need to be pulled down within the next few years; many of them had already been inadequate or on their last legs long before the war. In practical terms this meant the science block, the furnace buildings, the changing rooms, bath and gymnasium, the workshops and the music teaching rooms, the fives and squash courts, the armoury and the rifle range. There was not a hope that war damage compensation would amount to more than a fraction of the sum needed to rebuild to a standard that would meet modern requirements, or provide additional accommodation for the younger boys, which by then had become essential.

This last item was in fact made possible by the Altering Scheme which came into effect in 1948, allowing the Estates Governors to give to the college the proceeds from the compulsory purchase by the L.C.C. of property on the Estate. The new junior block, the first major piece of post-war rebuilding, came into use in the autumn of the same year.

The next year the Estates Governors were further empowered by the Ministry to make a grant to the school of up to £50,000 towards another urgent piece of rebuilding, the science block. In point of fact it was a cause for gratitude that the old block had been destroyed during the war, for it would have been totally inadequate in post-war conditions, and the need to start from scratch made it possible to plan a building which would be as efficient and forward-looking as its predecessor had been when Lord Rayleigh laid the foundation stone in 1906. For eight years, during and after the war, science had to be taught—sometimes, if it rained, with umbrella in hand—in makeshift accommodation, including a corner of the building which had been patched up to a state of semi-efficiency that did not, however, include the plumbing. As a result, the chemists working on the upper floor frequently flooded their physics colleagues working below—a process surreptitiously aided by boys directing tubes from the water-taps down the gaping cracks in the walls. When the new building came to be designed, E. W. Tapper (Bill to the masters, Ernie to the boys), the head of physics, who planned it and introduced many novel ideas, made sure that his department no longer worked below the chemists.

The foundation stone of the new building was laid in 1950, and two years later it was in use. The cost was £106,000, an enormous sum for those days. The result was one of the finest science blocks of any school in the country. With typically ruthless efficiency Gilkes chivvied the science staff to take possession before they considered that the building was ready. They grumbled, but in retrospect George Way thinks he was probably quite right to hurry them on.

The former Dulwich Covered Courts, which had been used as an armed forces storage depot during the war, were taken over in 1947 as a gymnasium, and land for playing fields was acquired on the east side of College Road, and converted to tennis courts and a running-track. £18,000 was spent on the reconstruction of the kitchen and dining-room and on the transfer of the music school to the old gymnasium, the cost being met out of the profits of the school shop.

But this was still in the future: in the mid-forties the dilemma remained of how to attract not only enough boys but enough boys of the right calibre. It was in the Education Act of 1944 that Gilkes, with characteristic boldness and vision, found the answer.

In 1942 the Minister of Education, R. A. Butler (as he then was), had set up a committee under the chairmanship of Lord Fleming to consider how best to bring together the public schools and the general educational system of the country. Two years later, following the committee's report, the Education Act of 1944 came into effect, setting forth a new concept of education. 'It was the first of our statutes,' writes Lester Smith, 'to deal with a great social service with a Welfare State outlook.' At the heart of this Act was the determination that no child should be prevented by poverty from having an education at secondary school level which would best suit his age, aptitude, and ability. Under the terms of the Act, any child who passed the common entrance examination of his local authority qualified for a free place at a secondary school, his fees being paid by the authority concerned. Not only day-schools but also boarding-schools were encouraged to take these children.

This measure was unpopular among the left wing of the Labour Party, which greatly disliked this encouragement of a meritocracy; but in the climate of the day the conviction that no child should be deprived of education through lack of money, and that to open the doors of the independent schools was the best way of achieving this end, was shared by most people, not least by the officers of the L.C.C., always a forward-looking body, and at that time the major Labour-controlled education authority in England. It must be remembered, too, that the country faced the prospect of a big post-war educational bulge, coupled with a very serious lack of anywhere for the children to be educated. The outlook was particularly grave in cities like London, many of them with large areas which had been reduced to a bomb-scarred wasteland, and where few of the schools had continued to function during the war.

So Gilkes went to see (Sir) Graham Savage, then Education Officer to the L.C.C., and told him that Dulwich was eager to take advantage of the scheme.

His reasons for embarking so wholeheartedly on the Dulwich Experiment, as it came to be called, were no doubt mixed. Partly he did so because it brought a heaven-sent chance of restoring the school to its former position, setting it on its feet financially and attracting boys whose scholastic achievements would raise it to a high academic level. His motives also quite certainly sprang from his own socialist convictions (of a non-party nature), for, although he was by no means so left wing as some of his critics believed, his views were certainly progressive rather than the reverse. 'There has set in the nation a tremendous flood-tide towards social reform,' he said at the Alleyn Club dinner in the summer of 1946. 'In the spirit of the new age which is coming, it is possible to choose as our new entrants the best boys, quite regardless of their fathers' income.' And the following year, in his report to the Governors, 'We have set before us a noble ideal and are well on our way to realizing it. In future no boy will be debarred by social position or poverty from entering Dulwich College.' He saw the Experiment in the widest possible terms as the forerunner of the educational pattern of the future, and as a step towards the creation of a society in which talent would be rewarded. It must be remembered, however, that the scheme was not quite so innovatory as it is sometimes thought to have been, both by its supporters and by its critics. As we have seen, ever since 1928, when the school ceased to be Direct Grant, there had been a steady annual intake of around twenty-five L.C.C. scholars; and in 1945, the year before the Experiment 'took off', there were 150 of them already at the school, out of a total roll of 650. This does not, however, in any way detract from Gilkes' vision and achievement.

It was decided, after keeping back twenty places a year for boys from abroad, to divide up the rest of the places which were available each year and offer them, not only to the L.C.C., but also to the various local authorities from whose area boys traditionally came to Dulwich, in proportion to the number from each area. They had first to pass at a satisfactory level the normal examination of these authorities (that is, the eleven plus), and afterwards the college's own English and arithmetic papers.

One by one Gilkes approached the nearby local authorities, and arrangements were made whereby a certain number of free-place boys would come from each. The authorities concerned welcomed with open arms Dulwich's willingness to take part in the scheme on such a large scale, for this meant they could send boys to a school with a fine reputation which had remained in working order throughout the war. From the college's point of view, one great advantage was that its own juniors were able to sit the examinations, as well as boys from preparatory schools and, *ipso facto*, the sons of Old Alleynians. Above all, the school would be allowed a completely free choice from among all the candidates.

The first of the boys were sent by the L.C.C. in the autumn of 1946; and in the next few years about ninety came annually from the L.C.C., forty from Kent, between ten and twenty from Surrey, and twenty from Croydon. These were all day pupils, but at first Surrey, Southend, Croydon, and East Sussex all sent a small number of boarders.

This big intake naturally altered the main age of entry. In recent years most of the boys had been coming to Dulwich at thirteen, apart from the small annual intake of L.C.C. scholars, who started two years earlier. Now the overwhelming bulk of the boys would be coming at eleven plus, the age at which, under the 1944 Act, the change from primary to secondary education took place. In 1945, as part of his policy of attracting able pupils, Gilkes had already lowered the age of entry to bring in boys at the age of ten and eleven, 'a reversion,' as he said, 'to our earlier practice. In my time most of us came in about that age. I did and my brothers did and all my children are going to. From the school's point of view that is the ideal age for choosing boys, because then you can examine them very simply and can regard them rather like empty bottles, making sure that the size and the shape are all right and not caring very much what is inside!'[1] The new scheme meant that entry at this age was very greatly increased. Moreover, in 1952 two further classes were established for nine-year-olds (who were, of course, fee payers

[1] A point of view with which his successor, Ronald Groves, would have disagreed. 'Anybody who has been connected with choosing boys at eleven,' he said, 'will know how difficult it is to decide between those who are just beginning to develop and have potential ability, and those who appear quite good at that age and may be early developers.'

for the first two years): opinions vary as to whether Gilkes wanted to wean these boys away from the Dulwich College Preparatory School or whether he wanted to make it possible for his own sons to come at this age!

Side by side with earlier entry went later departure. This was owing partly to the fact that more boys stayed on to do sixth form and university scholarship work, and partly because, with two years' national service facing them at eighteen, they preferred to remain for an extra year rather than leave at seventeen, as they might otherwise have done.

What no one had foreseen was the rapid and immense jump in numbers which this longer school life would bring about. In 1944 Gilkes had told the Governors that he envisaged a school of seven hundred boys, which was where it should remain. Two years later the figure to which he aspired as the optimum maximum had become a thousand. 'That is where I hope we shall stop and where I think we shall stop.' But this did not happen. For one thing, as the war came to an end it became clear that the vast and essential building programme could only be financed if there was a corresponding increase in the sum yielded by the school fees. It was a Catch 22 situation: continued existence = more boys = new buildings to contain them = still more boys to pay for the buildings and to spread the ever-increasing overheads. Oddly enough, it seems as if no one actually sat down with paper and pencil to work out just what would happen with this steady quota of boys from the local authorities, all of them coming considerably earlier and most of them leaving a good deal later. By 1951 the average school life had risen to around seven years.

Nor, perhaps, did anyone foresee what such an influx of small boys would mean (in 1946 one quarter of the entire school consisted of new boys). The *Alleynian* wrote despairingly of 'the hideous row which now pervades the school buildings and grounds. Nowhere can one find sanctuary from the din of shouting, screaming children!' This imbalance automatically righted itself as the years progressed, especially from 1951 onwards, when, as the only way of stopping further expansion, the intake into the lower forms was reduced.

In all the arrangements with the local authorities, as Gilkes pointed out, 'We have not surrendered one jot or tittle of our independence. I am still allowed to choose the boys who come to us through the local educational authority scholarship lists. I am allowed to reject anybody, and the candidates we get are sufficiently numerous for us to be perfectly certain that we shall get excellent boys.' Gilkes himself saw every boy: Brian Curtois, now the B.B.C.'s chief Political Correspondent, and one of the small number of boarders who were accepted under the scheme, remembers being interviewed by him at Southend, a tall, imposing figure with white hair.

If the scheme was welcomed in most quarters, there was also some opposition, not least from other secondary schools in the neighbourhood. One headmaster, writing anonymously in the *Times Educational Supplement* in 1949, said, 'The logical outcome of the Dulwich policy of the last two or three years is that the grammar schools of South London will be drained of all those leaders to whom they look for maintenance of their school standards, and of those few first-class brains whose presence alone ensures the retention in the grammar schools of men with the highest qualifications.' Gilkes himself was fond of claiming that he was getting the cream of all the schools within the Dulwich catchment area, which must have made a lot of them extremely unhappy. 'He made much too much of an ostentatious fuss about it,' a former master comments. One extremely justifiable grievance was that quite unofficially Gilkes had, as it were, a preview of the best candidates from the primary schools, before the grammar schools were able to interview them.

It was the Old Alleynians, however, who had the gravest misgivings of all, convinced as they were that the Experiment would alter the whole character of the school.

Once again the situation must be seen against the fall in academic standards, even taking into account occasional successes such as the excellent number of university awards gained in 1938—the fact that, for instance, out of 451 boys who left during the last two years before the outbreak of war, 147 had not reached a position in the school which enabled them to sit for School Certificate. What the Dulwich Experiment did was to enable Gilkes to select boys on the strength of their brains, and this, as he said on many occasions, he was determined to do. He also firmly believed that if the school were to be kept going it was essential 'to forget the past and weigh in with the future'. His failure lay in his inability to realize how much his attitude would upset a number of Old Alleynians who were deeply loyal to the school, and who had always assumed that this was where their sons would go. On the one hand he said to them, 'We need your sons and nephews and relations and the sort of continuity they bring; I want an increasing number of boys coming into the school who are sons of Old Alleynians . . . The unifying thread which runs right through and keeps the quality of the school unchanged is the solid masses of Old Boys.' As an Old Alleynian himself, and the son of a man who had been Master of the college for nearly thirty years, devoting the best part of his life to its well-being, Gilkes was certainly sincere when he said this. On the other hand, he proclaimed in no uncertain terms that, sons of Old Alleynians or not, they would not be accepted unless they measured up to the high academic standard which he considered essential.

Within the school itself the situation was not helped by the member of staff whom he appointed in 1951 to the new post of deputy master. Known as 'the Butcher', like Welldon before him, he was an excellent teacher and organizer, a powerful, shrewd and intelligent leader of men who managed to bring into being several useful reforms. He was also a strict disciplinarian of whom many of the boys were extremely frightened. He used to have three punishments: ''Old your *lapp*les, boys!' he would say in his Welsh accent (to their bewilderment), making them sit thus for half-an-hour or so; or he would set them to write out the Te Deum thirty times, or to 'do twenty cubes starting at 730'. He quickly assumed control of the administrative side, acting as intermediary between the Master and the staff, particularly so far as the heads of sides were concerned. He also managed to gain rapid promotion to several lucrative and influential positions over the heads of senior masters, which was naturally much resented. Nor did his colleagues greatly appreciate his habit of standing outside the common room at the end of morning break, watch in hand, ostentatiously noting those masters who were setting off late to teach. In the opinion of many of the staff of this period, it was to a great extent the appointment of this particular man, and their consequent inability to maintain direct lines of communication with the Master, that led to a widening gulf between Gilkes and the common room—a gulf which, as the months wore on, it became increasingly difficult to bridge.

Little of this filtered through to the boys, who in general speak of Gilkes as inspiring great awe and respect. Some of them found him pretty petrifying—he was certainly not a man with whom one would ever argue, and you could generally hear a pin drop in his presence—but to others he was warm, human, approachable, and always fair. He liked to feel that he knew them all, and even with the smallest would suddenly melt and show that he knew the boy's name. He had a matter-of-fact, down-to-earth quality which appealed to them: when he took Scripture lessons, for instance, he liked to interpret the Bible in everyday terms, relating some legendary Biblical journey to free-wheeling down Brixton Hill, or claiming that Moses was able to lead the Children of Israel across the Red Sea because he knew the best route, or that Samson didn't pull down the whole palace but only part of it, which he was able to do because it was badly cantilevered. Boys who took part in these lessons thirty years ago still remember them as clearly as if it had been yesterday. One parent of the day says, 'He was completely attuned to the realities of the school. I could have gone to him about anything.' Like his father before him, he used to walk round the playing fields every day and encourage the boys, his large grey poodle ('Ursa Major') at his heels.

Less popular was his insistence on a daily P.T. session, in which he himself generally joined; medical notes pleading exemption proliferated. He told one master that the P.T. was pretty useless, but that it enabled him to pick out boys who would make good prefects—that is, the ones from whom the others would take orders.

Under Gilkes the musical tradition of Dulwich continued to flourish, for he was passionately fond of music, played various instruments, and gave great encouragement to the building up of the choir and orchestra.[1] In this he was brilliantly supported by Stanley Wilson, who came as director of music in 1944 when Gayford retired after twenty years of achieving so much for music and drama. A music club was formed with the aim of establishing the school as a cultural centre of south London, and for a while concerts were given on Sunday afternoons. Although the club's life was brief, the distinguished performers at the concerts included Maurice Cole and Phyllis Sellick. In 1948 the annual House Music Competition began, and in the same year the School Service was held for the first time in Southwark Cathedral, with the whole school travelling in a special train from North Dulwich station to London Bridge.

By 1951 the choir numbered four hundred, about a third of the school. When the Royal Festival Hall was opened on 24 May as part of the Festival of Britain, sixty of the trebles sang in the first performance of Benjamin Britten's Spring Symphony, with the London Philharmonic Orchestra and Choir. In the same year, instead of the Christmas concert in the Great Hall, the full choir performed the first half of *Messiah* in Southwark Cathedral.

The next year saw the first of the annual concerts at the Festival Hall. Once again *Messiah* was chosen. Every single boy, tone-deaf or not, took part in some of the choruses, joined for the rest by the main choir, smaller but still substantial. Many of the solos were sung in unison by sections of the school. Masters performed some of the recitatives, and a boy treble sang one of the loveliest arias of all, 'I know that my redeemer liveth'. *The Times*, in its (perhaps just slightly tongue-in-cheek?) report of the concert, described it as 'a completely home-made performance ... This division of labour,' it went on, 'made the undertaking of the oratorio practicable and involved the maximum number of participants. The accompaniment was equally indigenous but not

---

[1] The story goes that one day he stopped a new member of staff and asked how the flute was coming along. 'Flute?' was the surprised answer. 'I don't play the flute, I play the viola.' 'Oh bother,' said Gilkes, 'I've appointed the wrong man!'

quite so satisfactory . . .' The next year, when the concert celebrated the coronation of Queen Elizabeth II, it was followed by a grand ball in the Festival Hall. Gilkes planned to make concert and ball an annual event, but the second part of the project came to an end a couple of years after his death in 1953. The concert, however, has continued to this day, one of the great events of the college calendar, Dulwich being the only school to fill the Festival Hall every year with boys, parents, Governors, friends, and melody.

Stanley Wilson, like Gilkes himself, died quite suddenly in the autumn of 1953, still a relatively young man. He was an inspiring person to work under, however atrocious you might be at music, and boys who were in the choir at that time had the chance of going through several major works during their school years.

Drama, too, saw a great renaissance. The House Drama Competition, like that for music, was inaugurated in 1948, and Edward Alleyn would have had cause to be proud of the energy and skill that masters and boys brought to the performance of the plays which they read and staged. Drama at this time was in the hands of Philip Vellacott, whose activities spread far beyond the college: he formed the Attic Players, and won an international reputation as the translator of many Penguin Classics and the author of broadcast talks and plays. When he came to the school he was beginning to make a name for himself with his translations of Euripides, and one Founder's Day he put on his own version of *Ion*. Over the years he was to be responsible for about twenty-four productions of Shakespeare, some of them of a very high standard indeed. A colleague charmingly describes him as 'someone who thought and spoke naturally in Greek (the best and liveliest Greek) and who dropped into English from time to time in order to explain to the rest of us what he was finding so hilarious about the latest developments of Dulwich life.'

Once more the societies became an important facet of the school, warmly encouraged by Gilkes, who was keen on restoring what he felt had been lacking in the decade before the war, 'the importance of things of the mind'. In 1948, in fact, he could report to the Governors that twenty-one societies had 'raised their heads again'. Though some of them were ephemeral, in the way of school societies, many had a satisfying hold on life.

By the early fifties the college had all the pupils it could cope with (and indeed had to turn away two applicants out of three); finances were on a stable basis; the academic standard was extremely high, and the coveted Oxbridge awards, once so sparse, were beginning to reach double figures. It is a sad irony that Gilkes himself, the main architect of this remarkable success, saw only the early fruits of his work. For in the autumn of 1953, while on holiday with his family, he had a heart attack and died instantly, at the age of fifty-four.

Fig. 5.3   The Queen Mother reopening the picture gallery in 1953, with Mrs Gilkes, Christopher Gilkes, Lord Gorell, and the Captain of the school, Hector McLean

At some point between 1947 and 1950 Gilkes had consulted his doctor because he was suffering from disturbed vision: the diagnosis was congenital malignant hypertension, a form of high blood pressure for which there was then no treatment, and which causes headaches, confusion, nervous irritability, and depression—and can, indeed, result in a complete change of personality. He had, the doctor told him, a limited lifespan remaining to him. So, as he strove to build up the college once more into a living entity, he did so in the certain knowledge that he had only a small number of years for the task. Couple with this the fact that he was not a man who could bear to be thwarted, and perhaps one can find here the explanation for the controversy which surrounds the latter years of his mastership.

Though it seems unlikely that he was ever an easy individual to get on with (a relative describes him as 'a first-class person for making a nuisance of himself'), as a boy and younger man he must have possessed an equanimity which later deserted him. A report in the *Alleynian* of Gilkes as a schoolboy on the fives courts describes him as 'playing hard and with a contented geniality which it is hard to ruffle'. At Stockport he used to give parties for the staff at which he was full of *bonhomie*. Then there are the two remarkable testimonies from people who knew him while he was at Uppingham and Stockport. A Governor of the latter, an Oxford academic, wrote when Gilkes applied for the mastership of Dulwich:

> What I admire most, I think, about Mr Gilkes' work as headmaster is the impression of ordered freedom which the school conveys. One seems to get at the head through the members, and to realise his strength and character in the health and activity of the houses, the societies, the games, the school magazine, the boys especially interested in the arts, and so on. The place seems to run itself in a happy kind of way, yet of course without wise oversight it could not run itself. Similarly I have noticed how Mr Gilkes, with instinctive tact, has made the old boys and their association feel that they have a natural place—and a very significant place—in the life and work of the school.

Still more revealing is a letter from the Rev. R. H. Owen,

who was head of Uppingham while Gilkes was teaching there:

> The Old Man was one of the most serene men in face of difficulty that I have ever known. Chris has inherited a good deal of his father's serenity. The father was my hero, and those who knew the nobility of the father must not expect it exactly repeated in the son. But he is a sterling fellow. His character demands respect and gets it. If a headmaster has a touch of genius about him, it is an enormous help in inspiring boys. When Gilkes left me, I had not seen any touch of genius. The epithets I probably used in recommending him for Stockport were sterling, sound, full of common sense. On the other hand, I have met a number of his old Stockport boys at Oxford, and they have spoken of him as a *great* headmaster ... It's a big responsibility recommending anyone for the headmastership of one's old school. I somehow feel that no one can be quite good enough for Dulwich. But I have searched my schoolmaster memory, and of the men I know personally who are not already headmasters of one of the great schools and who are not fighting, there is only one man whom I would prefer to Gilkes as Master of Dulwich ... I believe that Gilkes would prove a good and sound Master of Dulwich, and that he might prove a great one.

This estimate of his qualities is echoed by so many of the people to whom I have talked—boys, masters, Governors, Old Alleynians. 'Nothing could beat him, and he surmounted any difficulty,' one of his staff commented. There was a directness about him which made a great appeal to many of those, especially the boys, with whom he came into contact. Sir Graham Savage, who had many dealings with him in connection with the L.C.C. scholars, commented to me that he always found Gilkes a cheerful, pleasant person, and praised his ability to get on with the local authorities. And when he died his wife received an enormous number of letters from people who had known and admired him, or who had watched his work at Dulwich.

It must have been immensely difficult to return to the school where his father was still revered as almost divine—and it must have been hard to grow up as the son of a man so revered. Nor can it have been easy to give orders to senior men who had known him as a schoolboy, or to deal with those who had seen active service and were used to command. And what enormous guts it must have required to keep the school going during the war . . .

His weakness lay in personal relationships with those who he felt were opposing what he regarded as necessary aims. He was a lonely man, confiding in practically none of his colleagues, not always scrupulous in the methods he adopted to put through cherished plans, and thin-skinned when it came to jokes against himself, though he loved to make jokes with the boys. (But here again there are inconsistencies. When the 'Oriental scholars' and the college boys jointly put on a show one winter, with music by Sandy Wilson, the *succès fou* of the evening was a parody of Gilkes' supervision of a chapel service, including his direction of the singing of the hymns, which Gilkes himself seemed to enjoy as much as anyone.) He cared little about the reactions of other people—which perhaps partly explains his apparent inability to understand how greatly they could be hurt by a cutting remark from him. It also explains his admirable disregard for convention, which at times sat oddly on someone in his position. He liked to shop in Brixton market, a sack over his shoulder, because the food was cheaper there; the kitchen staff used to put left-overs from the school meals into buckets, which he, or one of his sons, would then carry across to Elm Lawn for his chickens; on summer days he and his family would have breakfast in front of the house with the boys streaming past on the way to school, because it was nice and sunny there.

But he was a man who found it difficult to be patient or to brook criticism, especially, one imagines, when he felt the shadow of death beginning to hover over him. It was the staff—none of whom, so far as I know, realized how desperately ill he was—who bore the brunt of his ruthlessness in achieving his ends, and the consequent atmosphere of tension. 'It was like being back in the army,' one of them said. 'You never knew where the next landmine was coming from.' With the Governors too his relations were often stormy, and no doubt they worsened when Lord Soulbury was replaced by Lord Gorell (who was told, when he accepted the job, that he had taken on the most difficult chairmanship in England).

Gorell was a distinguished literary figure, but very bad at holding together a Board of Governors. Moreover, Gilkes' increasing tendency, as he became more and more isolated, to rely on his deputy head created its own difficulties.

'In spite of all these adverse conditions,' Eric Handscomb says, 'I *personally* found him always courteous, though somewhat aloof—perhaps still remembering himself as a school prefect when I was yet a junior. I consider that a lesser man would have thrown in the sponge during the difficult war years, and that his Dulwich Experiment probably saved the school from extinction.' This evaluation is echoed by James Cobban, who taught classics at the school before and after the war, and who said at an Alleyn Club dinner in 1967, 'In the dispassionate light of history it will be made absolutely clear that it was the vigour, often maybe the ruthless vigour, of Gilkes that saved Dulwich.' It is interesting, too, to read what the Inspectors who came to the school in 1952 wrote: 'Dulwich College as it is today reflects in great measure [the Master's] aims, his personality, his outlook. He has brought to a heavy task boldness, inflexible determination and a clear understanding of major policy.'

His whole ideal was the welfare of the college as he saw it; and he almost certainly killed himself in trying to make that ideal a reality.

6 The Dulwich Experiment

Ronald Groves (1954–66)
C. W. Lloyd (1967–75)

'The greatest social and educational experiment ever attempted by a public school'   (Evening News)

'SMALL in stature but large in understanding'—so one of the Governors described Ronald Groves, who in the autumn of 1954 became Dulwich's new Master. For some years he had taught at King's School, Canterbury, where he had been not only senior science master but also bursar with special responsibility for the conversion of buildings (and what could have been more appropriate, with so much rebuilding waiting to be done at Dulwich?). In 1943 he became head of Campbell College, Belfast, succeeding a former Dulwich assistant master, W. D. Gibbon. Hilary, his wife, was coming back to familiar territory when he was appointed to Dulwich, for she was the daughter of George Smith, and had spent her early years at the college, when the Master and his wife still lived 'over the shop'.

Ronald Groves found an unhappy school, for, though the Dulwich Experiment was beginning to show the first signs of the academic heights it was soon to reach, morale was at a low ebb. Twelve months had gone by since Gilkes' death, and during this period, with the deputy Master in charge, critics of the Experiment had not been slow to make themselves heard. Much needed to be done to restore goodwill. It took Groves about a year to restore harmony, an unenviable task to which he brought quiet efficiency, tact and determination. 'He was very greatly respected,' said one Old Alleynian who went to the college about this time. 'Even the kind of lout who didn't care a damn what his parents thought of his academic level would stand to attention. He seemed to know us all, too, which could be a bit disconcerting for the younger ones.' And one of the assistant masters remarked, 'In any gathering he emanated an air of authority. He was quite tough with his staff, but he probably needed to be; and toughness was always combined with humanity. He was extremely shrewd, and knew what people's weaknesses and strengths were.'

It was fortunate for the school that both he and the bursar were skilled in finance, for in this direction also a good deal needed to be done. One necessary measure that was quickly brought into effect was the raising of the fees, which were still extraordinarily low—lower, in fact, than those of any comparable school in the London area. With the approval of the Ministry of Education, in 1955 they were increased from £75 to £105 a year, and in 1956, to keep pace with a rise in the Burnham scale and the superannuation fund, by a further £12. From this time onwards the salaries of the teaching staff kept steadily ahead of Burnham, for the first time in the history of the college comparing well with those paid at other independent schools.

Changes were also made in the Foundation Scheme. One of these, which had come into effect just before Gilkes' death, provided for an extra Governor, so making it possible for the headmaster and staff of the college and of Alleyn's each to have a representative on the Board instead of being obliged to share one, as had formerly been the case—which, since the interests of the two schools were by no means identical, had sometimes created difficulties. In 1962, after much discussion between the various beneficiaries of the Foundation and the Estates Governors, who were anxious to modify the Foundation Scheme in such a way that more money would be available for the development of the Estate, the Scheme was altered so that it became possible for all the reasonable demands of the school for financial help with building and other needs to be met without recourse to Parliament.

Dulwich benefited from having as Chairman of the Board of Governors at this time an Old Alleynian who brought to the job immense gifts and professional skill: his inspiration was tremendous and his foresight uncanny. Hartley Shawcross succeeded Lord Gorell in 1959, receiving his peerage in the same year. ('Schools like peers for their chairmen,' one of his colleagues remarked drily. 'It's good for their public image, and they can bring influence to bear.') He was a first-rate chairman, decisive, brilliant at catching salient points, excellent at devising equitable solutions to knotty problems. He never missed a meeting if he could help it, arriving exactly one minute before it was due to begin and not pausing to chat afterwards: a benign smile, and he was out in a flash. He took an unfailing interest in what went on at Dulwich, and was never too busy to give help and advice.

With the school's finances on a sound basis, attention could be turned to the urgent matter of rebuilding. 'Groves was never happier than when the school rang with the sound of builders' hammers,' one of his staff comments. 'We must get the plant right, he would say, and then, whatever the system and the times, the future of the college will be secure.' The steady ringing of hammers throughout the fifties and sixties must have rejoiced his soul. Between 1955 and 1966 six classrooms were added to the junior block to relieve the congestion in the main building, so that the whole of the lower school could be taught in one place; there were new music-rooms and squash courts; changing rooms were built to replace the old ones, which a Government inspection in 1964 damned as 'old and deplorable' (Alleynians of the day described them in less repeatable terms); and a new swimming-bath was opened. Much of the gravel, such a scourge in the past because of its tendency to turn into liquid mud in rainy weather, was replaced by tarmac,[1] and the original wrought-iron gates, restored to their early glory, were put back into

---

[1] 'When my father was your guest at the first Alleyn Club dinner after the war,' Christopher Smith said in 1954, 'I remember him saying that when he came to Dulwich the first thing that gripped him was the charm of the place, and he certainly said that the next thing that gripped him was the mud.'

place at the College Road entrance. The pavilion was at last restored to its proper use, and the jungly spread of grass and trees between Dulwich Common and the boarding-houses was cleared, and gardens laid out in accordance with a plan suggested by Gilkes before his death. Ronald Groves, back from a visit to the United States, rechristened the cloisters 'the Breezeway' and decided to exclude the breeze by glassing them in. This caused some protest from those who rightly felt that the innovation spoilt the look of the centre block, but the boys whose only refuge this was in their free time, no matter how fierce the wind and rain driving in, can have felt nothing but gratitude.

All this rebuilding necessitated an extension to the heating plant, an operation which, carefully planned and organized, was rapidly carried out during one summer term and the following holidays—though some doubts were felt about the validity of the laws of physics as hot water poured over the roof of one boarding-house while the baths in the other were stone cold.

Much, however, remained to be done, not least to provide an adequate dining-room. Apart from the boarders and the lower school, the boys still had lunch in the Great Hall, where one antiquated lift hoisted the food from the kitchens below to one small serving-room provided with one hot cupboard. Over the years many plans were drawn up for new buildings commensurate with the immensely increased numbers in the school: echoing Booth's vision of the thirties, it was hoped to have an assembly hall to seat 1,500 people, which would also cater for drama, modern language and music teaching, private studies for the sixth form, practice rooms for the choir and orchestra, two gymnasia, and so on. There were endless discussions about the most suitable sites, and advice was sought from Sir William (later Lord) Holford, planning consultant to the City of London and Professor of Town Planning at London University. After a tour of the school in 1964 he commented to the Governors, 'With all respect to your predecessors, I have seldom seen so much architecture used to enclose so little space!'

In 1965 it was estimated that a memorial hall, dining-room

and kitchens, a physical training centre and Scout accommodation, computer rooms, workshops and the reorganization of the centre block would cost nearly half a million pounds. By the time Ronald Groves left in 1966 plans on the drawing-board were well advanced, and the Covered Courts, which had been causing some anxiety because of their rickety condition, had been demolished and replaced by the present P.E. centre. This was opened by A. E. R. Gilligan, giving Dulwich one of the best gymnasia and Scout centres in the country. There was talk of a footbridge or tunnel to make the passage across College Road safer, but in the end it was decided to trust to the good sense of the boys—and the tunnel anyway would have been impractical, partly because of the cost and partly because of technical problems caused by underground television lines.

One factor which did as much as anything, after the recent embattled years, to restore harmonious relations between the Master and the staff and amongst the staff themselves was the system of regular meetings to discuss the progress (or otherwise) of individual boys. The meetings were not new, but under Ronald Groves they developed in a way which brought many benefits. 'At first they were pretty terrible,' he says, 'because there were so many boys the staff were critical of. People were always being reported.' This situation became easier as the procedure whereby the boys were accepted was modified, giving the assistant masters a large share of the responsibility. It became possible—but only after a considerable period of time—for him to look down the table at these meetings, when dire penalties were called for, and ask blandly, 'Who picked the boy?' Someone would reply, 'I did,' and a friendly discussion would follow; or the man concerned might say, 'Well, Master, I interviewed him, and I didn't think he was right for us, but you over-ruled me'—and everyone would burst out laughing.

Another ingredient in the restoration of goodwill were the meetings which took place regularly between the heads of sides and subjects to sort out such matters as the number of periods per subject, the distribution of free periods, the allocation of 'difficult' forms, the setting and pairing of subjects, and other essential details. Again, these were not new, but during Gilkes' day it had become customary for the deputy master to chair them.

One of Ronald Groves' first actions was to abolish the post of deputy master, which he felt, in the situation he had inherited, to be a barrier between the staff and himself, though later, when Eric Parsley retired, he found it necessary to appoint a second master to bear some of the increasing pressure of work. There could be only one choice—Eric Handscomb, that amazing man who did the work of six men. 'As quite a young master,' George Way remarks, 'his efficiency had been tacitly recognised by Booth, who, whenever a masters' meeting came to some tricky point on the agenda, would interject, "Handscomb, take notes!"' 'He does the timetable in the holidays,' Ronald Groves said at an Alleyn Club dinner in 1961, 'he keeps the records, he is one of our panel of selectors of new boys, sets most of the questions, and is the only one who knows the answers to all of them.' Another colleague writes:

> He was (I suppose) a Modern Linguist, but I remember him as Administrator-in-Chief, the man who was secretary to the heads of sides. He had an immensely shrewd and perceptive intelligence, and despite his always quiet manner was greatly respected by everyone, and carried great weight in common room debates. His interventions were always on the side of sanity, and he could both 'cool' a situation and spotlight the essential issues. He also had a quick and unerring eye for the ridiculous. Dulwich owes a tremendous debt to Eric Handscomb.

These meetings between heads of sides were of the greatest possible value, Ronald Groves feels, in creating a happy atmosphere, enabling him to find out what people were thinking and what was happening in the school, and so prevent molehills from growing into mountains. 'He seemed to enjoy the more intimate "feel" of this smaller gathering,' says Eric Handscomb. 'If he had a fault, it was in listening too long and too patiently while Mr X and Mr Y argued the case for giving their pet subjects greater space in the timetable. It was a good fault: it might have been too reminiscent of his predecessor if he had asserted his authority sooner. There was a wealth of good humour and often entertaining comment at heads of sides meetings'—as, indeed, there still is.

Bringing the staff into the procedure whereby the local authority scholars were chosen contributed as much as anything to the feeling that everyone was working together. This process had formerly been solely in the hands of Gilkes and his deputy (increasingly the latter alone), and selection had been made almost entirely on the basis of academic ability. Now a system was devised whereby first Ronald Groves saw the parents and boys briefly, and then the boys were tested by a team of masters working in twos or threes. Fresh masters were brought in each year, and care was taken to involve those who were particularly critical of the scholarship scheme. What the selectors looked for was the boy who would make a contribution not only to the academic standard of the school but also to its overall life in the field of sport, hobbies or whatever. They were given comprehension tests largely devised by Raymond Wilson, one of the outstanding young masters, and himself an inspiring teacher, who helped to make the English department so exceptionally good at this time. 'None of these boys had an I.Q. of less than 115,' he says, 'and, once you start going for the all-round achiever, after about 110 his I.Q. becomes irrelevant: motivation is much more important. So our job was to find out how highly the boys were motivated in wanting to come to Dulwich.'

The interviews went on for about a fortnight. Each afternoon, the day's work completed, the whole team would cross the road to Elm Lawn, where, over tea provided by Hilary Groves ('Crumpets positively swimming in butter'), they reviewed the applicants. 'Groves had an enormously retentive memory,'[1] Raymond Wilson says:

> Often he remembered the parents by some small detail, perhaps of their clothing. 'I didn't take to her much,' he might say. 'She

---

[1] This I had observed for myself in our discussions about this book. Some comment of mine about the academic achievements of individual boys would produce the answer, quick as a flash, 'But he only got a place at Peterhouse—it was Bloggs who walked off with the scholarship', or 'Yes, he turned out to be a bit of a disappointment; he only got a 2–2 at Wadham'— and this about boys who had been at the school twenty years earlier.

had a funny feather in her hat. But he was all right: very anxious for his boy to come to us, and though there aren't many facilities in the house to read or do prep I think he'll manage to work something out. He's a bricklayer, a nice chap, sincere . . . I think the boy'll do.' He was absolutely practical about it, and the principle of compensation worked—that is, if two boys had equal claims but the first came from a bookish home and the second not, then the second was in.

One interesting facet of the selection was that Dulwich, unlike many public schools, has never had a Jewish quota: no one knew, when the boys were being interviewed, what their religion was, and this policy worked to the advantage of the minority groups. There has always been an excellent admixture of foreign boys, who have contributed much to the school and have never felt themselves to be outsiders. 'The American boys are the only ones who occasionally cause problems,' one master said, 'because, although much more advanced socially than our boys, they're behind us educationally, as a result of their broader based syllabus.'

From an academic point of view, the fifties heralded the most 'sparky' era the college has ever known. At the time of Gilkes' death the first of the local authority scholars were reaching the top forms and starting to go to university, and the great rivalry with other schools of high academic standing began. Each year the various league tables—O's and A's, state scholarships, open awards to Oxbridge—were eagerly scanned, and each year the results grew more impressive. In 1948 Gilkes had said that it was a good year when the school gained as many as seven open awards; in 1955 fifteen were won, and from this point onward Dulwich steadily climbed the ladder, reaching the top for the first time in 1960, and thereafter keeping pace with the most famous schools in the country. Between 1966 and 1976 more awards were won than by any other school—often with a considerably wider spread in the number of subjects in which success was gained. Similarly, whereas in 1952 it was estimated that about a quarter of the boys leaving would be going on to university or some other college of further education, by the 1960s this figure had risen to somewhere in the region of three-quarters.

Bright boys are tempting intellectual bait for brilliant teachers; and during the years of the Experiment Dulwich had the pick of the field so far as the staff were concerned. Gilkes and the Masters who followed him gathered together a number of clever, forward-looking young men for whom a post at the college held many attractions: they were teaching talented boys who wanted to learn; at few other schools would they have had the chance of working with so many pupils at an advanced level; they were by now well paid; and Dulwich was only a long stone's throw from the civilized attractions of London. As colleagues, too, they had a group of highly intelligent people with whom real conversation was possible. 'There was a quite outstanding crowd of young to middle-aged men, who kept you right on your toes,' one of them remarks. 'It was a very happy common room, with very little back-biting, whereas at my previous school there were so many elderly bachelors that they virtually took over the common room, and woe betide anyone who tried to occupy "their" (ie, the best) chairs.'

Though it is quite unfair to pick out individuals from such an exceptional group, some of them are mentioned over and over again by boys who learned from them and by colleagues who shared jokes and tribulations with them. Jim Gibson (known as Cathy after an Olympic swimmer of the day) is one: Gilkes—who didn't really believe in such a subject—took him on to organize the English department. He arrived to find that the only anthology of English poetry in the school consisted of about eight hundred copies of Palgrave's *Golden Treasury*, which he abstracted in twos and threes and took away to dispose of, replacing them with what the *Alleynian* called 'the best-stocked English bookroom in the country'. A colleague describes him as 'a missionary head of English. I liked him enormously. In the moments of relaxation from burning with a hard, gemlike flame (or whatever it is) he could be very funny indeed. He was someone of complete integrity and an outstandingly good teacher.' There was Ernest Heard, head of modern languages, whose department was particularly successful. As one boy of the period, now head of the modern language department of a famous public school, puts it, 'At the time when we were going into the E.E.C., Dulwich contributed as much as any other school to the teaching of modern languages, not least through the numbers of staff and boys who went on to other schools to run departments.' There was Frank Bamford, head of classics, who would thunder at his class, 'Don't sit there like so many buckets waiting to be filled!' A. S. Macpherson, head of German, was well known outside Dulwich classrooms, for his *Deutches Leben* series was probably more widely used than any other school German course—indeed, it was pirated by the Germans to help them during their occupation of the Channel Islands. For many years he was one of the most distinguished teachers of German in the country. David Baggley was an outstanding head of history, as was E. N. Williams, who followed him. 'The history results were amazing during this period,' remarks Charles Lloyd, Groves' successor, 'and the work at sixth-form level quite astounding.'

One of Ronald Groves' most successful ventures was a series of sixth-form lectures which continued for eleven years. He had previously started such a series at Campbell College, and was keen to develop them at Dulwich also. When Dr Williams (a distinguished writer and historian as well as an excellent teacher) joined the staff he took over from Groves the task of tempting top-rank people to come to the school and talk. The list of lecturers is remarkable—all the more so since they were paid no fee, their only reward being a large and attentive audience. Sir Charles Snow (as he then was) spoke about the two cultures; Sir Edward Boyle on the duties of a Departmental Minister; Lord Salisbury on the House of Lords; Professor Nikolaus Pevsner on recent trends in British architecture; Sir Gordon Russell on industrial design; and John Weightman on existentialism. Other speakers were Lord Shawcross; Lord Hailsham; Michael Stewart, later to be Secretary of State for Education and Science; Mark Bonham-Carter; A. J. Ayer, who delivered 'one of the most stimulating harangues heard at Dulwich for some time'; George Woodcock, General Secretary of the T.U.C.; Professor Asa

Briggs; Richard Crossman, who came several times, and was popular not least because he was refreshingly indiscreet; the Earl of Kilmuir, Deputy Chief Prosecutor at the Nuremberg trials; Professor Stuart Hampshire; Hugh Carleton Green, Director General of the B.B.C.; Alec Dickson, founder of Voluntary Service Overseas; Lord Attlee, who was extremely impressive; James Callaghan,[1] not yet leader of the Labour Party ('He answered many stimulating questions with a mixture of responsibility and gravity and impish humour, and was quite the most relaxed speaker since his colleague, Mr Crossman, similarly mesmerized the audience'); and Sir Isaiah Berlin (who 'created just the whirlwind impression we had been led to expect', and after a fascinating and skilful talk on the role of the writer in modern Russia 'hustled out as quickly as he had come, leaving the Sixth Form in a state of bewildered admiration').

The excellent results on the arts side were matched by those from the science block. In the between-war years Dulwich had not had a particularly distinguished record in this direction. However, the Second World War had created a demand for scientists, with the prospect of a good career at the end of their training; and the science staff took advantage of this by introducing the subject into the lower school and, as George Way puts it, 'unashamedly lacing the curriculum with the most spectacular experiments we could devise, rejoicing the hearts of the small boys who enjoyed blowing things up.'

Between 1952 and 1964 the number of boys specializing in science grew from 44% to 55%; even by the time Ronald Groves arrived the new science block was already becoming inadequate. It was fortunate that the Governors were able to take advantage of money made available by the Industrial Fund for the Advancement of Scientific Education, an

---

[1] Callaghan features in another context, as the father of an enterprising Alleynian who returned a borrowed French textbook in which he had adorned every male portrait with a pair of moustachios. Since this could clearly not be passed on to anyone else H. I. Alexander, who was then master in charge of the bookroom, sent the boy's father a bill for 2s 6d, which was duly settled.

organization sponsored by various industrial giants which had been set up in order to improve the teaching of science in schools. For the extension to the science block which was built in 1957 the Fund gave Dulwich £27,000, plus £2,000 for equipment; the remaining £15,000 was provided out of a loan from the Estates Governors. This was one of the Fund's largest projects, and the first to be put into use; at that time the college probably offered the finest scientific facilities of any school in the country.

The extension was opened by the President of the Royal Society, Sir Cyril Hinshelwood, Professor of Chemistry at Oxford. One of the most interesting guests was the man who was the moving spirit behind the Industrial Fund, himself an Old Alleynian, and arguably the most distinguished scientist and man of many parts that the school has ever sent forth into the world, Sir Harold Hartley—scientist, don, chairman of innumerable companies, president of the fourth World Power Conference, in the forefront, as vice-president of the London, Midland and Scottish Railway, of the most important technical revolution in the country of his day, the modernizing of our railways: in short, 'a sort of super-rolling stone' (as one newspaper put it) 'who believes in starting every new career from the top'. 'Just as he had brought to his activities as a university tutor,' *The Times* wrote in its obituary, 'the invigoration of his many contacts with outside interests; so to the public and official concerns of his later life he contributed the clarifying and liberalizing influence of a precise and disinterested scholarship.' He spent many years on the Board of his old school—to which, he said, because of the teaching of Harrison and Baker he owed almost everything—and helped it in innumerable ways.

In its splendid new surroundings the science side, having by then absorbed the despised engineers, reached its peak in 1962, when there were five upper sixths, six sixths, and six removes (at Dulwich the removes are equivalent to the first-year sixth forms), with twenty-four full-time scientists on the staff. Between 1955 and 1975 it contributed one hundred and thirteen to the grand total of Oxbridge awards: of one of the winners, the senior science tutor at Oxford who examined him wrote, 'His performance was quite phenomenal. It is twenty-five years since we saw any marks resembling these.'

Mathematics, too, with fifty-nine Oxbridge awards between 1967 and 1975, reached unprecedented heights, as well as having some astonishing individual successes (though it was a boy of an earlier era who surely achieved a Guinness record with 2,182 out of a possible 2,200 marks in the advanced and scholarship maths papers, scoring *above* the maximum in four of the seven papers because, apparently, he produced a better method of working than the examiners had foreseen). Several boys were selected for national and international mathematics Olympiads—in 1971 the school provided three out of the team of eight going to the Olympiads in Yugoslavia. Much of the phenomenal success of the science and mathematics was due to the inspiration and dedicated work of George Way, H. V. Styler, and Ray Payne.

In 1961 the staff had been augmented by the Rev. J. N. F. Earle, who in the same year published his best-selling and controversial *What's Wrong with the Church?* 'He was,' wrote the *Alleynian* when he left ten years later, 'one of the body of mathematicians who have raised Dulwich to its position of top mathematical school in the country at the present time . . . and the director and inspiration of this country's best-publicized and most successful school computer department.' There had already been a good deal of discussion about computer projects with Alan Cooper, head of the mathematical side, as well as meetings with outside bodies and with industry. The college had, in fact, been offered its own computer, but because of the size of it and the cost of maintenance, and in view of the rapid changes taking place in the whole field, the offer had had to be refused. Nevertheless, Ronald Groves felt that the project must go on, seeing it not only as useful to specialist mathematicians, but as a great chance to try to bridge the gap between the 'two cultures'—arts and science. Linguists both ancient and modern, he believed, would find a real interest and outlet in the logic and language of computing; ultimately, too, every boy would need to know something about computing as part of his general education.

When Nick Earle had established himself on the staff, he needed little persuasion to add to his other enthusiasms the job of developing this project. Since the school did not yet have its own computer, the scheme (which was, he believes, probably the first of its kind in the country) was run through Cybernet Time Sharing Ltd, which sold time on its machines to businesses without a computer of their own. Dulwich was offered free time, and this meant that for the price of a telephone call the boys had access to an extremely complicated system, thereby saving many thousands of pounds (in 1972 this time cost £2.50 a minute). But it was not all philanthropy; many of the boys who caught the bug worked for Cybernet in the holidays, providing highly skilled labour at a modest rate of pay.

By 1968 a course on the part played by computers in modern society was part of the curriculum of every sixth-form boy. 'All sorts of programs get written by all sorts of people,' the *Alleynian* reported; 'programs to do maths prep, programs to prove Physics masters wrong, programs to tell you the time of day, programs to draw Christmas trees, and the inevitable programs to play battleships or cricket with.'

As with so many aspects of the vigorous life within the school, this venture into computer education was made possible by the size and quality of the sixth forms. This was true, too, of the Liberal Studies course which was introduced in 1964. Liberal Studies was a concept very much in the air in the educational world at that time, as part of the conviction that it is essential, in our increasingly specialized world, to bridge the gap between the two cultures by interesting the science side in the arts and vice versa. Weekly lectures to large groups of specialists in either culture were followed by discussions among small groups, the excellence and versatility of the staff and the size of the school making it possible to devise courses using home-grown talent: with around ninety masters, at least half of them with Oxbridge degrees, and together covering a very wide field of interests, almost any subject could form the basis of a course, from astronomy to computing, the history of art, philosophy, ideas in music, navigation, and book-binding. The masters could ride their particular hobby-horses to their hearts' content, and the boys were unrestricted by exam syllabuses.

With so much going for them at Dulwich, none of the staff—whom Ronald Groves chose with great care and insight—dreamt of leaving except for promotion. And this was the snag, for, since these young masters were both ambitious and sought after, they tended to be offered excellent posts at other schools. The turnover was disconcertingly swift: at the time of Groves' retirement it was calculated that, of the assistant masters who had served under him, twenty were at that time headmasters, and most of the others who had left did so to become heads of departments or of other educational establishments. The boys, with their usual percipience, understood the state of play. 'We always know who's going to leave and who's going to stay,' they said to one master departing for a professorship, 'and we knew you wouldn't be here very long.'

The memories of one member of the staff, who overlapped Gilkes and Groves, give a vivid impression of the school at this time:

A throng of boys in black jackets and trousers, emerging from, or disappearing into, parts of the buildings that I never fully explored in my seven years there. A large, vigorous, articulate and lively staff—one that was basically friendly but kept you on your toes. Boys of good academic ability, some very able indeed with whom you needed to be two laps ahead in your teaching. Being worked *hard*, in teaching and administration, often with little margin to spare, and a sense of relief in being able to collapse into one of the leather armchairs in the splendid masters' library and just go to sleep. A sense of all sorts of things 'going on' in the school community life of which one was never fully conscious, merely because one was too busy keeping up with one's own immediate concerns. (For example, I myself never knew a great deal about the Arts, Music or Games; and hardly ever entered the Science Block; and though for some reason I *may* once or twice have reached the top floor of the North or South Block, I can't remember doing so. I myself lived very largely on the ground floor of the South Block, and in any North Block room always had an uneasy feeling I was 'abroad'!) Despite all the hairy problems that my years there saw, my abiding memory is of a splendid staff, energetic, able, committed and enthusiastic, who rode the storms that they themselves to some extent created. And of a very good crowd of boys, some of whom I remember well as individuals and about whose later careers I wish I knew.

In 1961, when he was a little past the halfway mark in his mastership, Ronald Groves, in his annual report to parents, made the point that the academic level had been won, 'so to speak, in our stride, rather unobtrusively against the background of the multitudinous activities that go on all the time at Dulwich—societies, games, lectures, field-days and the like'. Certainly the societies flourished and multiplied, though it became increasingly difficult to combat the lure of activities outside the school, 'the glamour of "pop" music, the lowering of the age for "dating" and the high wages earned by unqualified teenagers', as the *Alleynian* put it. To combat this, all the societies were drawn together under one umbrella organization, the Union, which came into existence to co-ordinate the various activities and to whip up interest, a thankless task which it performed with a degree of success that tended to depend on the enthusiasm or otherwise of the secretary and of the master who was president. Chess was popular, and in 1966 Dulwich won *The Sunday Times* chess competition against some seven hundred other schools (this was not the first time it had done so). The following year Raymond Keene, one week after leaving the college, beat Mikhail Botvinnick, for thirteen years the world champion, in an international championship at Hastings; in 1972 he became British amateur chess champion; and he is now an international Grand Master (the second English player to gain this distinction), and one of the best-known chess theorists in the country.

As always, there was music. When Stanley Wilson died in 1953 he was succeeded by C. H. Johnson, who inspired the formation of the Chamber Music Society and encouraged the development of the Madrigal Group. One of his first assignments was to finish rehearsing the choir for a performance and recording of Berlioz's *Te Deum* under Sir Thomas Beecham.

Like his predecessor, Cecil Johnson died while still comparatively young, and in 1957 Alan Morgan took his place—a
stroke of immense good fortune for the school. Appointed
shortly before Gilkes' death in 1953, he had been instructed by
the Master 'to make the boys open their mouths and SING!'

The annual concert at the Festival Hall continued to
attract capacity audiences, but in 1964, when the hall was
closed, another venue had to be found. The Fairfield Hall
provided such an excellent substitute that it was decided to
hold the Christmas concert there in future instead of in the
Bath Hall, one of the most popular occasional items being
Arnold's Toy Symphony, with the Master, his wife, and some
of the assistant masters playing the solo parts. This has always
brought the house down. Other highlights were tours in 1963
and 1966 by the Madrigal Group to Belgium and Germany.
The boys recorded madrigals and part-songs, performed in the
Bremen Musica Antiqua Festival, made a tape of folk-songs
and nursery-rhymes for use in German schools, and gave a
concert at an 'approved' school in which every item was a hit,

Fig. 6.1   Rehearsing for a Festival Hall concert

from 'There's a hole in my bucket' to the Egmont Overture played on two pianos. Concerts were also given in the Queen Elizabeth Hall and the Purcell Room. An outstanding musical pupil of this era was Alan Hacker, one of the finest clarinettists of our generation. Others were David Greer, now at Queen's University, Belfast, and the composer Anthony Payne. The biannual chapel concerts began in 1962 with a performance of Bach's *St Matthew Passion* and have continued ever since. The intimacy and appeal of the setting have helped to make these performances memorable occasions.

At the height of the Dulwich Experiment, just over 86% of the boys at the College were local authority scholars; and in 1958, of the twenty-three open awards gained to Oxford and Cambridge, all but two were won by these scholarship boys. But even in Gilkes' day there had been intimations that the number of local authority places was likely to become smaller, partly because of the growing feeling that comprehensive schools were the future shape of our educational structure, partly because, as the post-war building of schools got into its stride, places were once again available in state schools.

In 1961 the L.C.C. informed the Governors that, instead of the eighty-five places which they had previously reserved each year for new entries, the number would be reduced to sixty in the following year and forty-five in 1963. This was alarming news, and early in 1962 Lord Shawcross, Ronald Groves, and the Clerk to the Governors went to County Hall to discuss the situation with the Chairman of the Education Committee. As they pointed out, when the arrangement had come into force the L.C.C. had undertaken that no substantial variation in the number of pupils sent by the Council each year would be made without proper notice. The whole understanding on the part of the Governors had been that the L.C.C. regarded the arrangement as a permanent one, and this was why the main entry had been lowered from 13+ to 11+. (Here the Governors were perhaps being a trifle disingenuous, for there was in general no permanent commitment on either side with any of the local authorities—though, as H.M. Inspectors recorded after their visit in 1952, 'the position with regard to the London County Council is in this respect rather different in that 425 places in Dulwich College are shown in the Authority's Development Plan as part of its provision for secondary education'.) The sudden cessation of such a large number of pupils would present the college with immense difficulties, especially since contact had long since been lost with most of the preparatory schools which had formerly provided the bulk of the entry. To this the L.C.C. replied that, with London's population on the decline, it wasn't going to be easy to fill their own schools, and to pay for children to go to Dulwich would create an *Alice in Wonderland* situation. They had a point, as Lord Shawcross said, adding, 'It's clear we're not going to win this one!'

Nevertheless, the Governors took their case to the Minister of Education, who, though sympathetic, had no powers to help. In the end a compromise was reached: the L.C.C. reduced their number to fifty a year, while Kent, Surrey, and Croydon, which did not have London's problem of schools waiting to be filled, for the time being continued to take the same number of places as they had done in recent years.

At the time Ronald Groves felt that this was a somewhat inequitable way of winding down such a brilliantly successful scheme, but with the passing of the years he has come round to the view that the reasoning was justified and the decision inevitable—even though the number of local authority scholars was only a drop in the ocean of the total population of children attending London schools. 'I wish there could be a wider recognition of the experiment that Dulwich has made,' he wrote in 1964. 'If there is anything in this idea of integrating schools into the State system, Dulwich has tried to do it and to be fair to everybody.' He himself would have liked to see all three Foundation Schools (the College, Alleyn's, and James Allen's School for Girls) working more closely together, so as to economize in such areas as classics, in which college pupils in the highest forms are given almost individual attention—a marvellous opportunity for the boys concerned, but basically a wasteful state of affairs that could have been ameliorated by the pooling of resources.

One idea was in fact mooted (by Stuart Maclure, editor of the *Times Educational Supplement*) for a degree of integration between the college and the five comprehensive schools with which, by the mid-sixties, it was surrounded, together educating some five thousand children and providing a cross-section of all the educational needs of the neighbourhood. Why not, he suggested, devise a scheme whereby the college would become the centre of a number of activities in which all these schools could unite—the arts, perhaps, and sport, since the comprehensive school pupils had to travel long distances to play games? The plan came to nothing, and it would have required immense goodwill, vision, and drive on the part of everyone concerned to bring it into operation, as well as a large sum of money which it might not have been possible to find. But perhaps a unique opportunity was missed for bringing together schools from the independent and the state sectors, at a time when the climate was riper for such an experiment than it had ever been before or is likely to be again. And perhaps, too, the bond thus formed would have helped to defuse the occasional confrontations between the boys from the college and the local state schools.

In 1965, with a Labour Government pledged 'to reduce the socially divisive influence the [public schools] now exerted', a Public Schools Commission was set up to advise on just this problem of integrating the public schools and the state system. The Headmasters' Conference and the Governing Bodies Association for Independent Schools established a joint working party to prepare information likely to be required by the Commission, and Ronald Groves was persuaded to accept the post of adviser to this body. At the end of the summer term of 1966 he relinquished the mastership which he had filled for twelve years with such distinction and success, and to which he had brought not only strength of purpose, a policy of conciliation, and a first-class brain, but also a valuable shrewdness and ingenuity which he never shrank from exercising for the good of the college. A brilliant teacher—'amusing, riveting, fascinating', in the words of one of his assistant masters—his main regret is that the Friday afternoon prefects' periods which he took, and which in George Smith's day had covered a wide range of educational topics, gradually turned into discussions on how the school should be run, how caps should be worn, whether hair should be long or short; though he did manage, in the midst of his duties as Master, to keep his share of the science scholarship teaching. But, 'You do what you're good at, and latterly I had to become so closely involved with the rebuilding—it would have been disastrous if we hadn't achieved then all we managed to do.' Whatever his own reservations on this score, he left the school an infinitely happier and more united place than he had found it, and was regretted alike by masters, parents and boys—who had always, as he said, been so incredibly reliable and intelligent.

In one matter, however, he had to admit partial defeat. In 1961, in his annual report to the parents, he had written, 'It has been my constant effort since coming to Dulwich to reduce the numbers somewhat. Ironically, a measure of my success could be that whereas this term we started with 1,390 boys, in my first term there were 1,391.' Well, perhaps after all he could claim a small triumph, for when he made his adieux in 1966 the number of boys had sunk to 1,363.

In the autumn term of 1966 there was once again an interregnum during which the duties of acting master were carried out by George Way, who had succeeded Eric Handscomb in 1961 as second master, and who is described by his colleagues as a man of infinite goodwill and honesty, the hardest working man on the staff. Under his caretakership things went on smoothly until Charles Lloyd became Master in the new year of 1967.

For Lloyd, the decision to take over the mastership had not been an easy one. He had been headmaster of Alleyn's for three years, having previously been head of Hutton Grammar School; he was happy there; and obviously, when the invitation came from the college Governors to move from one Foundation school to another, various difficult factors were involved. He was concerned at the possible upheavals caused to Alleyn's by having two headmasters within such a short space of time. Moreover, he had embarked on an extensive rebuilding programme, which he had hoped to see through. Nor was it easy to transfer his loyalty in this way—though once the move had been made he felt himself fortunate to have been so translated. After his acceptance of the post was made public the local press ran an article with the headline DULWICH COLLEGE IS TAKING ALLEYN'S HEAD, and 'Thank goodness we've got a pub at last!' the boys said. Lloyd remembers with much amusement the congratulations of one member of his staff at Alleyn's, who told him with deep sincerity, 'It would have taken a great man to refuse it'!

Lloyd found such a trim and orderly ship that, he felt:

> ... anything I did could only be for the worse. The staff were absolutely united, and the academic standards so high that it was rather like driving a spirited coach-and-four: I felt that I was there to keep it running as smoothly as possible in every department. It would have been fatal to say, 'Here's a place to try out my ideas', or to make changes which would have harmed the traditions of the school. Dulwich is bigger than its Masters: they come and go, but the school has so much driving force of its own that it rolls on regardless, and the individual Masters can't make a vast amount of difference.

Some changes, however, he did feel to be necessary, and one of the most important was the creation of a middle school. With close on 1,400 boys, this was an advantage administratively. More important, however, was the consideration that boys going up from the lower school at the age of thirteen or thereabouts tended to find themselves lost in the huge wilderness of the upper school, all the more so since, instead of the fair degree of regimentation to which they had been accustomed, they suddenly found themselves expected to cope with quite a large degree of freedom. So the boys of thirteen, fourteen, and fifteen were put into the south block under the care of Stephen Howard, perhaps the most outstanding assistant master of the post-war years. A great scholar and inspired teacher, he accepted reluctantly the job of running the middle school when it was created in 1970, just as he had shrunk from taking on the headship of the classics side ten years earlier, not because he shirked either, but from doubt of his own abilities.

Howard was involved in tragedy in 1972, through no fault

of his own, when three boys fell to their death during a climbing holiday on Snowdon. He was shattered, and only with great difficulty could Charles Lloyd persuade him to stay on. 'However you look at it,' he said, 'I'm coming back with three fewer people than I started with.' By a terrible irony of fate, Howard was himself killed six years later, also on a climbing expedition. His loss at the school is still felt, by colleagues who relied with complete trust on his unobtrusive goodness and practical idealism, and by the boys whom he taught with such learning and wisdom, and who always knew they could go to him with their troubles. 'His influence threaded itself through the school,' a prefect said. 'He was such good value in conversation, and his fund of knowledge was amazing—he could finish off a Shakespearean or a Greek quotation at the drop of a pin. He was wise without being overbearing or bumptious, and you don't often find that.'

Another important innovation was the holding of regular open meetings with the staff, a democratic forum at which the masters—especially the younger men who found it difficult to raise their points at the more formal staff meetings with ninety-odd people present—could put forward matters about which they felt strongly. These open meetings really originated in the remark of one young master who asked, 'Can't we have a chance to discuss things like whether or not ballpoint pens may be used?' Ballpoint pens probably never actually came on the agenda, but a multitude of other things were discussed, from Saturday morning school to the abolition of boxing and caps, and whether or not spelling is important. There was no time limit and sometimes the meetings went on for hours, giving everyone a chance to let off steam; there were tremendous arguments between the old and the young, the length, passion, and quality of the discussions reflecting the involvement of the staff.

'As schoolmasters they were the best bunch of men you could possibly have,' Charles Lloyd says:

They had immense knowledge and experience of teaching. I never tried to vie with them in their own disciplines, for I always felt it was essential to create circumstances in which these men could get their very best out of the boys. You can only run Dulwich through the staff. But I used to feel that, after listening to what they said, I could summarise the arguments better than anyone else in the room, and that they recognised and respected this. The biggest compliment I can pay them is that once a decision had been made, even if it wasn't a popular one, they were a hundred per cent behind me.

The introduction in 1971 of weekly boarding was another change. By then, as in so many areas of life at the college, a great wind of liberalism had swept through the boarding-house system. In 1966, according to an article in the *Alleynian*:

> One could be quite severely punished for walking through a door in front of a prefect, or for having one's jacket undone. A new member of a senior boarding-house could often be baffled by the intricacy of the 'asking permission to . . .' ritual, which could involve having to ask one prefect if you could address him, having to apologise to the House Captain (who [sic] you had not noticed) for not having asked him first, then asking him if you could address the prefect, before you could finally address the prefect (with the utmost deference) . . .

A few years later the prefects had been swept away altogether in the two senior houses.

Perhaps just because Dulwich is largely a day-school, the boys feel nowadays that the atmosphere in the boarding-houses is very free and easy, and therefore much more 'livable with' than in a boarding-school proper. 'There's a lot to be said for it,' one boy remarked:

> If your parents have to go abroad you can switch to being a boarder with the minimum of upset. It helps, too, in your last year, when you're working for exams, because there aren't so many distractions as you would get at home. There are all the games and other facilities the school provides—drama, music and all the rest of it—and I suppose the boarders contribute quite a lot to the life of the school too. Of course you miss out in some ways. It's not always easy to cope with the lack of privacy, and you lose contact with the things going on in your area and don't have friends there, except your parents' friends, which makes you a bit isolated in the holidays. On the other hand, there isn't the fag of a long journey every day, and there's always something interesting

going on, and companionship which you wouldn't get as a day-boy. And it forces you from quite early on to mix with people from all sorts of different backgrounds and ways of life.'

A third area where reform seemed to be needed was in the part which formal religion played in the school. The sixties were a time of religious doubt and crisis in all schools. In 1961 the *Alleynian* had talked of the 'boys who are passing through a phase of juvenile agnosticism[1] during a crucial period in their development as human beings, and who attend prayers, and mumble what is to them a repetitive ritual, while their thoughts are elsewhere, and their eyes are staring self-consciously at their shoes.' Gradually changes were made which would satisfy both the boys who were convinced Christians, many of whom felt that it was difficult for services to be really sincere if some of the participants were unwilling or unbelieving, and those for whom such services meant little or nothing. It was no longer compulsory to go to chapel, except for the boarders at the beginning and end of term: instead, the boys were given the option of listening to a religious or philosophical talk. The pattern of assembly, too, received radical treatment, especially for the senior school, becoming less conventional in form and more challenging in content. 'You can't say, "Let us pray" to a row of sceptical boys,' remarks John Boxley, whom Ronald Groves had appointed as chaplain, and who was responsible for many of the changes which were introduced under Charles Lloyd. The old library was fitted up so that it could be used as a chapel, making it possible to hold mid-week communion services in which anything up to a hundred boys took part—as they still do. As a result, the committed Christians were far more involved, while those with genuine religious doubts no longer felt disgruntled because they were being forced to participate in something alien to them.

Parallel with this went an extension of Voluntary Service,

---

[1] 'I had a very informative discussion with my housemaster,' one small boarder wrote to his mother. 'I was surprised to find that he openly admitted to be an agnostic. He, like me for one, is not sure but is prepared to go to chapel for forty minutes a week to think about it.'

to which, again, all schools were then moving, as it became increasingly recognized that for many boys playing games is not necessarily the be-all and end-all of free time. At Dulwich Voluntary Service had started in 1963 for boys in the sixth and upper sixth (later the fifth and fourth forms were included), and it was offered as a choice on Wednesday afternoons instead of games, and on Field Days as an alternative to the Combined Cadet Force. Armed with garden tools, paint brushes, or simply themselves, a party of forty to sixty boys set off (as they set off today) to tend old people's gardens, paint their walls, or visit the sick and elderly and handicapped. One summer eight of them drove down to Rapallo to remove quantities of volcanic rock so that an extension could be built on to a kindergarten for the village children.

The best part, they say, is visiting places like special schools and hospitals, because there is more human contact. Continuity is important, too: one man whom they visit regularly at the present time is a severe spastic, and the boys involved with him go back with great fidelity, and arrange for him to be brought to the school for sports days and concerts. A small band of them regularly collect old newspapers, which are sold to raise money for some cause that they themselves choose—the Wildlife Fund, Save the Whale, the British Heart Foundation, Friends of the Earth. Of course, most schools run projects of this kind, but in general they are not so big an operation as they are at Dulwich. Obviously, some of the boys volunteer in order to get out of games; but for many of them these projects spring from a real desire to help others, and a recognition that, knowing themselves to be privileged, they have a debt to society which they want to repay.

Then there was the development of the sixth-form centre, so that the older boys would be better able to feel that this was their own territory, and where they would have more freedom to work in peace and to organize their study periods con-structively. At first it tended to be a bit of a white elephant, but gradually the boys began to make greater use of it. A sixth-form forum was set up, and Charles Lloyd came to some of the meetings, to listen to discussions and try to allay the growing discontent which characterized the rebellious sixties. 'The Forum provides the sole direct means of communication between pupils and the Master,' said the *Alleynian* in 1970; and Charles Lloyd was bombarded with all kinds of demands, from a relaxation of the smoking ban (quickly knocked on the head) to grievances such as compulsory school uniform, lunch, prefect-power, and the coffee machine. The forum led to some popular changes—it was, amongst other things, largely responsible for the introduction of soccer on a limited scale, 'So long,' Lloyd said, 'as I can't see it!'—but gradually it degenerated into disgruntled carping about trivialities (the jam in the doughnuts was a favoured topic), and attendance grew sparse.

Dulwich was fortunate—especially in view of its situation on the outskirts of London—in emerging from the sixties revolt as well as it did. The first signs had, of course, come long before: in 1955 Ronald Groves was deprecating long hair in his letters to parents—he sometimes expressed the fear that he might be remembered as Ronald ('Get-your-hair-cut-boy!') Groves—and winklepickers made their unlawful appearance in his day. But this particular form of self-expression was almost as old as the century. Christopher Gilkes is said to have kept a pair of scissors in his desk for severing unruly locks; in the twenties George Smith had had trouble with 'sartorial efflorescence'; and even Gilkes *père* had written in his diary:

> I was obliged to notice throughout the term departures from the school rule about dress, as to the wearing of black coats. I hope that the departure will no more occur; I thought it right to send a circular to all the parents, as well as to speak to the boys: waistcoats of different colours were also worn. The matter is of more importance than appears at 1st sight to everyone . . .

As the decade progressed the mood of rebellion became more open and articulate. An editorial in the *Alleynian* in 1967 declared:

> It has become increasingly obvious that people at Dulwich no longer accept the imposed values of even five years ago. The prefect system is no longer a synonym for divinity, and authority

does not receive unreasoning obedience; rugby is yielding its exalted position to drama and music, as the need for self-expression overcomes the desire for corporate expression. However, this heartening growth of individuality creates its own problems. The traditional values were at least dependable. Each cog in the vast machine knew what was expected of it in its oblations to the system and knew and feared the consequences if it transgressed in any way. Now everything is uncertain—individuality is easily perverted into stupid insolence and at the same time there always remains a veneer of tradition to which lip-service is paid by nearly everyone.

It was an uneasy time, and in the late sixties every headmaster lived in fear of drugs. 'A school's reputation is very important,' Charles Lloyd says, 'and it can be ruined overnight.' He feels Dulwich was remarkably fortunate in having only a very small drugs problem, unlike so many schools. One reason, certainly, was the innate good sense and sophistication of the boys. Probably, too, they were so caught up in the busy life of the school, with everyone functioning at high speed and little time to be bored, that they were not easily susceptible to temptation.

Nevertheless the college, a large and flourishing independent school in an area with a great deal of social and educational deprivation, was a natural target for such bodies as the Schools Action Union and the National Union of School Students. The number of Dulwich boys who took part in the activities of these bodies was extremely small, and they 'kept their heads low', as one of them puts it. One or two wrote pieces for *Voice*, the magazine of the Schools Action Union; they flouted, as a matter of principle, the rules with regard to such things as uniform and compulsory games; they slipped into other boys' desks various small protest magazines; and they took a minor part in the propaganda for two N.U.S.S. demonstrations (though not in the demonstrations themselves). One of them writes now of his:

> ... annoyance about a whole set of features of school life that were irksome, infuriating, irrelevant, or a waste of good time that could have been spent on getting an education. In theory, I could see the system was unfair; then, I had plenty of friends outside the school, and could see no moral reason why I deserved to have a

whole range of school facilities that were so much better than theirs. I wasn't better than them, I was just cleverer. Being clever and active brings a whole range of awards for your whole life— rewards that you collect for yourself. Why should you start off with free access to the squash courts, the swimming pool, the music facilities, denied to people outside who could have used them better while you were getting on with your academic thing?

One of the occasions chosen for a demonstration (at various times there were twenty-seven of them) by local members of the Schools Action Union was the Founder's Day celebration in 1969 which marked the 350th anniversary of the birth of the college. 'DOWN WITH THE PUBLIC SCHOOLS!' and 'LLOYD IS OBSOLETE!' the banners proclaimed, but the rebels were quickly sent packing.

This anniversary was a splendid, long planned for occasion. The Queen Mother visited the picture gallery for the second time since the war, for in 1953 she had come down to open it after it had been rebuilt, when she had also toured the school. Gilkes, noticing then how rough the gravel was, had arranged to have it tarred and gravelled, but the weather was very hot, and the tar started bubbling through. Quickly a drugget was laid on top, but the effect, as one of the masters who watched the proceedings comments, 'was like walking over a waterbed or the bouncy floor in the House of Horrors. However, the Queen Mother took it in her stride (so to speak), showing no awareness of anything unusual.' The experience must never-theless have been somewhat traumatic, for on the second occasion—when it had been pouring with rain, and a roll of hession had hastily been laid over the resulting lake—she turned to Charles Lloyd and asked, 'You haven't got that awful drugget again, have you?'

There was a grand ball at the Festival Hall, as well as the usual concert; Dr Michael Ramsay, Archbishop of Canterbury, conducted the service in chapel on Commemoration Day; and later in the summer a splendid dinner was given, the menu repeating, so far as was possible, that served up at Alleyn's inaugural banquet. Appropriately, the Founder's Day play was *The Jew of Malta*, in which Alleyn had acted one of his finest roles.

The celebrations coincided with the completion of a considerable programme of rebuilding. The arts and crafts department, the Scouts and the maintenance staff had all been bundled off to far-flung parts of the school while what was for some time called 'the Composite Block' was built. Partly paid for by Old Alleynians, this consisted of the Christison Hall, the memorial cloister and the rebuilt art and crafts and design and technology departments, which made possible a great expansion into pottery, printing, metal and woodwork, and provided far better facilities for technical studies. Lord Shawcross had laid the foundation stone of this complex in the summer of 1967, and the buildings gradually came into use during the next couple of years. In 1969 they were opened formally by the Duke of Edinburgh, who in his speech paid tribute to Dulwich's unrivalled 'social niche', to its work in technology, and to the importance for industry of science-teaching in schools such as Dulwich. The Duke, coming on from Alleyn's, arrived twenty minutes before schedule, with the reception committee still not properly organized; and the boys' school-made hovercraft, on its maiden flight, narrowly avoided chopping off his leg. The new computer centre had come into existence rather earlier as a tribute to Sir Harold Hartley, the funds being raised amongst his eminent friends. In 1968 it was opened by Sir Harold himself, then in his ninetieth year, somewhat deaf but otherwise as sprightly as ever.

Rebuilding of the centre block had still to be tackled, but eventually the old kitchens and boarders' dining-room became the present sixth-form centre, study area and library. Freed at last from its function of doubling as the dining-room, the Great Hall was redecorated to live up to the more elegant role it would play in future. There was much deliberation among the Governors about what should be done with regard to the honours lists that entirely covered its walls. To refurbish them would have cost an astronomical sum, but some of the Board were unhappy about sanctioning any other form of decoration, until Sir Jack Westrup put an end to the discussion by declaring, 'Well, I'm the only one of you whose name is up there, and *I* don't care, so what are *you* making such a fuss about?' Advice was sought from the Victorian Society, and after the honours lists had been photographed for posterity a large, patterned Victorian wallpaper was chosen, promptly dubbed 'Dante's Inferno' by the boys—some of whom regretted the disappearance of the lists, study of which had been a valuable antidote to ennui during a tedious sermon or lesson.

The whole of the sixties rebuilding programme, which cost nearly three-quarters of a million pounds, was to a large extent made possible by the substantial increase in the endowment that the college was now receiving. In 1967 the passing of the Leasehold Reform Act enabled tenants on the Estate to buy their ground leases, and, as in the early nineteenth century, this brought in considerable sums of money, and a corresponding increase in the annual revenue which could be passed on to the various beneficiaries. The college, which had always been regarded as having the first call on the Estate, received the lion's share of the endowment, and in 1969 its income from this source was nearly £40,000. Alleyn's, on the other hand, received only one-fifth of this sum—little more than half the amount passed on to the schools in the 'outer parishes', St Olave's and St Saviour's School and the Central Foundation Schools, which also benefited from Alleyn's legacy.

The two latter had not, of course, been part of the original bequest, but had been brought into the Foundation under the Scheme of 1882 in order to satisfy Edward Alleyn's wish that his endowment should be used to further education in the parishes in which he had such a lively interest. In the years since the Scheme was passed, however, the whole educational scene had changed, and these schools were now receiving an 80% grant from the Department of Education for capital expenditure, while their running costs were met by the local authority. It was hoped that they would allow the Foundation to buy them out, thus making it possible to put into better order the distribution of the income and give Alleyn's a fairer share of the proceeds. In the event the Central Foundation Schools turned the scheme down, and, as the lawyer whom the college consulted wrote, whatever the history of their inclusion in the Foundation might be they were now 'a fully-fledged Beneficiary (at law) with the College; and it is difficult to see why their Governors should really agree to forego their rights except in return for some other real benefit such as a capital sum which in the circumstances would have to be very large.'

So nothing came of this idea, or of other projects which were considered by the Board for keeping the three main schools of the Foundation viable at a time when the future of education seemed to be in the melting-pot. They could, it was suggested, be integrated; the college could introduce co-education; or their sixth forms could be amalgamated. But discussions on these possibilities fizzled out, and in 1971 the Governors decided that the college should remain what it had been throughout its (post-Reconstitution) history—highly selective, independent, and with no association with the other two schools on the Foundation.

Another knotty problem was the fact that the college and Alleyn's shared the same Board of Governors, as they still do. This had been continuously and severely criticized for years, not least by the L.C.C. Inspectors in 1938, by Lord Soulbury, who a few years later remarked on the 'absurd position of one Governing Body controlling two competing schools', and by successive Masters and Governors who had to struggle with this anomalous situation. In 1974 Charles Lloyd set before the Governors a comprehensive and far-seeing plan for reorganization which would give the college and Alleyn's separate Boards, so that each would have:

> . . . a governing body whose exclusive concern it is and whose deliberations can take place without the Governors constantly having to assess their possible effect on other schools of the Foundation . . . Because the present Board of Governors is concerned with two schools and also the Picture Gallery, and because the members of the Board are all busy men, the amount of time which can be devoted to College matters is limited. Agenda items are almost inevitably bursarial items concerned with finance, salaries and buildings. Little is said about education and yet education is really the end for which finance and buildings are the means. Moreover, although the Royal Academy

[since October 1940 the meeting-place of the main body of Governors] is a convenient venue for Governors' meetings, meetings should more properly be held in the College board room which was built for that very purpose. Some Governors never visit the College except once in every two years . . .[1]

I recognise that it is difficult for the Board to consider this matter of separate Boards for Dulwich and Alleyn's objectively and I appreciate it may not be in the best interests of Alleyn's to have a separate Board now. This, however, underlines the substance of my argument. Under the present system it is not possible for the Board to formulate policy for one school without having to take into account the interests of the other. The present arrangement takes its origin from the latter part of the nineteenth century when there was an Upper and a Lower School at Dulwich. The two schools have now been independent of one another for nearly a century and are individual schools each in its own right. Recent changes in the administration and organisation of education in both the maintained and independent sectors, together with the greatly increased pressure upon the head of a school, make it imperative now that this dichotomy should be recognised. In my submission the creation of two separate Boards for the two Dulwich schools is long overdue.

Ways of ameliorating this difficult and complex problem were discussed, but nothing was done, though to some extent the situation was helped by the creation of a small separate committee for each of the schools.

The matter had become of particular urgency because of the decisive move of the local authorities away from sponsored entry. I.L.E.A. (which in 1965 had assumed educational responsibility for Inner London) had decided to take

---

[1] The Board of Governors of Dulwich College and Alleyn's is something of a curiosity in that many of its members have no particular association with either school (though that is not to say that a great number of them, over the years, have not worked very hard on behalf of both). Several are appointed by eminent but distant bodies or individuals: the Archbishop of Canterbury, the Lord Chancellor, the Universities of Oxford, Cambridge, and London, the Royal Society and the Royal Academy. Throughout the present century, too, there have been a varying number of representatives of the L.C.C. There are also, of course, Governors more closely connected with the school, including Old Alleynians. But the general composition of the Board makes for a certain remoteness.

no places at independent or Direct Grant schools after 1970, and, though for the time being the other authorities had continued to send boys, clearly they would not do so indefinitely. It was essential, therefore, that Dulwich should award more bursaries of its own, to keep up not only the academic standard but also the numbers. So in 1971 eight further scholarships had been established, providing a total of twenty each year for boys entering between nine and fourteen. A one-form entry at 13 + had also been initiated, which helped still further to reforge the links with the local preparatory schools. By 1972 fewer than a third of the intake were local authority scholars, and, though it was still some years before there were none at all, in effect the Dulwich Experiment was winding to a close.

Charles Lloyd's tenure came to an end in 1975, when he reached the retiring age of sixty. He is remembered as a big personality who commanded respect, a first-rate administrator with a rare ability to listen constructively to every side of an argument and then make his own decision, and an immensely witty speaker and conversationalist. His goal for Dulwich, one of his staff commented, could perhaps be summed up as the pursuit of excellence. When I asked him about this he replied:

> Yes, I think I was given to saying that, but I believe I used to go on to remark that one rarely achieved it, but that schools such as Dulwich make it more attainable than most. As I see it, the trend of those years was the pursuit of excellence in all its forms, based on careful selection without reference to the parents' ability to pay, a first-class staff, and unrivalled facilities for games, music, societies and the arts.

In 1949, when the Dulwich Experiment had been in operation for nearly three years, Gilkes wrote, 'Socially the school represents a cross-section of Greater London south of the river'. It is unlikely that the extent to which this was true will ever be ascertained with any accuracy. Nor, probably, with so many imponderable factors, will it ever be possible to judge the extent to which the Experiment made the school accessible to boys from really poor homes.

However, some light is thrown on the subject by an analysis of the background of the boys who left between the years 1953 and 1959, most of whom would have begun their life at Dulwich during the first six years of the scheme—that is to say, between 1946 and 1953. Among the fathers there are practically no diplomats or politicians, not many lawyers, architects, creative artists, scholars, princes of the church or of industry, few names which were household words. Repeating the pattern which had predominated ever since the days of A. H. Gilkes, many were local government officials, civil servants, businessmen, servicemen, merchants, teachers, doctors, dentists, engineers.

What the Experiment did was to reduce the preponderance of these fathers, who were overtaken by those following occupations rather lower in the social scale. During the seven years under review the greatest single category was composed of skilled artisans of one kind or another—including a great many policemen, who seem to have had a particular predilection for sending their sons to Dulwich. There was a much smaller group of manual workers, and a considerable number of shop-keepers. The grey area of categorization is entered upon when we count up the substantial proportion who called themselves 'clerks', or perhaps 'accountants', which could cover a large range of occupations, not least because some of the men concerned may have described themselves in this way as a result of social pressure. This did in fact happen in a different context, to one of the college porters who had entered his son for university, and who was advised to call himself a clerk rather than what he really was at the time, a docker. (He refused to do so, and his son was accepted just the same.)

The totality of fathers covered an extraordinarily wide spectrum of society—surely no other school can have had anything comparable at this period. But the concensus of opinion of those who were most closely connected with the Experiment seems to be that at any rate during the early years about half the intake consisted of middle-class boys and half of boys from a working-class background (if one dare use these meaningless terms nowadays). However, this percentage almost certainly shifted a little over the years, for later on a number of middle-class parents whose sons had failed to win a local authority scholarship sent them as fee-payers.

It is unlikely that many boys from really poor households came to the college as they had done in the 1920–28 Direct Grant days, when a high proportion were from elementary schools, for, even with their tuition fees and travelling expenses paid, the incidental costs would have been too great. Nor would conditions at home, for some of these boys, have been conducive to concentrated work in the evening, or to staying on at school when their siblings and friends were out in the world earning good money. Moreover, a number of the primary school headmasters in deprived areas—though by no means all of them—were far from happy about the scheme, and did not always make it easy for potential parents to hear about it.

Nevertheless, despite these reservations, two aspects of the Experiment are unquestionably of immense significance. The first is that it opened the doors of a new world to a very great number of boys who would otherwise never have had the chance to discover their potential, no matter how ambitious they were or how hard they worked. (It must also have opened new windows to their parents.) The second, extremely important, aspect is that backgrounds ceased to matter; the social mix-up was tremendous, and produced a total freedom from class and money consciousness.

Of course, the boys often felt strange at first. One of them, now the educational correspondent of a big daily newspaper, was a policeman's son whose mother was determined that only the best—i.e., the college—was good enough for her boy. He recalls how strange it all felt in the early days; how the quality of the jacket which you wore (there were various qualities) inevitably marked you out; and how he loathed the elocution lessons at which the boys had to recite 'How now brown cow'. On the other hand, it made him feel at home to play football with a tennis ball. Another, today a lecturer at the London School of Economics, was the child of a broken marriage: his father was an educated Cypriot and his mother

a splendid uneducated Irishwoman who also had great
ambitions for her only child, and who did anything, from
being a scrubbing-lady to running a Butlin's camp, so that he
should have the best possible opportunity. He speaks today
with deep gratitude of the trouble which four or five masters
took with him, thereby making it possible for him to develop a
strong sense of personal worth. 'The school gave me roots,' he
says.

A third, in this case from a middle-class background, one of
three brothers all of whom were at the school, praises the
Experiment as a complete leveller. Only now, looking back,
does he recognize the backgrounds of his friends and what
their fathers did. He grew up unaware of class, race, or
colour—and for him personally this is the most important
facet of the school. 'The difference of background, attitude
and experience was phenomenal.' Even while they were at
Dulwich, he says, the boys felt they were part of an interesting
experiment, that other public schools might copy them, and
that whether they failed or succeeded mattered a lot in terms
of the impact which it might have on the world at large.

Yet another, the son of a Camberwell publican, also stresses
the fact that you were surrounded by people from all walks of
life, and no one was slotted into any particular category:

> The product of Dulwich College at that time is a professional
> person, whatever background he came from, and many of those
> who were there during the Experiment are only just now
> beginning to reach the peak of their careers. When I went to
> Guy's to study medicine I found at least fifty other Old Alleynians
> there, and there were just as many at King's College Hospital and
> Southampton General. The Experiment will come into fruition
> during the next ten years.

One man in his forties, now a doctor (and the first member
of his family to become one), says:

> My father was an insurance manager, and most of the boys when
> I was at Dulwich were the sons of shop-owners and clerical
> workers. I can't think of anyone in my form from a professional
> background, except one, whose father was a doctor. We were all
> rather in awe of the school, especially as when I was there the

seniors were all pre-Experiment boys from a rather different, middle-class background and were 'as to the manner born', while the juniors had come from the ordinary level of local authority schools. Basically very few of us had been to prep schools, and at first the difference was overwhelming—we'd no idea, for instance, what 'preparation' was: it had always been just homework to us.

I think we all appreciated that the standard of work was going to be very high, but most of us were never conscious of pressure. We knew we should have to work extremely hard, and that the exam results were going to be very important for us. But far from feeling inferior as scholarship boys we used to despise the fee-payers—'What a stupid lot they are, not bright enough to get here with a scholarship as we all did!'

We were streamed quite early on, so we used to go all the way up the school with the same group. I've kept the friends I made there ever since.

This is a point which many of the local authority scholars stressed: 'You keep your Dulwich friends for the rest of your life.' They agree, too, that the product of the Experiment tends to have a particular Monty Python–Goon Show type of humour which is a tremendous bond.

Of all the dozens of people with whom I have discussed the Dulwich Experiment, almost to a man they have praised it for its value from the social aspect, and for the opportunity it gave to bright boys to follow careers which were satisfying to them and useful to their fellow human-beings. 'Of course it was élitist,' said one man who was closely connected with the college for much of the thirty or so years during which the scheme was in operation:

And of course it'll be splendid if one day we can all send our children to state schools and know they'll get the intellectual climate, the academic chances and the extra-curricular activities which boys have at Dulwich. But until that happens parents will continue to want the best education for their children that they can have, and heaven knows the country needs people who're highly educated. So why condemn a scheme which, at no extra expense to the tax-payer, enabled some thousands of bright children to have an excellent education that has benefited society as well as themselves? Fair enough, it's against the present egalitarian climate that five per cent or so of our school-children should have advantages which are barred to the rest; but the Experiment children were helped not because their parents were rich but because they were themselves bright, and because they worked hard so as not to throw away the privilege that had been given them.

He would certainly agree with James Cobban, formerly Chairman of the Direct Grant Schools Joint Committee, that 'to put it bluntly, we are landed for the foreseeable future with a dual system in this country. Anything that would open the opportunities the independent schools have to offer to a wider section of the community should therefore be encouraged.'

An interesting footnote comes from Charles Lloyd, who at the Alleyn Club dinner in 1974 said that, when the B.B.C. wanted to do a programme on 'Pressure, and whether we should train children or let them do as they please', they asked him for his comments. 'We particularly want someone from Dulwich,' they told him, 'which, of all the great schools with a truly academic standing, is the most democratic.' Lloyd wasn't quite sure what they meant, and pursued the matter further. The producer replied, 'It probably has as wide a social range as any other school of comparable standing in the country'—and what could one ask for better than that? Perhaps, if we ever do achieve equal opportunities of education, the Dulwich Experiment will act as a blueprint.

7 Present and Future

D. A. Emms (1975–)

> '*The crowd, and buz, and murmurings*
> *Of this great hive, the city.*'
>
> (Abraham Cowley)

THE ending of the Dulwich Experiment has led to many changes in the school. In 1978, for the first time since 1946, not one of the new boys was a local authority scholar; and though there are, of course, still a number of them making their way up the college their ranks are steadily dwindling with each year that passes. The Experiment, quite apart from the sociological aspect, had been a priceless asset when support of this kind was most badly needed; its demise brought into being a situation calling for a great deal of creative thought, adjustment to new needs and problems, and a bold, realistic determination to decide in which direction the college was to move.

No one understood the difficulties better than Charles Lloyd's successor, David Emms, who after Oxford—where he was a rugger blue—and ten years at Uppingham became headmaster successively of Cranleigh and of Sherborne. He took up his post at Dulwich in the autumn of 1975, bringing with him a reputation for total dedication to the demands of the job, and a humanity which always makes him put people first.

In some respects the most urgent problem of all resembled

that which had faced Christopher Gilkes thirty-five years earlier: how to maintain the academic standard for which the school had become renowned, while yet ensuring that numbers did not drop disastrously at a time when all schools, state and independent, were concerned about falling rolls because of the decline in the birthrate.[1] The knowledge that their sons would receive an excellent education has for most of its existence been a major reason why so many parents have chosen Dulwich, for, as Auriol Stevens writes, 'The inculcation of academic skills is one of the only purposes of schooling on which virtually everyone agrees ... Certificates are demanded by our society as its only available measure of ability and application, and schools which fail to help those of their pupils who can gain these accoutrements to do so, fail them utterly.'

A similar point of view was expressed by Lord Wolfenden, who became Chairman of the Board of Governors in 1973 after a lifetime in education—headmaster successively of Uppingham and of Shrewsbury, Vice-Chancellor of Reading University, Chairman of the Headmasters' Conference, Director of the British Museum, among a host of top appointments. The college has benefited to an incalculable degree from his wise counselling. He said during an *Alleynian* interview:

> If I lived in the neighbourhood, and had a son who I thought was potentially clever enough for the school, I would have no hesitation in sending him to Dulwich. I think the primary standard we have to judge a school by is its academic achievements, and of course Dulwich's are first rate. I think that a school must provide other things too. The quantity and quality of things going on around Dulwich is staggering, and I am all for encouraging boys to develop any interests they have to the full; but ultimately a school is where one goes to be taught.

Now the automatic procession of clever boys would no longer be waiting at the gate. How were they to be replaced?

---

[1] The official estimate (1980) is that the drop in the school population may be as high as 24% over the next three years or so.

Clearly it was impossible to maintain the standard by reducing the numbers to those of the pre-Gilkes era: this would have been intolerable from the point of view of the staff, many of whom would have had to be made redundant, and nonsensical anyway, since the overheads would have remained much the same while the receipts from fees plummeted—it would, in fact, have been a quick and foolproof path to suicide. On the other hand, to keep up the numbers at the expense of drastically lowering the academic standard was a bleak prospect, particularly for masters in the more rigorous disciplines, such as classics. 'Unless the material is good,' one of them said to me, 'you can't do anything with it, even if you have the best staff in the world. They all love their subjects, and want to fill the universities with the right kind of boys trained in the right way.' It is true that, apart from the years around the turn of the century, only since the Experiment had Dulwich become one of the *top* academic flyers. But nothing in life flows backwards—at any rate if it wants to survive—and with few exceptions everyone felt that to lower their sights appreciably would be disastrous, not least for the staff, most of whom had had the rewarding experience, during their years at the school, of teaching exceptionally bright boys, and had done so with success and fulfilment.

One possible solution was to open the school to girls at sixth-form level. This had many advantages, not least that nearly everyone, masters and boys, welcomed the idea, which was in any case in line with the general move towards co-education in the independent sector and at universities too. The pros and cons were debated for some years, until in 1980 the Governors decided against it, at any rate for the time being, on the grounds that the three Foundation schools were by now providing a nice balance of the sexes, with one for girls, one for boys, and one for both (since in 1976 Alleyn's had begun to take girls, and by 1980 its intake was fully co-educational).

In 1981 the Government's Assisted Places Scheme came into effect, and the college decided to take part in it, though, in common with most independent schools, the Governors and staff felt serious reservations about the project. With so many cuts taking place in the educational and social services, it was a sensitive moment to introduce a measure which was highly unpopular within the state sector of education. Moreover, since the Labour Party had declared its intention of abolishing the scheme forthwith if it came to power, there was the possibility that a lot of children would be stranded mid-stream in their school life. Thirdly, though its funding by central Government was favourably regarded, there was uneasiness because the local authorities and primary school heads were not to be consulted in the selection of the boys. Nevertheless, it was felt to be essential that Dulwich should participate in the scheme, both because its seven or eight competitors in the area were doing so, and also because of its century-long tradition of educating the less privileged members of society. The present scheme involves a 'means test', so that the better-off parents must contribute to the fees; however, as in the Dulwich Experiment days, boys from very poor homes will once again be able to benefit, though it may be more difficult for information about this scheme to reach them.

Everyone agreed, however, that the number of scholarships and bursaries awarded by the school must be increased, in order to replace to some extent those previously offered by the local authorities. To this end an appeal was launched in 1979, one object of which was to provide these bursaries, so far as possible giving them to boys from less advantaged backgrounds. The first scholars under this scheme were admitted in the autumn of 1980, and the success of the appeal seems to show that a growing number of boys will come to the school as a result of it.

Much has been done, in the last few years, to provide up-to-date equipment to help in the process of learning, so that, when the boys leave school, they will have acquired the best possible skills to face our increasingly competitive world. Early in 1979 a new language laboratory was bought—at the time of its installation it was the most modern in any school in Europe—to replace the smaller one which had been acquired in the sixties. 'Basically, the atmosphere of the lab is fun,' one boy wrote in the *Alleynian*, 'and quickly reduces inhibitions for that reason. I was already in my "A" level year when it was installed, and only wish that I had had the use of its facilities at an earlier stage. But it is for the senior students, perhaps, that the lab is most exciting. It has helped me to appreciate French and German as living languages rather than academic subjects.' This is exactly the attitude which the modern languages department wants to encourage—the opportunity to make the lessons more lively and varied without sacrificing academic standards, and to give the boys individual attention so that the bright ones will not be held back, while those who are slow to learn will gain confidence to join in the proceedings without their 'rather beastly friends' (as one master put it) overhearing and making fun. There are many visitors to the laboratory: producers on the B.B.C. schools programmes like to see what use is being made of their lessons, and heads of departments of other schools and places of education from Europe as well as from this country come to inspect it. One rarity is the full-time technician who is always at hand to ensure that everything is in perfect working order.

The boys' interest in design and technology has been steadily growing for several years—many of them now opt for technical subjects—and an extension to the existing centre was built in 1980, providing what are arguably the best-equipped workshops to be found in any school in the British Isles. A television and video system was another purchase, its first assignment the agreeable one of recording an enchanting performance of *Toad of Toad Hall* by the lower school on Founder's Day, 1979, before it settled down to the more sober task of enriching the educational resources of the school.

In 1977 Cybernet, which had provided free thousands and thousands of pounds' worth of computer time, decided that they must put a limit to this in future, so the next year the college bought its own computer, then the biggest system owned by any school in the country. This led to a rapid increase in computer science as an academic subject, as well as giving the boys a greater opportunity to use the terminals for all kinds of in-school and out-of-school activities, projects, and hobbies.

The computer is now indispensable, not only for teaching but also for administrative purposes—form lists, examination results, finance, addressing envelopes . . . It is also used, in a minor way, in preparing the timetable. For many years this daunting task was in the incomparably skilful hands of Eric Handscomb, who had no mechanical aids. He comments:

> In any case, at Dulwich there are so many constraints, and the distances to be covered are so vast, that this exercise in logistics must still be done by squared paper, pencil and rubber. For instance, things are just falling into place when one realises that Mr. X, who has a gammy leg, will have to move between periods from a junior schoolroom to the top of the north block; or that Mr. Y, ageing and somewhat tetchy, has been timetabled for a class in the room next door to the form conducted by Mr. Z, whose lessons verge on the riotous.

Difficult it may have been, but his colleagues rejoice in claiming that they never caught him out: just when one of them gleefully thought that 'Handscomb had slipped up at last', he smilingly pointed to some variable that gave him game, set and match.

Nowadays the task is more complicated than ever, not least because the number of A-level combinations has risen from fifteen in 1967 to forty-six in 1979. So a computer helps to a certain extent, though the work still has to be done mainly by human hand and brain, and absorbs many hours throughout the summer holidays, involving an immense amount not only of mathematical juggling but also of careful thought, for the results will affect the teaching lives, for good or ill, of over a hundred men and women (a small number of women having, in the last few years, been appointed to the staff). Until the whole programme has been run through once it is all a bit of a nightmare—and one year disaster nearly did strike, when the long roll containing the embryonic timetable was left on the train, presumably travelling backwards and forwards for a week, before someone read the label and an unknown hand hurled it out on to the platform at West Dulwich station.

There will never be agreement about the competing claims of academic schooling and of 'education for life', and probably there is no 'right' answer anyway. Primarily, as Lord Wolfenden said, we send our children to school to be taught; but all the same we don't want them, when they leave, to be cornucopias of knowledge and not much else. The difficulty lies in finding the right balance between the two extremes. Dulwich is particularly conscious of this dichotomy because of the years of the Experiment, when the accusation was sometimes made that the boys were educated to a very high level at the expense of much else that a school should provide. It has been called philistine and arrogant, forcing its pupils into a mould and encouraging them not to think, respecting cleverness but not intellect, placing the emphasis on the individual rather than on the community.

Were the boys, like hothouse plants or battery hens, subjected to an academic pressure which was ultimately to their detriment, and is there still a tendency in this direction? Every range of opinion is voiced by the common room:

> If boys are pushed too hard they will simply react later on—it's against their own interests to bring them up to a false level.
>
> It doesn't follow that the less bright boys won't work as hard and be as rewarding in a different way as the clever ones. Teachers should be able to cope with dull boys as well as bright ones.
>
> If you put clever boys in the hands of able masters, you're bound to get pressure.
>
> What are staff *for*? To educate the whole man, not to teach calculus to first-year university standard. Remember Walter Oakshott's[1] marvellous remark, 'Then [i.e., before the war] we taught boys; now they teach subjects'. In any case, what do you mean by clever? And having defined it, do you want to fill your school with clever boys? I personally would want a mix.
>
> If the school becomes a bit of an academic backwater as it used to be, it can't be helped.
>
> Boys educate one another—this is what accounts for the heady atmosphere and for any academic over-pressure rather than the staff or the selection principle—they push one another on.

This is an aspect of the school to which David Emms has given much thought—to the need (since no institution is

---

[1] Successively Highmaster of St Paul's and Headmaster of Winchester.

perfect) to encourage a greater degree of 'soul', as it were. In common with many of his staff, he would like to see more concern for pastoral care, in the fashionable phrase, so that the weaker boys, the shy ones and the under-achievers do not fall through the net. 'What is important in a school with such high academic expectations,' one parent said, 'is to make the boy of medium ability feel that he really counts, and only the staff can do this by getting to know him as a fellow human-being.' David Emms would passionately agree with the comment of one of the masters that the school will live or die by the degree to which it provides a caring image.[1]

It is particularly important, in such a large school, that the younger boys should have a sense of belonging. Towards this end the lower school now has its own magazine, house system, and Assembly; in 1979 it put on its own play for the first time—an irresistibly witty and accomplished performance of *Joseph and the Amazing Techni-Color Dreamcoat*; and in the following year, also for the first time, it had its own prize-giving. There is a tremendous spirit of rivalry and keenness among these young boys, and the staff take advantage of this to organize competitions for drama, music, and poetry-speaking. In the lower school the form-master is especially important, and many of the staff there have presided over the same form for years, helping their charges to become used to the pattern of work and the work-load, which is probably more rigorous than they have been accustomed to.

These small boys can be a delight to teach, for they have an unselfconscious spontaneity and warmth which can be very touching. David Emms relates how one golden autumn day, when he was talking to a lower school Assembly, he quoted

---

[1] Under the heading of pastoral care must be included the concern for the boys to be found in the sanatorium. Here wounds are bathed and bound up and aspirin and cough mixture dispensed. Even more valuable, in the cosy atmosphere round the tea-table, over brimming cups and home-made scones, friendly chat, sympathy, and understanding are there for anyone who seeks them, from boys big and small and masters from every discipline to passers-by like myself. It is a refuge of warmth, especially for the more introvert boys who may sometimes feel overwhelmed by the size of Dulwich, and by the impression one has of a river in spate rushing tumultuously on.

'Season of mists and mellow fruitfulness'. 'Who wrote that?' he asked. 'Yeats, sir!' 'Shelley, sir!' 'Shakespeare, sir!' He promised a small prize for the right answer, and was later confronted by three of the boys who had meanwhile looked it up. He fished in his pocket, a bit nonplussed, and produced 10p each, which he gave them with the remark that he hadn't much on him at the moment. One of the boys tried very hard to return his award, saying, 'Oh, I think you'd better have this back, sir—I'm sure you'll need it!'

Recently a scheme has come into operation whereby volunteers among the prefects are allocated to each of the lower forms to organize games, prevent bullying, and provide someone to whom the boys can talk as they might not to a master. The degree to which this works depends a great deal on the interest and involvement of the prefects concerned; but it is going increasingly well as both sides come to recognize the benefits of the experiment, as the prefects' faces become familiar, and as they themselves feel more involved and bear greater responsibility for carrying out the routine lower school duties.

This project is in line with David Emms' conviction that much depends, so far as the future happiness and prosperity of the school are concerned, on the strengthening of the prefect body. As in every school, prefect authority, strong until the fifties, was much weakened in the sixties, mirroring what was happening in the world at large. One lasting result is that many boys nowadays are unwilling to become involved or to use the responsibility they have been given. Some of them are not happy to be chosen as prefects because they resent the amount of time the duties take up, or because they feel they don't always get enough back-up from the powers that be. There is a reluctance—again typical of the age—to step in front of the ranks, as it were.

When I discussed this with some of them, comparing present attitudes with those of earlier days, when it was the 'form' to struggle for pre-eminence, to be simultaneously captain of the school and of rugger and cricket, editor of the *Alleynian*, a fine athlete, and eventually an Oxbridge scholar, one of them replied, 'No one would dare to be all that

Fig. 7.1 David Emms, with one of the Vice-Captains, Andrew Sikorski, and
the Captain, Stephen Swaffield (1980).

nowadays!' No doubt this is true: qualities of leadership are
no longer prized as they were, and there is a feeling among
some of the boys that it is immoral to lead, or to belong to
what they think of distastefully as a policing body. They may
be reluctant to punish,[1] or to report serious offences such as
smoking; and they are not altogether happy about the few

[1] It is difficult to think back to the situation of not so long ago, when the
captain of the school had power to beat. One of their number, in the fifties,
left useful notes for his successor on this subject of beating, advising him, at
the beginning of term, to have a few practice wallops on a cushion.

privileges which the prefects enjoy, such as not having to queue for lunch—'Pretty anti-social,' one of them commented. Others find it hard, at sixteen or seventeen, to accept the transition (as one Old Alleynian put it) from 'reckless and relative indiscipline to the assumption of responsibility and leadership'. Certainly a good rapport between staff and prefects is vital if the latter are to have a sense of involvement; they must, too, if they are to behave like adults, feel that this is how they are being treated.

Nothing of this kind can be achieved quickly, especially in a school like Dulwich, which is so much *sui generis*. But lately there has been a change, and David Emms comments:

> Although all these things have been true in the past, and some of them are still true, I feel there is a growing willingness to take responsibility. I think the new system of lower school prefects is working in this direction, as the boys who have been accustomed to recognize the authority of 'their' prefects while they were still young and impressionable make their way up the school. And I sense a growing understanding of the need for a strong prefect body among the prefects themselves, and a realization that they have their own contribution to make to the general happiness and orderliness, that it is *their* school and that much can be achieved with their help.

Nearly all parents—those 'unfortunate biological necessities', as one master smilingly described them to me—have a great need to feel part of, and welcome at, their children's school, and so often they don't, not least because it is appallingly difficult not to have the sensation of being a schoolchild oneself again, on the mat before the head for some horrendous crime. Dulwich moved more slowly than some schools in opening its doors to parents, and in recognizing that education is a two-way process in which neither home nor school can work effectively without the support of the other. This lagging behind the times was in part a direct result of the Experiment, which meant that for many years the school had no need to go to the market-place for customers. Moreover, many of the boys then came from backgrounds where, in those days at any rate, it was less usual for parents to become involved in their children's schooling. A lot of them, grateful for the chance that their sons had been given, must have felt far too diffident and uncertain of themselves and their 'rights' to venture through the imposing gates of the college. To bridge this gap there has been a great expansion of parents' meetings, at which not only academic progress (or the reverse) can be discussed, but personal matters as well. There is a real feeling among the parents I have talked to that the masters are concerned not just that the boys should do well at their lessons, but about their welfare as people also.

Another innovation which David Emms regards as particularly fruitful was the creation in 1978 of the Friends of Dulwich College, an association formed to bring parents, Old Alleynians, and local residents into closer relationship with what is going on at the school, and to provide a framework within which they can support it. Social events are organized, both so that the parents may get to know one another and to raise money for much-needed equipment—minibuses, scouts' tents, seats for the playing-fields, games for the boarding houses, a contribution towards a micro-computer. A sports club, to which is attached a social club, offers members the games facilities of the school. There is a careers panel of expert and knowledgeable fathers, and a section which helps with the increasing expense and problems of transport. But the main purpose of the Friends is to reduce what is sometimes considered to be the 'chilly image' of the school, to help people feel affection for it and to understand that, despite its size and enormous catchment area, it is *their* school, that they belong to it and it to them.

Extra-curricular activities are as lively as ever. The modest drama competitions between the six Athletic Houses (on the mysterious principle that drama and music somehow rate as minor sports) have developed into ambitious productions, with outside adjudicators and adventurous plays. In 1971, it is worth noting, had come the first breath of sexual equality, when girls played the female parts in an open-air production of *Hamlet*.

Many hundreds of boys take part every year in a variety of dramatic productions, from inter-house and inter-form competitions and plays by virtually every dramatist writing in the

English language, to a stunningly accomplished performance in 1979 of *Guys and Dolls*. This involved nearly fifty actors (including girls from James Allen's Girls' School and Mary Datchelor's), almost a hundred backstage helpers, sixteen members of the staff, and scenery of a professionalism and effectiveness which many a West End theatre would admire. A musical was a new departure for the school and, interestingly enough, paralleled an equally successful and adventurous production of *West Side Story* at Cranleigh School during David Emms' headmastership there—probably the first time anything of the kind had ever been attempted (and permitted!) at a public school. This was followed later in the year by the performance of *Joseph and the Amazing Techni-Color Dreamcoat* by the lower school to which reference has already been made. There was a delightful freshness about this show, and a degree of involvement, that made the play a memorable experience both for participants and for audience. In the spring of 1981 the college took a play on tour to schools in Canada and Massachusetts—the first time this had been attempted with drama.

All the work for the drama productions is done outside school hours, and the boys bring an immense degree of enthusiasm—many have to be turned away from the minor productions for lack of parts—and are often far bolder in their approach than the staff would dare to be. It is, too, an excellent way of bringing masters and pupils together on an equal footing, or even with the boys top-dog, when the staff act as stagehands. Another benefit is the degree to which introvert boys can be drawn out of their shyness by taking part in the plays. One fifth-former who was able to mix very little, but who was in the chorus of *Guys and Dolls*, was amazingly liberated by the experience, which transformed his attitude to the school. 'I love it,' he said afterwards, 'especially the games and the drama. There's so much going on, and I've got so many friends. Every time I walk around there are fifty or sixty people I know and can say hello to.'

Mention has been made of the appeal which was launched in 1979, partly for the establishment of much-needed bursaries. The rest of the money was used for a new 'multipurpose' building, the Edward Alleyn Hall, which is available for drama all the year round—therefore freeing the bath for its proper role during the winter—as well as for concerts, exams, and many other purposes. The money from the appeal was augmented by funds from the endowment. During the last few years the college has been fortunate in being able to depend a good deal on help from this source, thanks to careful and far-seeing investment by the Estates Governors, through which the funds of the Foundation have been put on a very secure basis. It is now usually possible for the college, faced with an expensive building project—the nightmare of all schools at the present time—to rely on the endowment for about half the sum needed. The excellent state of the college finances owes a great deal, also, to an Old Alleynian, Sir Robert Lawrence, who in 1973 became Deputy Director of the Board of Governors and a year later Chairman of the Finance and General Purposes Committee. Thanks to his excellent chairmanship, and his insistence that the books should balance, the heavy overdraft which the school had previously borne was transformed into a healthy credit balance.

And always, often unobtrusively in the background, there is music, now with more space to expand, since the extension to the music block in 1977. There are promenade concerts in the lower hall by the chamber orchestra; performances by the Madrigal Group, not only in the school but in the Purcell Room; overseas tours and broadcasts; chamber concerts; a brass group; and the two concerts every year at the Fairfield Hall and the Festival Hall. All the singing and orchestral playing is voluntary, and one enormous advantage, which probably no other public school has to the same degree, is that with such a young entry (now extended to include a form of eight-year-olds) there are 150 trebles in the choir. The boys would like to have an 'official' pop band, and envy the renowned one at the neighbouring school of Kingsdale; in default of this they have groups of their own, and one of the most popular societies is the Roc Soc, which gathers a turnout of eighty or more every Monday when the boys listen to pop records.

The forty-odd societies come and go, ranging from the serious to the fringe–lunatic, but mostly providing a rich field of extra-curricular interest. Some of them are viewed by the masters as a useful adjunct to the teaching, others as a good way of letting the boys blow off steam in various idiosyncratic directions. 'The great thing,' says the president of one of them, 'is to have continuity, and to let the boys do the things they want to do. It's important to do everything *through* the boys, to give them a sense that they are doing the running; it should be a kind of guided democracy. We like to have outside speakers, but they have to be picked with caution, for few audiences are more merciless and cynical than a roomful of schoolboys, who instantly detect incompetence or flannelling, or being talked down to.'

During his years at the college there is practically no aspect of the many-sided life within its walls to which David Emms has not given much thought. One interesting project that has thus come into being concerns the valuable library which the college is lucky enough to possess. During the war the muniments and manuscripts had been sent for safety to the London headquarters of the Midland Bank, and in 1948, when they were back home again, Sir Jack Westrup was asked to report to the Governors on the general state of the archives. He discovered that they were stored all over the place, wherever a niche could be found: in a cupboard in the main room of the library, in the bursar's room, in the room above the library where the masters play billiards. 'It would appear,' he wrote, 'that no serious attempt has ever been made to maintain these books in a proper condition. Many of them are falling to pieces as a result of prolonged neglect.'

In 1964 the annual budget for the Masters' Library was still only £250, and Her Majesty's Inspectors reported that, though the library had 'considerable antiquarian interest and is frequently consulted by scholars from other parts of the country and abroad, it makes little contribution to the educational life of the school'. Perhaps stung into action by this criticism, the Governors voted £1,000 towards the cost of repairing the archives, and managed to get a grant for the same sum from the Pilgrim Trust—though this was a drop in the ocean, for it was estimated that at least £25,000 was needed to allocate a muniments room where the documents and books could be safely stored, as well as for the services of a qualified archivist.

But adequate funds to pay for the costly job of keeping the books in good condition and displaying them in surroundings worthy of their quality continued to be unavailable, though an attempt was made over the years to repair some of them. Not until 1979 were serious efforts made to treat with proper respect the priceless legacy which had been started by Edward Alleyn and augmented in later years by other well-wishers. Then a small committee was formed to look into the matter, and for the first time real cognizance has been taken of the value, in terms both of money and of historical importance, of the collection. Plans are being made for the proper preservation and housing of the books, so that they can be seen and appreciated and so that scholars may consult them in greater comfort than is possible at present; and for the improvement and extension of the boys' library and sixth-form study area.

Many factors have come together to create, in Dulwich College, such an interesting and unusual school, which can be fitted into no stereotyped pattern. It has, I think, always been an innovator, never afraid to strike out on fresh paths, and always successful when it has done so. It has been bold in its syllabus—in Carver's day covering a wide field of 'new' subjects, in branching out into practical science in the late nineteenth century, in plunging eagerly into computer science. There was the early acceptance of L.C.C. scholars, later to expand during the Direct Grant period in the twenties and to culminate in the Dulwich Experiment, when the college, to an immensely greater extent than any other school, followed the recommendations of the 1944 Education Act and threw open its doors to local authority scholars.

Then there is the curious anomaly that Dulwich, which has always been largely a day-school, has modelled itself on the traditional English boarding-school, with most of its games fixtures against boarding-schools, and with the emphasis on moral values and loyalty to the school that we tend to see as one of the most fundamental ingredients of a boarding-school education. This pattern has been superimposed on boys who for the past fifty or sixty years have come from an enormous catchment area, and whose backgrounds span a very wide spectrum of society. They are lively, wide-awake, South London boys, with (as a one-time master puts it) sometimes a certain prickliness, an 'I-defy-you-to-teach-me attitude' which one grows to know and love. The contrast between Dulwich and the conventional public school was drawn in vivid terms by one Alleynian who went on to Winchester and afterwards taught at the latter:

> The difference is absolutely colossal. In the thirties and forties Winchester was a kind of 'ideal university', with a staff of quite astonishing devotion and erudition. The boys didn't have to worry about their future, since the whole purpose of the school was to enable them to find the optimum route up the ladder. At Dulwich the boys know that nothing is going to be laid on for them. But it's the attitude to leisure that shows the most striking difference: there's a wonderful sense of individualism compared with the purposeful sense of using leisure time at Dulwich, and a sense of social security. The Dulwich boy knows that he's going to have to fight for his place in life.

This judgement highlights an extremely fascinating aspect of Dulwich—a certain ambivalence about what kind of school it really is. This 'crisis of identity' brings its own problems, but is also, it seems to me, one of the reasons why it has never become complacent, has never stagnated. The comments of some of the staff reflect this constantly changing pattern. One of them said:

> It's a very lively school, and the best of the boys are extra-ordinarily interesting to teach, with a healthy streak of independence. Their collective instinct is very shrewd and they sum up the masters very accurately: you can't bluff them, and there's never any chance of being off-form or complaisant—they jump on you at once. There's a feeling that everyone *ought* to do well, and they have a rather mercenary attitude: if you give them

good value they appreciate it, and they don't mind the discipline once they know they're getting value. They see it quite cynically as a straightforward bargain. They're as bright a lot as you'd find in any school—the difference in backgrounds is partly responsible for this, with some of them from a genuine working-class background and some from an extremely well-heeled middle-class one. This has kept it from becoming depressingly right wing. Their attitude and experiences vary tremendously, and with such a mixture there's no room for an awareness of social categories or prejudice about what colour a boy's skin is or what creed he follows. There's no snobbery or bullying, and boys of different age-groups get on well together. The young ones especially are very committed and lively. And they are amazingly open: they carry on their conversations whether there are staff around or not—they don't think of deceit.

The boys themselves talk about how much they enjoy the school, the scope and variety which it offers, the easy relations with the staff. 'It's a good-natured place,' one of them said, 'and there aren't any personality clashes between boy and boy or master and master. There's no feeling of hatred for the masters, either—and no bullying and no fights [which obviously amazed the speaker]. You can talk to anyone without a sense of intimidation or threat. The masters treat you as human-beings when you get older; you can have discussions on any topic without minding what you say. Most of them want to get involved, and really do mind about the boys.' 'It covers such a wide spectrum of society,' was the comment of one of the less conforming sixth-formers, 'and this makes it a far more enjoyable place. I don't feel ashamed to have gone to a public school as I might if I'd been, say, at Eton.' They compare the free and easy atmosphere of Dulwich with the 'cloistered public-school feeling of the normal boarding-school. With some of them it's like going into prison. Dulwich is different because of the size, the position, the quality of freedom without being lax; it comes up better on sports, music, the general atmosphere and the academic results. The troublemakers should be made to go to a comprehensive for a fortnight, and then they'd realize how fortunate they are to be here!'

And what of the wives? If schoolmastering is total commit-ment, as many teachers deeply feel, what happens to their womenfolk, left alone, or coping with children, for many solitary evenings and weekends? Of course, there are the holidays and half-terms; yet these are by no means as free as one would imagine, but are often filled with school duties, from checking textbooks and preparing for the next term's work to taking parties of boys abroad to ski or to enjoy culture, or on camping expeditions with the Scouts and the C.C.F. If a man has a boarding-house the situation is compounded, unless his wife enjoys the job as much as he does—and many wives find pleasure and fulfilment in helping their husbands to run a house. But in general, schoolmastering, like politics and journalism, militates against family life, for during term-time children tend to see little of their fathers, who are looking after other people's children. Moreover, as I observed during my research, within the walls of a school a very special relationship is set up between master and pupil, an ebb and flow in which no outsider can participate. This relationship, and the degree of involvement on the part of the teacher, is surely unique to teaching; for in no other profes-sion does one have such continuous, close contact with other human beings during their formative years. No wife, however devoted and understanding, can share this bond.

But here too the situation is changing, in tune with the revolution that is going on within marriage itself. Husbands no longer automatically expect to find warmed slippers awaiting their weary home-coming feet. Their wives very likely go out to work, as much from economic necessity as from the desire to follow a career of their own, and chores and child-minding are shared on a fifty-fifty basis. It will be interesting to see, in the years to come, what effect this new pattern has on traditional attitudes, and on school life.

'Dulwich is unique'—this has been said to me so many times. And following its history over the past one hundred and twenty years I have been fascinated to trace the part which each successive Master has played in shaping it into the school it is today. The fact that any of them has made any difference at all would be disputed by some of those who have been most closely connected with it. 'Apart from Christopher Gilkes,' one assistant master said, 'the school continues without change, uninfluenced by heads who come and go.' And another: 'Each school has its own personality and indeed its own momentum: it forges ahead like some great tanker. Each new head arrives at Dulwich with a reputation for being a "new broom", yet in the end the school remains recognizable as the same place as it was fifty years ago.'

This, however, seems to me only partially true. Of course, no headmaster can work in isolation, and the longer I spent observing Dulwich the more I realized what an immense contribution is made by the teaching staff, most of whom carry on, in their own particular fields, a range of activities which adds in an incalculable degree to the richness of life there. Nevertheless, what happens in and to the school while a particular man is in charge must reflect to a greater or lesser degree his personal vision of what he wants it to be; and it has been immensely interesting to trace, in historical perspective, how the peculiar characteristics and ideals of each of the Masters of Dulwich College have influenced and guided the path which the school took. With men of a different calibre it might have gone in quite another direction and have become a 'polite backwater', as someone put it, instead of what it is today—a city in miniature, not over-concerned with other people's feelings, aware of itself, perhaps, as a collection of individuals rather than as a community, but teeming with life and a sense of purpose.

The modern headmaster, to the regret of most of them, is an administrator rather than a teacher, since, as T. W. Bamford puts it in *The Rise of the Public Schools*, 'He is responsible not only for the teaching, but for the building, the estate, the staff, the boys and health, besides the reputation of the school in the public eye'. He needs an iron nerve, the ability to make decisions and carry his staff with him in doing so, an understanding of the strengths and weaknesses of this staff, compassion, and the capacity to be absolutely tough when the welfare of the school depends upon this quality.

How does David Emms visualize the years ahead? He would like Dulwich to keep those features for which our public schools became renowned—the friendly competition in games, the commitment which he himself feels so strongly, the sense of 'belonging' that would encourage more boys to take part in school activities after the bell has rung at 3.40. He would like to bring the Governors into closer contact with the school. There is need within the college for a greater awareness of the critical eye to which it is uniquely exposed, because of its vast catchment area. The chapel—the first building of Edward Alleyn's Foundation, and one that has played a central role in the day-to-day existence of the college for three hundred and sixty years—means a great deal to him, as does everything that worship within its walls stands for; and he would like it to be more closely integrated into the lives both of the day-boys and of the boarders.

Perhaps his greatest wish is that Dulwich, while keeping up its academic standards, should be 'a school about boys', showing a recognition of them as individuals with individual needs and contributions to make. 'It is important to be relaxed with them and perhaps take risks in our relationship with them, to show them that examination marks and grades are not the be-all and end-all of school, so that when they leave they will take with them something positive, memorable and lasting in human terms.' He feels very strongly that cynicism, which is no more absent from Dulwich than it is from the rest of our society, is a destructive force, and one that neither boys nor staff can afford to cultivate. And he sees, as one of the most vital facets of his own task, a continual striving to show his concern, to ask young Jones, who is twelve, why he didn't do better in the last match, or congratulate him on his exam results. 'This is one of the best ways, perhaps, in which young and inexperienced staff can be helped to see that their job isn't only to educate—or rather, that education involves far more than classroom work'—echoing, fascinatingly enough, the advice which George Smith, half-a-century ago, gave to Eric Handscomb, 'not to let teaching interfere with his real work'.

The future of all independent schools is uncertain, and

Dulwich has its own large share of problems. But at the end of the day I am left with the impression of a school which, under David Emms' bold and far-seeing guidance, will continue to offer in the years to come, as it has done throughout its past,

Fig. 7.2 'A school about boys . . .'

immense opportunities, where the staff can find fulfilment, and the boys an unusual degree of involvement and satisfaction. 'They say your schooldays are the happiest time of your life,' one boy remarked—quite an ordinary boy, in the sense that he was not especially distinguished either in work or in sport—'and that's what they've been for me.'

8 Games and Field Sports

'*The new boy, donning the Dulwich cap for the first time, may well deem himself a potential hero—if not, indeed, a hero* ipso facto—*for he stands dazzled in the descended glory of past years which scintillate with innumerable grand deeds and grander men. Prick the lists of sports where you will, and you will prick a famous Alleynian. Whether it be King Cricket, Rugby football, hockey, athletics, Badminton, shooting or even the games of maturer life, Dulwich has made for itself a glorious place that many schools might envy.*'

(Westminster Gazette, 1922)

In the second half of the nineteenth century the attitude in public schools towards the use of free time began to change drastically. Gone were the afternoons of careless freedom: organized games took their place as an essential part of education, the indispensable basis for the building of moral character and patriotism. This attitude had, of course, much to do with Britain's role of empire-builder.

Many years later the 1944 Fleming report was to criticize this emphasis on games, which it regarded as having been 'elevated to a quite disproportionate degree of importance [while] depressing the regard which should rightly be paid to the intellect, and to the talents of the boy who is artistic, musical or skilled with his hands'. Perhaps one of the greatest services which A. H. Gilkes conferred on Dulwich was his insistence on the need to establish a proper balance between games and the other aspects of school life, a balance which has survived for many years. 'The work and the games go along together,' one boy said in 1980, 'and that's why I've always had such a marvellous time here.'

A. H. Gilkes, himself a fine athlete and a good cricketer and footballer (at Oxford he had been captain of the Soccer XI), certainly regarded games as immensely important—but for the contribution which they made to inducing health, forming character, and building up the whole man: as, in fact, one indispensable facet of a rounded education, a point of view which was not at all typical of the public-school headmaster of his era. What he distrusted was the effect which a wrong attitude might have, by inculcating selfishness, competitiveness, and self-aggrandizement. He also greatly disliked any publicity being attached to games, and would (somewhat unrealistically!) have preferred to confine all matches to the home ground.

P. G. Wodehouse has his own entertaining comment on Gilkes' tendency to put a damper on athletic prowess—as, indeed, he did on distinctions achieved in any field, in the classroom or out of it, if he felt they were gained for the wrong reasons. 'So you scored 100 against Tonbridge did you, my boy?' he imagined Gilkes as saying. 'Well, don't forget we all have to die one day, and I expect the bowling was pretty poor anyway.' 'When you are forty years old,' he did in fact say to one pupil, 'it will please you more to remember that you were in the sixth form than in the 1st XV.'

Within this framework he believed deeply in fostering any aspect of the school's activities that tended to promote its corporate identity—swimming, cricket, football, the Rifle Corps, the gymnasium, the carpenter's shop, fives, music. He regularly watched games practice, played every year in the Masters v. Boys cricket match until 1899, and at matches would walk up and down the touchline, clad in tall hat and tail coat, no doubt frightening the smaller boys out of their wits. One of his first requests to the Governors was for a grant to drain the football grounds, famous then and later for the special quality of their mud, and rendered even worse, it seems, because for some years the drains were laid the wrong way. There were endless bitter letters on the subject in the *Alleynian*, one of them recording the comment of a visiting team that 'half Dulwich's matches are won by the superior ease with which the natives can support themselves on liquid mud'.

The reporter from the *Ludgate Monthly* who visited the college in 1893 recorded that he chatted to Gilkes, 'who was very busy superintending the laying of drain-pipes over the football ground. It was Wednesday afternoon and the boys were playing "footer".' The vast playing-fields were alive with the boys, with masters playing tennis and some of them golf. For the latter, however, there were too few hazards for proper play, though 'brick walls and hedges were used to diversify the flatter portions of the links'—an interesting mental picture!

At the time this article was written there were eight football pitches, and the cricket fields extended over some twelve acres. About two-thirds of the boys played football and a rather larger number cricket, for neither participation in nor watching of matches was then compulsory. 'The very name of coercion is odious,' the *Alleynian* commented in this context, and one boy of the period wrote, 'I didn't play rugger, which my mother thought a dangerous game; I did gym instead.' However, once a boy had volunteered to play any particular game he was expected to continue to do so. Gilkes trusted to the boys' natural loyalty and devotion to their school, but sometimes they let him down. In 1900 he wrote in his diary, 'As the term went on there seemed to grow up an impression that the football games were not attended properly. I spoke to the boys about the whole matter of keenness in work and also in play, pointing out how necessary this is, both as a matter of loyalty to the school and in the development of individual character. I hope what I said may do some good in this very important matter.'

Gilkes, like Carver before him, believed in basing the physical organization of the school on the principle that so far as possible the management (or mismanagement) should be in the hands of the boys, and the general running of the games was entrusted to the Field Sports Board, which was composed of the school captain and the captains of cricket, football, gymnastics, the baths, fencing, fives, athletic sports, boxing, and shooting. The only masters who had any authorized status with regard to games were the captain of the Rifle Corps and the treasurer of the Sports Board.

In an age when the tradition of inter-school games was being established, one of the great strengths of Dulwich was the contribution of the boarding element, which, though comparatively small in numbers, exerted on the life of the school an influence out of all proportion to its size. Inter-house competitions began around the mid-1890s, when E. M. Everett became housemaster of Blew House. Another reason for the degree of excellence in games-playing at the school, particularly in cricket and rugger, was the influence of the Dulwich College Preparatory School, which has always had excellent facilities and grounds, and of its remarkable head-master, W. R. M. Leake, himself an Old Alleynian, who in 1889 came back to Dulwich to teach before going on to the Preparatory School in 1909. He was a magnificent games player, in the 1st XV for four years and the 1st XI for three, a rugger blue, a county player and an international. He also edited the excellent book *Gilkes and Dulwich*. 'Both as boy and as master he made a tremendous impact on the college,' S. C. (Billy) Griffith writes, 'and I remember the affection and respect we had for him when I was at the Prep.'

Then there was the fact that the local residents took a tremendous interest in the games. Spectators turned up in their thousands: Gilkes wrote in his diary that at the first athletic sports which he watched there must have been some ten thousand people present. In Carver's day the sports had been something of a free-for-all, especially since there was then no fence around the grounds and so no means of keeping anyone out. In order to discourage audience participation Gilkes introduced 'unclimbable railings and admission by card', in the words of R. J. Mackenzie, who regretted the change, which, he records, made the athletic sports 'private gatherings of a somewhat sombre character'.

As time went on the staff became far more closely involved

in sporting activities than they had been, replacing the senior boys who had often been delegated to take games on Saturday afternoons before themselves playing in matches, often a pretty exhausting test for them. There is no doubt that the coaching and the example of many splendid members of the teaching staff who have run the games at Dulwich have been an inspiration to the boys, and the personal achievements of these masters a source of great pride, especially to the younger ones.

It was in 1920 that the school was divided into athletic houses, each named after a famous Elizabethan. They were the brain-child of W. D. ('Scottie') Gibbon, an assistant master who was a brilliant rugby coach. Before this, competitions between the day-boys had been organized on an inter-side basis, and the events which had created the greatest interest were the boarders v. day-boy matches, or the prefects against the rest of the school. Now Sidney and Drake, Marlowe and Raleigh, Spenser and Grenville brought in Big and Little Sides XVs and XIs. Each house produced four or five teams, and these happy, and at times chaotic, games were a sight that most Alleynians of the day will not easily forget. Another lasting memory will surely be of the 'Dump'—the boys left over from the house matches, who were lumped together in one team and captained, perhaps, by some stalwart rugger player who had ambitions but not the skill to shine at cricket. The new rivalry made a good deal of difference to the general keenness.

The boarding-houses had their own trophy, the Gordon Bowl, which had been presented to the school by A. G. Gordon, who was a pupil at the end of the First World War. 'This was a tremendous help to "esprit de corps",' George Way says:

> Before the war it was competed for by all four boarding-houses, but after the inception of junior houses it was confined to the two senior ones, Blew House and Ivyholme. This reduction in scale merely intensified the fierceness of the competition, especially as the sole 'enemy' was only just over the fence and could be glared at almost eyeball to eyeball from dormitory to dormitory. The elation in the changing rooms after a victory, and conversely the

temporary despondency after a defeat, had to be seen to be believed. Nevertheless, the rivalry between the houses was a very healthy one. Many boys found their closest friends in the 'other place'; and both houses were united in the pride they derived from the disproportionate numbers they jointly contributed to school teams—sometimes quite half the 1st XI or 1st XV. I cannot help feeling that much has been lost in recent years now that the boarders have no Gordon Bowl competition.

Though no one seems quite certain, it was probably after the creation of the Athletic Houses that a larger degree of compulsion to play games came in; certainly it was in full swing in the late twenties, and the boys were required to watch the 1st XV and 1st XI play. In the fifties watching matches on the home ground ceased to be obligatory, not least for the mundane reason that it became increasingly difficult to provide the boys with lunch on Saturday and this made a considerable difference to the matches. Sometimes there would be up to 1,500 people watching and cheering, with a crescendo of sound that could be heard as far away as the Old Alleynian rugger field half-a-mile or so distant; to play without a supporting (or opposing!) audience makes an enormous difference to the player.

Games themselves are no longer compulsory all the way up the school, though everyone must play rugger up to the fifth form. But after that there is a choice of eighteen sports—such a wide range is one of the many advantages of a big school—or Voluntary Service can be undertaken instead. Since the war the range of minor sports, which at one time tended to concentrate on boxing, shooting, fencing, and gymnastics (or athletics), all reflecting the importance attached to military preparedness, has been immensely increased and diversified, in line with the present liking of boys to 'do their own thing' rather than participate in team games; they also want to learn sporting skills which will be useful to them when they leave school. The attitude to sport is, of course, also greatly affected by the media: boys want to play games they see on television, such as soccer, or they are taken by the sudden and transitory craze for such activities as jogging and skate-boarding.

Then there is the fact that Dulwich is primarily a day-school, and boys (especially with the thought of exams weighing heavily upon them) are reluctant to stay on after lessons have finished, especially as many of them have long journeys to and from school—though no longer than in earlier days, when they might have to ride, walk or cycle from many miles away. It is difficult to fit a comprehensive games programme into a busy academic syllabus.

Nevertheless, the tradition of sport at Dulwich is far too well established, too integral a part of the ethos, and with a record of too great a distinction, for games to vanish: the value of sport is vigorously recognized, and the great majority of boys find a variety of games which they enjoy and at which they are successful. One master who has played a leading part in the organization of the games for many years says:

> We are very, very fortunate in having on the teaching staff, as we have always had, so many men who give up a great deal of time to encourage and help boys in their various spheres. Today, in many schools, games are relegated to the background, and P.E. instructors do their best, often without many thanks, to inculcate enthusiasm. Thank heaven, Dulwich remains as it was in this field, and there has been a noticeable and welcome return in recent years to the attitudes that held sway until the late sixties. Long may it last!

A second comment comes from Billy Griffith, one-time Secretary and President of the M.C.C., who feels that much was lost when it became no longer compulsory to watch 1st XI and 1st XV matches, and who would deeply regret it if compulsory games faded away.

> The unique spirit of the school owes a lot to the games, and to the Corps as well. As a small boy, and even when I was at the Prep, I looked forward enormously to watching the school matches. We used to line up hours before the start to get a 'good place', and from this sprang our love for everything connected with school activities. I can't get away from the thought that team games, as opposed to activities which boys carry out as individuals, mean vastly more to the very young—say those from eleven to fifteen— and I think it is important that their enthusiasm at this age, and the competitiveness that so many of them show, should be

encouraged as much as possible. The fact that I was a games player didn't in the least affect my enjoyment of the Corps, with the many activities, such as camps, which it involved.

His views are echoed by David Emms, whose hope is that the ending in 1980 of Saturday morning lessons, far from harming Dulwich's reputation on the sports field, which plays such an important part in the school's popularity and in far-reaching traditions of loyalty and pride, will work for the good of the games, not least by encouraging more parents and boys to watch the matches.

MAJOR SPORTS

Rugby Football

No one knows when the first game of football was played at Dulwich, but certainly it was before there was agreement about the rules (or laws, as they would be called nowadays) and while there was still no referee, which often led to heated discussions before, during, and after matches. One letter in the *Dulwich College Magazine* in 1864 suggested that a committee should be appointed to which decisions could be entrusted about 'minor points' such as the size of the field and the number of players. 'In this way a clear understanding would exist with reference to touching down in goal, running with the ball, and other points.' At Dulwich, moreover, it is said that there was at one time a brick wall running along one touch-line, which cannot have helped!

The first recorded match of the Dulwich College Football Club took place in 1865 against the City of London School; Dulwich won 1–0. Soon inter-school matches were being played regularly, Merchant Taylors' and Tonbridge being favoured opponents, as they were to remain for many years, though at one point the Tonbridge match was discontinued for a time—some boys had been caught smoking. Epsom, one boy records, yielded the hardest and pleasantest match, though not invariably the latter; in 1878 the fixture terminated in a dispute, 'and thus ended the most disagreeable and quarrelsome match we have ever played'. The early matches against St Paul's were equally productive of fierce battles and high tempers.

M. G. Glazebrook, who was at the school between 1867 and 1872, wrote to R. J. Mackenzie, at the time when he was working on his history of the college, 'I was the radical who got football disestablished in favour of Rugby football, who introduced the use of football jerseys, and later on designed a school uniform.' A contemporary, H. A. Bone, tells us that the football uniform was first worn some time before 1879. 'This was originally a very thick scrubby jersey of a pinkish grey with blue trimmings and what was meant for a heraldic rose (from the college arms) on the breast.' By 1873 the 1st XV were wearing jerseys in what were now established as the school colours, blue and black.

Under the captaincy of Arthur Meredith, one of those astonishing all-rounders who seem to be so rare today, in 1873 and 1874 Dulwich was able, as the *Alleynian* put it, 'not only to drop the adventitious aid of masters'—it was then quite a

Fig. 8.1   Classical XV, 1895/6
   (*standing*) Carmichael, Wright, Hindley, Selfe, Christison, Maxwell, Drake-Brockman, Leake, Grant, Powell
   (*sitting*) Gibbon, Cross, Browne, Werner, M. E. Clark, A. C. Clark

normal thing for them to play in the teams—'but to defeat all the public schools in and around London then playing the Rugby game'. But it was still something of a free-for-all: every Thursday the 1st XV and sometimes the 2nd XV took on anyone who wanted a game, and eminent club players and even internationals came down to take part.

In 1903 the first football game on foreign soil took place in Paris against the École Albert le Grand, the ground unfortunately being littered with large flints and stones, and the following year there was a return match at Dulwich. Sometimes those international matches attracted crowds of about three thousand people.

The golden age of Dulwich Rugby football dawned in the years before the First World War. In 1910 the school won all its matches, and five members of the team (E. G. Loudon-Shand, D. G. Donald, J. E. Greenwood, C. N. Lowe, and W. D. Doherty) afterwards became internationals; in 1913 these five all played in the Varsity match—three of them for Oxford and two for Cambridge.

During the war, when every able-bodied master was away on active service, the sporting activities of the school were left to a generation of stalwarts such as H. V. Doulton, all of whom did a remarkable job. After the war Dulwich provided the captains of both Oxford and Cambridge in the Varsity match of 1920, the first to be played since the end of hostilities, when Greenwood captained Cambridge and Loudon-Shand Oxford (while Greenwood and Doherty were captains of England and Ireland respectively). Three years later Lowe broke all English international records, having played twenty-three times for England; and *The Daily Telegraph* saluted him as 'the greatest of all modern three-quarter backs'.

Not till 1922 did Dulwich and Eton meet at rugger: it was the first time Eton had been to London for such a match, and 2s 6d admission fee was charged, the proceeds going to St Dunstan's. A large crowd watched while Dulwich won 19–3. By this time the game was so popular that on half-holidays, when house matches were played, the thirteen pitches were mostly being used twice each afternoon.

Between the wars the standard of Rugby football remained

comparatively high in terms of inter-school rugger, without perhaps attaining the heights of success which were reached by several teams after the Second World War. A number of blues and even internationals emerged during this period, such as Arthur Heppenstall, who made a great impact as a mature footballer and subsequently came near to international status; K. J. Stark and E. C. P. Whiteley, both of whom played for England; and D. H. Frankford, who was regarded at the time as the best three-quarter Dulwich had ever produced, and who would undoubtedly have played for England if he had not been struck down by a crippling disease.

Once more, during this period, the school was very fortunate in having several rugger-playing masters. There was W. D. Gibbon, who took over from Doulton; R. T. Rees ('Beaky'), virtually in charge between 1922 and the Second World War; and various other young masters who did a great deal of hard work at levels other than the 1st XV—G. W. Parker, for instance, a Cambridge rugger and cricket blue, who played full-back for England while he was on the staff. Nor must the head groundsman be forgotten. He was a remarkable character called Lance, who would point an admonishing finger at the sky above, daring the storms to break, and produce fast wickets and (slightly) drier rugger pitches.

Whole coachloads of supporters used to follow the 1st XV to away matches and stand in rows to cheer, which tended to make the rival teams feel they were beaten before they had even started. In 1947 J. F. Monkford's XV won all their matches, including Bedford at home (Bedford, then as now, being the great match of the year); and in 1954 ten coachloads of Dulwich boys saw their school beat Bedford on the Bedford ground by 9 points to 3, the first win at Bedford for thirty-three years. At this time an old Oxford blue, E. C. C. Wynter, was in charge of rugger, and he did much to raise the standard of forward play. He was followed first by David Knight and then by two Welsh rugger internationals, John Gwilliam and Brian Richards, and in these years winning matches became the norm. Gwilliam was helped by A. H.

Cooper, who ran the XV for a couple of years after Gwilliam left. Until that time the picking of the teams had still been left to the captain, but when Gwilliam and Richards took over they assumed this responsibility.

A number of county and club players subsequently emerged from the ranks of those who had played their rugger at Dulwich during this period: John and Alan Evans, Mike Bushby, Chris Howland, Ian Coutts—an outstanding double blue who subsequently played rugger for Scotland—and P. W. Cook, who twice played for England.

The game continued to have its good seasons, and during Charles Lloyd's mastership the school won every match over a period of three-and-a-half years, though the tactics were somewhat ruthless, and the main interest seemed to be in winning. There have since been some reasonably good years when the wins have balanced the losses, and some peaks such as the 1975 season, when the Dulwich team reached the final of the Rosslyn Park 7-a-side competition for only the second time since its inception in 1940.

Fig. 8.2   Line-out

Cricket

As with rugger, there seems to be no record of when cricket was introduced at Dulwich. The game was slow in developing, owing to the miserable conditions in which it was played—sometimes on Peckham Rye, or at the Crystal Palace, or even at Lords or the Oval, but generally behind the Greyhound, to which the field opposite the picture gallery was before long added. The upper school cricket club came into existence in 1860, and a year later, when the site for the new building had been agreed upon, the Governors authorized the levelling of an area for a cricket ground north of the present pavilion 'at a cost of not more than £20'.

In 1868 a contract was entered upon, for the sum of £50 per annum, 'for the very careful maintenance, in good order, of the two acres to be actually used for cricket by the Upper and Lower Schools'. Messrs Smith, the contractors, stated, however, that it was 'impossible for them to undertake any care of the rest of the fields for that amount, beyond turning sheep in whenever they have the opportunity of doing so'. The sheep must have continued to be 'turned in' for a number of years, since in the 1890s there were still complaints about them in the *Alleynian*. 'I imagine sheep are not essential for the good of a cricket ground,' one aggrieved correspondent wrote. 'I do not think Lord's or the Oval find it necessary to keep a flock.' The complaints were unjustified, however, for in the nineteenth century sheep were thought to be excellent for the purpose, and they were certainly used at Lord's.

The earliest match on record was played against the Dulwich Union Club 2nd XI in 1864. In this year and the next, sad to say, Dulwich lost every match. But soon things began to look up. 'Ten years have now passed away since the School first entered the New College,' an *Alleynian* editorial commented in 1879:

> Nor is the universal improvement more remarkable in anything than our games and School institutions. From the arrival of Shepherd dates a complete reform in the history of our cricket. With plenty of room to work, he has succeeded in giving us one of the finest grounds in England. Given a few days of sunshine, and we can now get a wicket which is unsurpassed, if indeed

equalled, by any other ground near London . . . Each season has
seen a steady improvement, and last year we were able, for the
first time, to play the M.C.C.

There were regular fixtures with St Paul's, Merchant
Taylors', the City of London, and Tonbridge. 'Our great
school match,' one boy had recorded some years earlier, 'was the
match with Tonbridge, and they were usually too good for us.'

William Shepherd was a remarkable man. Quite tiny (he
was only 5 feet $5\frac{1}{2}$ inches tall, and weighed just over 9 stone), he
had been coach at Oxford and the Oval, amongst other
places. As a bowler he had a unique delivery which was
variously described as the piston, the corkscrew, and the
handsaw, and which gave the impression that he was extract-
ing the ball from his waistcoat-pocket. He was engaged in
1872 as groundkeeper and coach at Dulwich, and super-
intendent to the sports all the year round; and there he stayed
for twenty-three years. When he arrived, he said in later
years, the cricket ground was not much over an acre, and was
very rough. Few of the boys knew which was the correct end
of a bat to hold, and there was neither a roller nor a mowing-
machine. He drained, levelled and returfed the grounds, and
made them into a superb playing-field. Among the many
famous cricketers whom he coached at Dulwich was M. P.
Bowden, whom he described as the best boy wicket-keeper he
had ever seen.

In 1881 the Governors authorized the erection of a new
pavilion at an estimated cost of £1,350. Treadgold Snr, who
was in charge of the games field for twenty-five years, said
when he retired in 1928, 'Only the very oldest Alleynians will
remember the picturesque old thatched cricket pavilion—an
open shed, with a little brick wing for Shepherd and his flock.'
(It is not clear whether he was using the word literally!)

At the turn of the century, when cricket came under the
aegis of James Douglas, an Old Alleynian who had returned
to teach, several cricketers appeared who subsequently
became well known, such as N. A. Knox (said to be one of the
fastest bowlers even as a schoolboy), J. H. Lockton, and K. R.
Nunes, the first West Indies Test captain.

'At Dulwich,' *The Times* wrote in 1921, 'skill in cricket has tended to run in families—an eleven drawn from the families of Douglas, Wells, Knox, Gilligan and Gillingham might make a brave showing as a "Gentleman of England" team.' It was in 1911 that the names of the three Gilligan brothers first became familiar. Their father was himself an old Brixton Wanderer: he began to coach his three sons as soon as they were tall enough to hold a bat, and when the family went down to Bognor Regis for their summer holidays he organized great cricket matches on the beach. It would be difficult to assess the effect that A. E. R. Gilligan, one of the great schoolboy athletes of his day, has had upon generations of Dulwich cricketers. Not only did he captain the cricket XI (and later England), but he played in the Rugby side and was joint winner in 1914 of the Public Schools Gymnasium Shield. His brother Frank played for Essex, and his brother Harold for Sussex and England. Arthur Gilligan captained the first 'Test' at Birmingham in 1924, breaking all Test Match records by taking 6 wickets for 7 runs in the first South Africa innings, and in the whole match taking 11 for 80. He was a charming, immensely popular man, 'modest in victory, cheerful in defeat', as the *Alleynian* put it. 'He was the kind of person,' Billy Griffith comments, 'whom only Dulwich could have produced. When his brother Frank was headmaster of Wanganui, I feel his prowess in cricket did much to influence New Zealand's attitude to this country.'

The present pavilion was built in 1934, and was opened by the Rev. F. H. Gillingham, an Old Alleynian and himself a noted cricketer. In his speech he remarked on the many pleasant associations which the old pavilion had had, and said that he was sure that 'the odours which arose from the subterranean passages, which were known by the name of "changing rooms"', had been of great service in preparing him for his work in the slums! After the ceremony a cricket match was played between the School XI and a team of Old Alleynians composed entirely of county players.

The pavilion clock was a gift from C. M. Wells, another all-rounder. He played in the 1st XV for three years and the 1st XI for five, was a Cambridge double blue, and played rugger for England and cricket for Surrey.

As with rugger, it is difficult to over-emphasize the contribution made to the splendid games results by the masters concerned, such as H. V. Doulton and R. T. Rees, and above all by C. S. Marriott, known far and wide as 'Father' but at Dulwich often as 'Doggie', who ran cricket at Dulwich for a quarter of a century, from 1923–48. During this period he played for England—the kind of success and example which make a profound effect upon boys. Many Alleynians owe their devotion to cricket to his influence. 'As a batsman he would not have been considered for the school team he coached,' the *Alleynian* obituary commented. 'As a fielder he was liable to muff the easiest of chances' (indeed, he used to be likened to the Ancient Mariner, 'He stoppeth one in three'), 'but as a spin bowler he is still considered to be one of the best ever to have played for England.' One colleague remarks on the strange fact that 'although he produced so many first-class cricketers for Dulwich, few if any practised his particular skill. This was because his curious winding-up action, producing much above average speed for a spinner, was quite impossible to copy. Many will rate him as the finest in the long line of outstanding cricket masters at Dulwich, not least for his remarkable enthusiasm.' He was a great favourite with his pupils, who would travel miles to see him play for Kent in the summer holidays and so many of whom he coached to excellence through sheer single-mindedness and devotion to the game. One of the last old-type schoolmasters, he was sometimes a bit of a liability when his cricketing days were over, for if he didn't like the play on an exam syllabus he might take his English class through another one. 'I'm not very fond of *Julius Caesar*,' he would say, 'so I've done *Macbeth* instead.'

'Father' Marriott had as professional a fine coach in Bill Brown, another delightful character, who came from Lord's. Later he was joined on the staff by G. W. Parker and by Billy Griffith of Cambridge and Sussex, who afterwards kept wicket for England and was the first Alleynian to make a Test hundred, and the first player to make his first hundred in first-class cricket in his first Test match—an achievement which is unlikely to be repeated. When Billy Griffith came to Dulwich as a master in the late thirties he was returning to his old school, where as a boy he had once been congratulated by P. G. Wodehouse on making the best catch P.G. had ever seen. Another fine cricketer of the period was D. R. Wilcox, who played for Essex while he was still at school and later captained Cambridge and Essex. Geoffrey Rimbault, who captained the side in 1926, was high on Marriott's list.

During this period, however, pride of place must go to Hugh Bartlett, and to Trevor Bailey, whose devastation on the cricket field was almost comparable with his performance while fire-watching. Hugh Bartlett is perhaps the only boy to make two double centuries on two successive Saturdays in school matches, and the only instance in Dulwich cricket of a player who captained the side three years running. In 1938 the school had an unbroken cricket season—the first for some seventeen years—thus achieving the prized reward of an extra-large photograph in the tea-room. The captain then was A. C. Shirreff, who was a 1939 Cambridge blue and later played for Kent, Hampshire, and Somerset.

P. G. Wodehouse, then living in Le Touquet, who often flew over to watch the matches and sometimes to write reports for the *Alleynian*, treated this particular team to dinner and the theatre. Occasionally he found the strain of watching matches more than his nerves could stand, and had to betake himself to some secluded spot from which it was impossible to see what was happening. He once forewent the chance of earning fifty thousand dollars or so by writing the lyrics for a musical because, he said, 'the cable putting up the offer arrived just when the Dulwich team was going great guns, and I couldn't bring myself to miss the Haileybury match.' Sometimes he was less enchanted: in 1939 he reported a match against St Paul's which Dulwich, instead of winning easily as they should have done, lost in a miserable fashion. 'This frightful game,' he wrote, 'probably the dreariest ever seen on the school ground.' The superb Bailey on this occasion won equal disapprobation, Wodehouse describing him as having 'been in a sort of coma for about an hour and twenty minutes'.

Somehow the major sports kept going through the war, and in 1941 Bailey and Mallett created havoc on the cricket field.

One year St Paul's was bowled out for under 40, and King's College School, Wimbledon, for 10. In the latter match Kiddle, whom some regard as the best bowler of the three, achieved 8 wickets for 3 runs, which may well be a public-school record. As a bowler he was in the eyes of many people a far better prospect than Bailey or Mallett, but, alas, he was killed in the war.

A succession of good sides followed after 1945, and this lasted for the next twenty years; many excellent players emerged who later gained blues. 'The weather seemed more consistent, the pitches flatter', says Chris Howland, who captained the Cambridge team and later became a member of the M.C.C. Committee. 'Bill Brown taught us how to bat properly, and on compulsory days the grounds were flooded with cricketers. It was miraculous that injuries were few and far between, and memories linger of jolly, noisy games with bowlers who began their runs under the chestnut trees and appeared at the last moment from behind the branches and the umpire, so that surprise and deception made up for inability to bowl length and line.'

Cricket has had a long spell in the doldrums in recent years, for nowadays examinations tend to cause havoc. But Nick Cosh and Roger Knight have led the way in outstanding performances. Roger has followed in the footsteps of his father, David, who was a wartime rugger blue at Cambridge and a near miss for cricket. After Cambridge Roger played cricket for Gloucestershire and Sussex, and he now captains Surrey while teaching at Dulwich. If the present record sometimes lacks glamour, Alleynians can cheer themselves with the thought that in the thirty-five years following the Second World War Dulwich produced more cricket blues than any other school.

Hockey
The suggestion that hockey might be played at Dulwich was put forward in the *Alleynian* as early as 1910 and quickly squashed (though, from the article in the *Westminster Gazette*, it appears to have been played in the 1920s). 'We should like to point out,' the editor wrote witheringly, 'that hockey would

have to be played on the cricket ground, which, in the Lent Term, is of course out of the question.' Nothing more seems to have been heard of it until 1945, when Philip Thomas, himself a distinguished player, was appointed to the staff, and Christopher Gilkes suggested that he should 'have a go'. Even so, it still had to wait until 1953 before it was introduced as a minor sport, and its advent was accepted with some reluctance by the rugger and athletic lobbies. The groundsmen also had to be persuaded of its virtues, since Dulwich mud is not easy to manipulate as a surface for hockey. Paradoxically enough this opposition, by arousing a good deal of discussion, tended to increase the popularity of the game among the boys.

At first it was played only during the last four weeks of the Lent term, on pitches to either side of the old Covered Courts, which were pretty frightful. 'However,' Philip Thomas says, 'what we lacked in facilities we made up in enthusiasm. Over the latter years of the fifties and in the early sixties we had some very successful sides and one or two unbeaten seasons. We had to be successful if we were to establish hockey within the school as a game to be reckoned with, and ourselves in the hockey-playing world as a school which played the game well.'

In 1960 Dulwich took part in the Oxford Public Schools Festival, winning the first game, against Gresham's. Tours overseas followed, first to Brussels and in later years to the annual Dutch schools' tournament at the Hague, where in 1974 Dulwich was the first British team to win the tournament. The college now goes to Oxford and to Holland in alternate years.

In 1972 hockey became the third major sport. More and more boys played, and in the last two years the first team have lost only three games. Today there are several pitches and an all-weather pitch, indoor hockey is played in the P.E. centre, and an Old Alleynian, Ian McIntosh, is now captain of the England indoor team.

Sri Lanka Tour, 1978
The traditional links between Dulwich and the Far East, which go back a century or more, were further strengthened

in 1978, when a combined tour of the three major sports—
rugby, cricket, and hockey—went to Sri Lanka and Thailand,
the largest project of the kind ever to have been organized by
an English public school. The idea had its origins in an earlier
rugby tour, when a team which included a number of
Dulwich boys had gone to the island in memory of a gifted
young Sri Lankan Old Alleynian, tragically killed soon after
leaving the college.

The tour was so successful that Sri Lanka seemed the
perfect destination for a repeat performance, this time consisting solely of Alleynians and on a much more ambitious scale.
A very cogent reason for the choice of Sri Lanka was that it is
one of the few countries where all three games can be played
simultaneously. A vast amount of money had to be collected
to finance the operation, and this was achieved in every
possible way and with much ingenuity, including a mammoth
fête. Ninety people, including several masters, were lucky
enough to be in the party. Thirty matches were played, and
boys and adults returned home with indelible memories of
some excellent games, a beautiful and fascinating country,
and warm hospitality and friendliness wherever they went.

MINOR SPORTS

Athletics was the first minor sport to get going at Dulwich.
In 1864 a writer in the *Dulwich College Magazine* said, 'It is
often the complaint of cricketers and football players, that the
season from Christmas to Easter is too late for football and too
early for cricket. By the absence of any good game, boys are
compelled to stroll about the college, or to take some short
purposeless walk.' (A far cry from a few years earlier, when
the boys were encouraged to follow, in their spare time,
whatever 'purposeless' activity took their fancy!) 'At
Winchester, Rugby and the other public schools, this danger
is obviated by the formation of a club for "Athletic Sports",
and a great field day at Easter, when prizes for running,
leaping, etc., are given, concludes the season.' Whether in
answer to the writer's prayer or not, athletic sports came into
being two years later as an annual event, with running, high

jump, wide jump and pole vault, hurdle race, walking race, steeplechase, sometimes a bicycle race and even a three-legged race.

In order not to interfere with cricket, the athletics sports day was held in the Lent term, and the weather behaved accordingly. 'Have we ever had a Sports Day,' the *Alleynian* asked despairingly in 1926, 'when we have found it unnecessary to huddle round the fire in the Pav.; when the majority of the spectators have not come armed with rugs and thick gloves; when there has been no call for furtive glances heavenwards, wondering how soon it will be before it starts, and whether the "it" will be snow or sleet?'

Between the 1860s and the 1960s little changed: the pole-vaulting record set up by the school in about 1883 was still the pole-vaulting record until 1979—which was in a way remarkable since the first was achieved, according to the usage of the day, with a bamboo-pole and landing into sand, and the second with a fibre-glass pole and landing into foam rubber. There were few school matches, and the events were very limited: they still consisted of the 100 yards, $\frac{1}{4}$ mile, $\frac{1}{2}$ mile, 1 mile, long jump, high jump, and putting the shot (but minus the bicycle race and the three-legged race, which must have lent variety in earlier days).

However, in 1965 a full range of events was introduced to supplement the traditional ones—discus, javelin, triple jump, and so on. The track was relaid, many more school matches were played, and the young boys, who had formerly not had the opportunity to compete, were encouraged to do so. Training and practice began to be taken seriously, and as an activity athletics was moved forward into the summer term. Dulwich entered for more competitions—the Southwark Schools, London Schools, and English Schools—and was chosen for London to compete in the English Schools Championships.

The most brilliant individual performer in post-war years is Trevor Llewelyn, who represented Great Britain Seniors in Tokyo in 1978 and broke the Welsh National High Jump record, clearing 7 feet $1\frac{1}{2}$ inches.

Boxing classes were started in 1879 by the Corps, and soon caught on. Members of the football XV were particularly advised to learn the art, 'for it is extremely hard,' the *Alleynian* advised, 'to tackle a man if he has a good reach and can box well.'

Boxing, fencing, and **gymnastics** all came into play in the Quadrangular Tournament, an annual event in the Lent term between Bedford, Dulwich, Eton, and Haileybury which began in 1921. After a while, when gymnastics faded at Dulwich, the Quadrangular was confined to boxing and fencing, and in this form continued with undiminished enthusiasm for many years. One former Dulwich Experiment boy comments that it was highly satisfying to clobber the daylights out of Lord Blessington-Thring of Eton—'It was our one chance of getting our own back on high-born gentlemen in a friendly way!'

In the sixties a number of schools, including Eton, gave up boxing, and the Quadrangular was discontinued. Boxing itself, however, continued at Dulwich for a few more years, until it came to an end in the latter part of the decade, **judo**, **badminton**, and **basketball** taking its place. One of the best boxers the school has ever produced was Terry Adams, a particularly brilliant all-rounder: not only did he play in the 1st XV, but he put the shot for the athletics team and was the finest swimmer in the school. He later captained the Oxford boxing team at the same time as another Old Alleynian, Adrian Hobart, captained the heavyweight division at Cambridge.

Fencing, which had a rush of popularity when the fives courts were bombed in 1944, also continued after the Quadrangular came to an end. In the thirties it had reached a very high standard, when two boys, 'Charlie' Chan and A. G. Lehmann, represented their country while they were still at school. There were some marvellous teams in the late fifties and early sixties, and in 1962 Dulwich won the Public Schools Championship.

Fives, first mentioned in 1874, quickly became popular, though it was some years before courts were built, and in the meantime the boys played in the cloisters. Soon an inter-boarding-house cup was being competed for—though the

Alleynian frowned on the unpleasant custom of some boys of 'bagging' courts by 'throwing in an old shoe before breakfast or even of leaving a glove in all night'. The first inter-schools match was played against St Paul's in 1894. Eventually the college had ten courts, and acted as host for the Public Schools Championships. Until the outbreak of the war it was one of the top schools in Rugby fives, but the courts, destroyed by a bomb, were never rebuilt, much to the regret of generations of boys.

The **squash** courts were also flattened during the war, and squash, which had always been a firm favourite, was played at the Dulwich Cricket Club; but after the war the courts were rebuilt as part of the Christison complex.

Golf: 'In the autumn of 1891,' according to a contributor to *Gilkes and Dulwich*, 'the golf fever, which had come South, invaded the College staff; some greens were made on the College grounds and a club formed, which was the precursor of the Dulwich and Sydenham Hill Golf Club.' Perhaps golf had been played earlier too, and by the boys, for S. H. Fry, who was at the school in the 1880s, had a brilliant golfing career; amongst other distinctions, he was runner-up for the Amateur Golf Championship in 1903, and he played for England between 1902 and 1909. He was also a wizard at billiards and snooker, winning the Amateur Billiards Championship on many occasions.

The great Dulwich golfer of modern times is Peter Oosterhuis, who won a whole string of championships while he was still at school. In 1966 he won the Berkshire Golf Trophy, defeating several Walker Cup players. *The Times* wrote of his performance, 'A new name came to the front in amateur golfing yesterday, and in dramatic fashion. The giant, young schoolboy . . . who is still at Dulwich, was known to a select few as captain of the England boys' team last year, but no one was quite prepared for the way he took a grip on this major event . . . A boy only just eighteen in a first-class field making the game look ridiculous . . .'

Soccer was played in the very early days at Dulwich, for, as has already been mentioned, at some point around 1870 (before we have the *Alleynian* to chronicle events for us) it was 'disestablished' in favour of rugger. Despite this, in 1883 it was still—or perhaps again—being played, though it was much looked down on. It must be remembered, of course, that A. H. Gilkes was himself a distinguished soccer player. But 'Dulwich is a rugger school and will remain so,' the *Alleynian* wrote firmly three-quarters of a century later.

Times change, and pressure from within the school led to its reintroduction in 1969 as a Lent term sport for some of the upper school boys. This was a slightly *ad hoc* arrangement, but a few matches were played. In 1975, however, it officially became a minor sport. Not everyone approves of it, but there is no doubt that it appeals to a great number of the boys.

Two teams are at present being fielded, and now that Saturday morning lessons have been abolished it seems likely that Dulwich soccer will flourish in the years to come, for it will be much easier to find a wider range of fixtures and tour.

Swimming began in 1883, though at first the boys had to use the Norwood baths. A year later, with money raised from subscriptions and a grant from the Governors, the college was able to build its own baths, the water being supplied by the Lambeth Water Works at a reduced rate, on condition that the Governors undertook 'that the concession should not hereafter be considered a precedent, and cited against them'. The baths were opened in 1885, and eleven years later Gilkes said in his report to the Governors that '14,042 baths had been taken in the summer term'. In 1893 the *Ludgate Monthly* remarked that the swimming bath was very large, and that in winter it was used in addition to the gymnasium for fencing, boxing, and so on. For many years it was unheated: the boys went into water at 45°F or lower, and the temperature was never higher than 65°–70°F.

During the Second World War the roof was blown off, but the baths (still unheated) were operational, though before plunging in the boys often had to fish out dead spiders and decomposing birds. The present splendid new baths were built in 1958.

Tennis was another sport which began very early, with the birth in 1880 of a Lawn Tennis Club. However, it soon fizzled out, as did a club instituted by the boarders three years later.

A proposal in 1907 that it should be played in the summer term came to nothing—to the relief of A. H. Gilkes, who wrote in his diary (apparently referring to his early days at the college), 'At this time lawn tennis was a very popular game in the country, and as in many other schools strong attempts were made to provide a home for it on the cricket fields. To my great satisfaction they failed.'

None the less, by 1934 the game was in full swing on the Old College Tennis Club courts, and in 1938—when it was constituted as a minor sport—the school joined the Public Schools Lawn Tennis Association. Athletics and tennis both received a great boost when a new cinder track was built on the east side of College Road, with six hard tennis courts in the middle.

C.C.F.

The Dulwich College Rifle Volunteer Corps came into being in 1877, founded by the Rev. C. G. Gull, an Old Alleynian who had returned to the college to teach, and soon it was attached to the 1st Surrey Rifles. By 1880 there were a hundred members and a band of twenty instruments, which, in addition to playing for the Corps, also performed at the Assault-at-Arms and the Master's annual garden party. The following year the Corps, clad in its uniform of porkpie hat, blue tunic and trousers, leggings and white haversack, paraded at Windsor Castle before Queen Victoria, along with 55,000 other volunteers. It was a beautiful summer's day, and picnics abounded in the Great Park. Among the contingents was a squad of the Shoeblack Brigade, 'stout, healthy lads', *The Times* commented approvingly; but the *Manchester Guardian* praised the Dulwich Company as the best of the lot. 'With head erect, eyes straight to the front, steady as a rock and straight as an arrow, we moved forward,' the *Alleynian* recorded, 'with a light springy step, past the thousands of supporters, from among whom we heard the cheering voice of many a friend, with a "well done, Dulwich", until at length we passed between the saluting base and the massed bands of the Guards.' Six years later the Corps furnished the guard of honour when the Prince and Princess of Wales, complete with a large retinue, paid a visit to the Crystal Palace.

In 1897, the year of the Queen's diamond jubilee, Her Majesty held another review at Windsor of the Public Schools Corps, and Dulwich was represented by three companies. 'How hot and red the little lady looked,' one of the boys who took part wrote, 'but most interested.' In the same year the Corps, led by its band, took part in the Lord Mayor's procession, for an Old Alleynian, Sir Horatio Davies, was Lord Mayor that year. (Sir Horatio had been one of the last poor scholars of the original foundation, and as a small boy, he said, he had seen Alleyn's bones when the founder's tomb was moved and the boys were allowed to view his remains.) On this occasion the Dulwich contingent was sandwiched between the bands of the Royal Artillery and the Engineers, and a long, cold, rainy march it was.

Shooting was an important part of the Corps' activities, and in 1878 Dulwich competed for the first time for the Ashburton Shield, the public schools' shooting competition, which had started seventeen years earlier. In 1886 the school was successful in winning the shield, which was brought home in triumph and hung in the Great Hall, as it was again in 1900. Some years earlier the Lane Shield had been presented by Captain Allen to mark the appointment of his son, G. F. C. Allen, as commanding officer of the Dulwich Rifle Corps. The trophy was competed for by Dulwich and Wellington, and was named after a distinguished Old Alleynian, C. H. Lane, who had returned to teach at his one-time school, and who later went on to Wellington.

A fascinating and startling contrast between the thinking of today and of a century ago is reflected by an editorial in the *Alleynian* of 1888, in which boys are urged to learn to shoot. 'What satisfaction is greater,' the editorial demands, 'than the confidence of personal ability to hit the mark aimed at, be it a bull's eye in the Bromley Range, a savage's eye in the wilds of India and America, or the ocular organ of a Bengal tiger?' (Perhaps our civilization has advanced a step or two after all!)

Shooting, which had a period in the doldrums in the thirties and forties—probably because it is such an expensive sport—has shown a welcome revival in recent years, and in 1977 F. O. Harriss won the Queen's Prize, a brilliant achievement. In 1980, for the first time for many years, a cadet pair shot at Bisley. It is also hoped to revive the Lane Shield. Stored away in the college are an enormous number of shooting-cups; perhaps before long some of them will see the daylight again.

1881 seems to have been the first year when the **Assault-at-Arms** took place, this being basically an annual event organized as part of the activities of the Rifle Corps and for many years held in the Great Hall before an audience of parents and boys. Everyone took part—Corps, fencers, boxers, the Scouts when later they came into being—and in 1894 the display consisted of physical exercises, a sword versus bayonet contest, vaulting the horse, fencing, boxing ('this most noble art of self-defence', as the *Alleynian* described it), sword feats, displays on the parallel and horizontal bars, bayonet squad exercises, a boxing mêlée and a single-stick mêlée. The Assault continued into the thirties but has only reappeared on a couple of occasions since the war.

In 1908 the Corps was converted into a contingent of the Officers' Training Corps, which had been formed a year earlier to provide officers for the Territorial Army and the Special Reserve, and in 1940 it was renamed the Junior Training Corps. 'Once war was declared,' George Way writes, 'Corps activities continued with added incentive, though many of the younger officers were soon called to active service. Field Days were red-letter days for the Corps. Led by the band playing its loudest, we marched to the station, for transport was then always by train. If our destination was Knole Park, the Sevenoaks population turned out in hundreds to watch the rare treat (for those grim war-time days) of our two-mile march through the town. Eventually, however, the venue was confined almost entirely to Epsom Downs, because the station there was the only place where tea could be provided for the weary troops at the end of the day.'

The Air Training Corps was started in 1941,[1] and two years later the first Dulwich College contingent of the Sea Cadets was formed. Nine years afterwards a party of twenty-five cadets lined one section of the funeral route of George VI, the only naval cadet contingent to do so.

By the end of the war the Corps had more than six hundred members, and in 1948 the Combined Cadet Force came into being, the Dulwich contingent being one of the very few which wears its own cap badge with the college coat of arms. Membership of the Corps has always been technically voluntary, but until recently woe betide anyone who did not join! Boys join in the third form, going straight into whichever section they prefer. The Corps has many attractions, especially for boys who are not particularly good at games. All three services lean over backwards to attract them. There are flying scholarships to the Air Force which are open to all three sections, and it is possible for a boy to win a pilot's licence even before he goes to university. In summer there are army camps—in derelict villages in East Anglia, for instance, where there are opportunities for 'storming' and for demonstrations. The Navy, too, arranges tempting expeditions when ships come into port.

These camps and courses do a good deal for the boys, especially when they find themselves sharing accommodation with non-Alleynians, so that they are not afraid to put themselves forward, as it were. They tend to shine on leadership courses, and when they come back to Dulwich often find it easier to accept responsibility.

In 1969 the B.B.C. did a radio report on Field Day at the college, and in recent years there has been a big revival of interest in the Corps.

---

[1] On one memorable occasion in 1943 the R.A.F. section had a Field Day at Biggin Hill, the officer-in-charge being David Knight, who had joined the teaching staff of his old school the previous year and who was in charge of games from 1969–80. He describes how 'one Dulwich master, F. W. King [none other than our friend Gilbert the Filbert], bravely but somewhat unnecessarily parachuted from a plane *after* it has landed, and one cadet, accidentally firing all guns of a Spitfire through the wall of a nearby hangar, caused a colleague who had been studying the propellor to faint and then to join the Sea Cadets!'

Sailing started as part of the C.C.F. Naval section training. It was not a sport, though a group of boys did try to start a sailing club in 1972. Nothing really got going, however, until 1977, when the Sailing Club came into being, establishing itself at Chipstead. Three Fireflies were bought, and later three glass-fibre Enterprises; more recently a Heron has been added. The college can now take part in races with other schools, and has joined the Croydon Schools Sailing Association.

SCOUTS

The 25th Camberwell (1st Dulwich College) Scout Group came into existence on 22 February 1929. An abortive attempt had been made to get a scout troop going two years earlier, but George Smith was not particularly enthusiastic and the project faded away. When Booth became Master he gave handsome support to the idea, providing a clubroom, tents, books, and other necessities, visiting the camps, and swimming in the icy water of Shere millpond when the Scouts camped there in 1930. H. V. Styler, who founded the Scouts, records that:

> He never let us down and stood up for us against carping, whereas Gilkes never really approved of us, though he tolerated the movement. 'There were no Scouts in my day at the college, and we got on all right without them!' He picked at us, rather, driving us from room to room, though he did at last find us a headquarters.

The tradition of Scout displays on Founder's Day was established in the thirties, and since 1950 Scout Open Day has been held regularly on that day.

For the past thirty years the Group has been over 100 strong (the highest number it ever reached was 178—over 250 if one includes the Old Alleynian Scout Group), and has consisted of three Scout Troops and one Senior Scout Troop. Since 1966 the latter has been called the Venture Scout Unit, and one of the keenest leaders was Stephen Howard. For a long time the Scouts had to put up with makeshift accommo-dation, but in 1965 it was decided to incorporate their headquarters in the new P.E. Centre. This was formally opened on Founder's Day 1966 by the Chief Scout, Lord Rowallan.

Service to the community has always been part of scouting, and the Dulwich Scouts have played their part in this concept. Many of them have gone on to hold warrants as Leaders in other Scout Groups after leaving school; the Venture Scouts have trained hundreds of boys for the National Cycling Proficiency Certificate; and the Group has helped a good deal in local scouting, especially in first aid, life-saving, and swimming competitions. The Scouts have helped at the national training ground for Scouts at Broadstone Warren Scout Camp, sold UNICEF Christmas cards and organized clothing collections. In 1976 a small number of them represented the Scouts of the whole country at the Commonwealth Service at Westminster; they have been on duty at the funeral of Winston Churchill and at the distribution of the Royal Maundy money; and since 1953 seventy-three of them have won the Queen's Scout Award.

One of the most popular activities, of course, is camping, both in this country and abroad. Every summer camp has a visitors' day, and many parents make long journeys to visit the camps. Other activities include canoeing, sailing, caving, rock climbing, orienteering, Air Scout training, parachuting, karting, miniature range shooting, dry slope ski-ing, and hiking.

On Founder's Day 1979 the Dulwich Group celebrated their fiftieth anniversary. One of the many interesting exhibits was a letter from a former Scout, who wrote, 'I was a very introvert, studious little boy, and it was scouting that showed me there was more to life than lessons and my engineering hobbies. It also gave me my first experience of leadership.'

9 The Alleyn Club

Pueri Alleynienses, quotquot annos, quotquot menses.
Fertur principum memoria;
Vivit fundatoris nomen, unicae virtutis omen;
Detur soli Deo gloria.

(The School Song)

IN 1907 the *Daily Mail* printed a long and fascinating article on 'old boy clubs', which were then still something of a novelty. The writer, who was by no means uncritical of these clubs, nevertheless commented on the importance that they had begun to assume in the social life of this country, and on the 'corporate pride of a new vitality' which they were starting to show. This spirit, he felt, was particularly noticeable in the larger day-schools, and perhaps the most remarkable example of them all was the club which had been started by the old boys of Dulwich College.

In 1874, the old Alleynian Club numbered fifty-four members. In 1904 they had grown to 460; today they number 624. Within a few years they will probably be 1,000. At their annual dinner they celebrated achievements of an immense range, from—as our foreign critic would observe—Mr Knox's twelve wickets for Gentlemen against Players to Lieutenant Shackleton's South Pole exploration. The roll of the year's honours covered distinctions at the University, in the Civil Service, the Academy, the Church, Education, the Law, Literature, Medicine, Public Works, Army, Navy, and other spheres . . .

The assembly at any one of these old boy dinners is a strange epitome of the activities of the nation, but the bigger day schools give the most striking example. Nothing has been more astounding of late than their pre-eminence in the honours lists even at the university. St Paul's and Dulwich have no single rival, and their eminence suggests the question whether they have not the secret of education which still escapes the older and more stereotyped public schools. Their old boys also perhaps touch life at more points, partly from the accident that they are in London where all men jostle, partly because they are not handicapped by inevitable expensiveness. They cannot be provincial, they may not be snobbish, they must be practical. Commerce and engineering come within their scope no less than language and science. Their old boys are continually within territorial touch—and 'great is juxtaposition'. They excel even in democratic games. I have seen . . . ten fifteens of Old Alleynians playing ten fifteens of present Dulwich boys, a great example of the virility of the corporate spirit!

The Alleyn Club had come into existence in June 1873, thirty-four years before this article was written. 'This Club,' the minutes recorded, 'originated at a numerously attended meeting of "Old Boys" of Dulwich College, which was held at the New Buildings, and at which it was determined that a Club should be formed and a Committee was appointed to carry that Resolution into effect.' The first meeting took place on Monday 21 July at the City Terminus hotel, the members then numbering thirty-three. C. C. P. Ray was elected as President—one of the original post-Reconstitution boys (he is listed as No. 33 in Ormiston's *Register*) and the son of Dr Edward Ray, medical officer to the college; and the secretary was C. H. Lane. The founders had intended that the membership should include all the Governors, masters and officers connected with the school, but, said Carver some years later, 'I put my foot down on that'.

The initial objective of the club was to keep up friendly intercourse between old pupils of the school and to form a benevolent fund to help former pupils or their families through temporary loans or gifts of money or in any other suitable way. There was a certain amount of disagreement about what part, if any, the club should play in helping the school itself, some members being strongly of the opinion that this was not its role; perhaps such an attitude was understandable in the early days, when the membership was quite small and the finances far from flourishing. However, the views of those who wanted a closer link with the college eventually prevailed, and in 1890 the constitution was amended and a rule added permitting funds to be used in support of 'any object which may be considered deserving of the same, and which is shown to be directly in connection with the Alleyn Club or Dulwich College'.

One of the earliest resolutions was that 'a cricket-bat be presented at the end of the season to that member of the 1st Eleven of the Upper School of Dulwich College who shall have obtained the highest batting average'; funds were also given for the improvement of the organ, for singing and art prizes, for sporting cups and medals, and for the Mission. The club campaigned vigorously, too, for Canon Carver in his fight to preserve the identity of the school. Letters of protest were written and delegations sent to the Charity Commissioners, and when Carver took his appeal to the Privy Council the club gave him 'moral support'—though just what this meant is lost in the mists of history.

The first dinner took place in 1874 in London, and until 1921 (when the number was reduced to two) there were four of these dinners annually. In 1878 it was decided that each member should be allowed to bring one Old Alleynian as a guest to the summer dinner, and that 'all gentlemen intending to be present should be requested to bring songs as a piano and accompanyst should be provided'. Gentlemen, of course, were at that time expected to be able to raise their voices mellifluously in solo numbers whenever the occasion arose; and at one meeting and dinner in 1899 Mr Gibbon sang 'Rule Britannia' while a cigar-box was passed round 'in which was collected £17.9.0 for the Lord Mayor's Fund for the relief of sufferers from the war'.

This was the Boer War, which had broken out in October of that year. In 1901 it was decided to donate a badly-needed new library in memory of the eleven Old Alleynians who had fallen in the war, in which 150 of them had fought, since 'the

Governors, though viewing the scheme with great favour, could do nothing in their corporate capacity' (though eventually they donated £500). The committee decided to aim at £3,000—a far more ambitious project than anything the club had so far embarked on—and in fact £3,600 was raised. The library was opened on Founder's Day in 1903 by Lord Davey, Chairman of the Board of Governors, the balance of £40 being put towards a portrait of A. H. Gilkes commissioned from S. Melton Fisher, which now hangs in the Board Room.

In 1891 it was decided that a register of the school should be kept, and a few years later the job of compiling it[1] was entrusted to the man who more than anyone else represents, for all Old Alleynians up to a very recent generation, the soul of the club: McCullough Christison, known far and wide as 'Slacker'. Christison was at the school from 1893–8, and from that time onwards he served it with single-minded generosity and dedication until the day of his death in 1972: as compiler of the Year Book; as honorary secretary of the club from 1906 until, when he reached the age of eighty-five in 1967, he asked to be relieved of the task; and as a member of the Estates Board from 1920 and of the College Board from 1923 (he was deputy Chairman of the latter from 1940 until 1968). No one, before or since, has ever served on these Boards for such a long time. His life and thoughts revolved wholly round his old school, and he is remembered with admiration, love, and sometimes with a touch of wry amusement, 'a dour Scot,' one Old Alleynian says, 'whose friendship I was fortunate enough to have for many years'. 'A shy, gentle man' is how a former member of the staff describes him, 'yet forceful underneath. I think the Masters were all a little afraid of him. Gilkes certainly gave himself away several times, saying "I don't know what Christison would have to say if he knew". One day, not knowing anything about assistant masters' free periods, he demanded from the Master to know why so-and-so was leaving the premises during school hours!'

---

[1] In 1922 this herculean task was passed to Lt. Col. T. L. Ormiston, who carried it through to the volume's publication in 1926.

Fig. 9.1   Alleyn Club dinner, 1936

It was fitting that when the new buildings, at first inelegantly known as the Composite Block, were erected in the 1960s, they were called after the man who in the course of the past fifty years had done so much for the college. One can imagine no act of recognition which would have pleased Christison more.

Under his secretaryship the membership of the club rose from 500 to nearly ten times that number, and branches flourished in many parts of the world. By the end of the last century and the first two decades of this one Old Alleynian dinners were taking place in India, the Argentine, Beluchistan, Burma, Australia, 'the Rock', Zanzibar, Ceylon, Baghdad, and Hong Kong; and soon they flourished too in Canada, Jamaica, South Africa, the Straits Settlements, Singapore, New Zealand, Malta, and many other places, as well as in several provincial towns of England, including Oxford and Cambridge. Many years later the Thai Old Alleynians entertained thirty members of the 1978 Sri Lanka tour to a sumptuous dinner in Bangkok.

Towards the end of the First World War a fund was started by Old Alleynians, masters, parents, and other interested people. Out of the money raised, £414 was used for the war memorial, and the rest was earmarked to give financial help to the sons of Old Alleynians who had died in the war. By 1934 eleven of these boys had been educated, there were no more claimants, and the money was invested to form a permanent scholarship fund administered by the Gilkes Memorial Trust, which had itself been set up in 1923 to establish and maintain exhibitions and scholarships. Later the fund was used to provide books for boys going on from the college to some form of further education.

Old Alleynians played their part at the time of the General Strike of 1926, 'thanks,' as the *Alleynian* put it, 'to the incentive given to the Old Alleynian Football Club by Mr E. T. Campbell M.P. (O.A.)'. Sir Edward Campbell (as he afterwards became) was at that time Assistant Commander of the Metropolitan Special Constabulary; and at the end of 1925, when the prospect of a general strike was probably very much in everyone's mind, he came round to the school gym one evening when the O.A.F.C. was training and offered £1 per head to anyone who volunteered for service. To a man the members stepped forward. As a result, the Old Alleynian Section of the Metropolitan Special Constabulary was in a position to function straight away. Headquarters were at Camberwell Police Station, and the average turn-out was in the region of eighty-five men. By the time the strike came to an end the O.A. Unit was 193 strong and included twenty assistant masters. The section continued to be active until the Second World War, and half-a-dozen or so of its members were awarded the Long Service Medal.

In 1932 the Old Alleynians' Endowment Fund was started to help former members of the school to continue their education at the college and beyond, should the need arise through misfortune or family bereavement. It came into being largely through the enthusiasm and inspiration of Sir Clement Hindley, himself an Old Alleynian, as an expression of gratitude for the subscribers' own good fortune in having enjoyed an excellent education; and through it many Alleynians, old and new, have been able to make their way in careers which would otherwise have been outside their reach.

Two of the founders and original trustees of the fund, C. F. Brown and A. P. Hughes, have now been responsible for its fortunes over many years. 'Robin' Brown was honorary secretary for twenty-six years and Chairman for six years until a year before his death in 1971. Alan Hughes was honorary treasurer for twenty-nine years, and has been Chairman since 1970. Many other Old Alleynians have served in the capacity of trustee, and such devoted service has made sure that the fund is still in existence and has maintained its relevance through changing times. The link between the fund and the college is still close; boys are helped by grants to partake in educational activities out of school, and parents are assisted with fees for schooling or for the further education of their sons by means of grants or loans.

The *Daily Mail*, in its 1907 article, had made the point that 'the work of the [Alleyn] Club, as of all old boy clubs that I

know of, is in large measure charitable. Dulwich does at
Walworth what Shrewsbury does in Liverpool.' In an era
when there was a strong feeling of commitment towards the
underdogs of life, the club was deeply involved in social
reform in the slums of Camberwell; and it was the hard work
and enthusiasm of club members which almost from the first
was mainly responsible for the flowering of the Mission that
A. H. Gilkes had established, by providing an Old Alleynian as
permanent resident in charge, as well as working staff and
financial support; by helping to organize the sporting and
social events which took place between the Mission and the
school; and by sharing the responsibility for the annual
expedition to Rye, where—thanks to the fact that the Christ's
College Boys' Club was just down the road from their own
premises in Walworth—the boys lived for a happy week on
the Cambridge University houseboat.

In 1905 an extension of this involvement with the Mission
had taken place when the Old Alleynian Guild was formed to
co-ordinate the efforts of O.A.s who were doing voluntary
social work, especially in south London. In the same year the
Guild took over a large boys' club in Walworth and ran it
until 1916. In 1921 the Guild was merged in the Dulwich
College Mission, and in the following year the Mission itself
adopted, as the main focus of its work, the Hollington Club.
This had been formed in 1893 by a group of young men just
down from Trinity College, Cambridge. First established as
an adult club in an empty and dilapidated baker's shop in
Hollington Street, at a time when to be both in work and
sober was a combination looked on with suspicion by the
district, it provided social services and after-school education
before the L.C.C. had even thought of evening classes. To
many under-privileged boys it gave a priceless entry to life:
'judges and solicitors came from the back streets of
Camberwell', one of these 'boys' said to me. Between the wars
the Mission, together with some three dozen Old Alleynian
volunteers, ran the Hollington Boys' Club.

It had about two hundred members, aged between ten and
eighteen, and there was always a waiting-list. There were
evening classes, a lending library, gymnastics, dancing classes,

clothes for the needy and porridge for the hungry. Each boy was examined and treated by a doctor, himself an Old Alleynian, and a medical record was kept throughout his membership. Every August two hundred of them went to Birling Gap, Eastbourne, for the only holiday they had, under ideal canvas conditions. Above all membership taught the boys a spirit of service; many of them came back as adults from the Men's Club, built by the Mission for ex-Club boys, to help in the work of the Boys' Club.

After the Second World War the number of O.A. field volunteers diminished and professional help was enlisted. The club premises became due for demolition, but the Mission committee gave the club a new lease of life by rebuilding in 1970 next door to the Men's Club, with financial assistance from the Department of Education and Science and the I.L.E.A. The gymnasium was provided by George Amsley through the London Federation of Boys' Clubs. Thus a vigorous programme of indoor and outdoor activities could develop, which continues today.

One interesting experiment was carried out between 1955 and 1958, at a time when few conventional clubs held much attraction for young people—the Teen Canteen at the Elephant and Castle, designed to help 'unclubbable' boys and girls. The Mission developed other pioneering activities, such as adventure playgrounds, advice bureaux, and a counselling service for youth.

Over the years changing social conditions and needs have inevitably weakened the link between the school and the Mission. It is a long time since the boys contributed regular subscriptions, and about ten years since the Mission ceased to be the college charity; however, most of the Mission funds have come from deeds of covenant from Old Alleynians, with occasional substantial legacies.

But of course, important though support for the Mission has been since the very early days, it has involved only a comparatively small number of Alleynians, past or present. In the main the Alleyn Club has stuck to its principal task of forging and strengthening the bonds between its members, with their shared memories of the school which helped to form them. The strongest link has undoubtedly been through the sports clubs: cricket, football, swimming, fives, squash, golf, shooting, chess—these are some of the ways in which friendships have been maintained or renewed, as well as through the Dramatic and Operatic Society, founded in 1927, which for forty years, interrupted only by the war, gave two performances each season, mostly at the Cripplegate Theatre. Every year 'Slacker' used to take a big party to this show, prefacing it with a grand dinner-party.

The Shooting Club, which was founded in 1890, was the first of the sports clubs to come into existence. The second, in 1898, was the Old Alleynian Rugby Football Club. At first it had no home of its own and led a miserably nomadic existence, playing on unsatisfactory grounds in Norwood, Sydenham, Merton, and elsewhere, until in 1905 the Estates Governors offered it the playing field on Dulwich Common, where it has been ever since. At a cost of £550 a clubhouse was built, with changing rooms which at that time were considered to be the best in London (but providing only lemonade, as no alcohol could be consumed on the premises); it was enlarged in 1923 and again in 1931, and replaced by a handsome new pavilion in 1961. The club, supplemented by present Alleynians, regularly fields five teams at weekends.

The Old Alleynian Cricket Club, on the other hand, was a latecomer, since it was not formed until 1927. For many years it was a wandering club without its own grounds (partly, perhaps, because of Christison's own predilection for rugger). Since 1950, however, it has played on the Dulwich Common grounds, mustering one, or perhaps two, teams every weekend throughout the summer. In 1950 it held a festival match there to mark the unique distinction in Dulwich history of having both the President (A. E. R. Gilligan) and the Secretary (S. C. Griffith) of the M.C.C. as Old Alleynians.

Until the present there has been no formal link between the Alleyn Club and the various sporting clubs, which has created a rather strange situation. The finances of the parent body and of the sports clubs are quite separate, and when the Rugby and the Cricket Clubs were in low financial water a few years ago they were obliged to go cap in hand to the

Alleyn Club to ask for the loan of £2,000. However, a step in the direction of union was made in 1979, when all the sporting clubs were integrated with the Alleyn Club.

Increasingly, over the years, more financial help has been given to the college by the Alleyn Club. During the Second World War it contributed £500 towards the Red Cross ambulance which the school bought, and raised over £1,000 for the Prisoners of War Fund which was run by Eric Parsley, the surplus being used to buy seats to put round the grounds at the school. And after the war the Dulwich College Trust War Memorial Fund was started amongst Old Alleynians to help with the rebuilding programme, at first with the idea of using it for a large and improved hall—longed for and talked about for so many years!—where it would at last be possible for the whole school to assemble. When this once again proved impracticable, the fund was amalgamated with the money then being raised by the college Governors, and used for the erection of the Christison complex.

In other ways, too, the Club and the school are being brought more closely together. In 1978 the annual dinner[1] was held for the first time at the college, partly as an economy measure but more with the idea that it was an excellent way of bringing Old Alleynians back to the school. This was a popular move which has led to an increased attendance at the dinners. And in the autumn of 1979 the experiment was tried of having an Old Alleynian reunion at the school, with a service in the chapel and lunch and tea provided (free of charge!), a rugger match to watch in the afternoon, and a tour of the new buildings for anyone who was interested, as many were. This first reunion was for O.A.s who had left the school before the summer of 1942. It was so successful—and

---

[1] This is the sole occasion at which the club's silver plate is seen: the loving cup in joint memory of C. H. Lane, the first secretary, and L. M. Thomas, who was President between 1878–81; the cigar box (perhaps the one which was passed round to collect for the Boer War volunteers) in memory of P. H. Clifford, a brilliant and formidable barrister who had taken a leading part in club affairs; and the President's badge and chain, presented by T. H. E. Foord.

not only socially, for afterwards one of the guests sent out of the blue a cheque which covered the whole of the expenses— that the occasion is being repeated in the following years for the benefit of old boys of a later vintage.

David Emms hopes that the day may come when:

> The ground on Dulwich Common can provide a club headquarters for those many Old Alleynians who have not had sporting inclinations, but who would welcome a gathering place, though the staffing and management of such a club would be a daunting undertaking in modern times. Certainly there is a growing feeling that, at a period when the independent schools have been increasingly isolated and under political attack, a strong old boys' association, with a great membership even wider than that of the Alleyn Club, would provide, as it did after its inception, an invaluable weight of moral support and encouragement for the college.

10 The Picture Gallery

'*I can still call up before my eyes all the main features of that delightful collection, and I am conscious that there I learned to feel the value of art.*'   (M. G. Glazebrook)

SINCE the picture gallery is one of the most priceless possessions of the college, it seems appropriate to include a brief account, not of the pictures themselves, about which I am in no way qualified to write, but of how the gallery itself came into being and what part it has played in the history of the school.

In view of John Benson's disastrous failure to build the original college in a workmanlike fashion, there is a certain irony in the fact that the first reference to a picture gallery states that it had fallen down—on 6 June 1661—accompanied in its collapse by five chimneys, the garret, and 'fower of the old women's rooms'. The cost of rebuilding was £150. This entry in the college records is something of a mystery, since in Alleyn's plans there is no mention of a gallery. He did, however, leave to the college, as part of his legacy, the pictures which he had been buying over a number of years. The purchase of many of them is recorded in his diary, but they were of only minor interest.

Sixty years after Alleyn's death another collection was added to them—that of William Cartwright, actor and bookseller, who died in December 1687; it is possible that he was the son of an actor of the same name who had been a friend of

Alleyn's[1]. During his lifetime his collection amounted to 239 pictures, but only about a third of them can be identified as having eventually found their way to Dulwich. The remainder were probably sold, lost, given away, or perhaps destroyed as being too gross (one of them, for instance, Cartwright lists in the catalogue that he compiled as portraying 'a woman in her smock, and her pimp holding a chamber-pot to her'). A number were stolen by Cartwright's servants after his death, in payment, they claimed, of an unpaid debt, and the college was put to some trouble and expense to recover at any rate part of their inheritance. Apart from the six pictures by John Greenhill, which make Dulwich the centre for students of this painter, the collection has no special artistic value, and in most cases it is not known who the painters were. However, it is of great interest from an art-historical point of view, and also because many of the portraits, such as those of the Cartwright family, are related to the history of the gallery and of the Foundation as a whole.

For a century these pictures, Alleyn's and Cartwright's, hung in the rebuilt gallery, a chamber 77 feet long and 15 feet 6 inches wide, situated in the upper part of the west wing. 'In the Gallery belonging to the College there are a great many pictures,' the *Gentleman's Magazine* wrote in 1745, 'the donations of different people. Some are very well done, particularly one representing some father of the Church, or religious hermit . . . Fair Rosamund though in faded colours still preserves charms enough to render King Henry's immoderate passion for her excusable; and the Founder seems to observe with pleasure these happy institutions he has made.' In about 1791 this wing was once again partially rebuilt—which was when Walpole complained that the rich plaster ceiling was being destroyed—and the pictures were apparently hung in various rooms of the college.

At about this time the train of events began which led to the establishment of the gallery as we know it today. Four people were closely involved in its creation. The first of them

[1] The elder William Cartwright, with others, leased the Fortune Theatre in 1618.

was Noel Joseph Desenfans, a French poet and dramatist who came to England to teach languages. He married one of his pupils, Margaret, the sister of Sir John Morris of Clasemont, Co. Glamorgan, and with the dowry which she brought him was able to embark on a profitable career as a picture-dealer, for, though initially he is said to have known nothing about painting, he was guided by taste and education. One of his earliest *coups* was the purchase for a modest sum of a Claude, then an immensely popular artist, which he sold to George III for £1,000.

In 1790 King Stanislaus II of Poland commissioned him to buy pictures for a national gallery in that country. It was a propitious moment to start such a collection, for the French nobility, fleeing from the Revolution, brought with them as many of their treasures as they could to put on the market in England. To Desenfans' dismay, when he had accumulated nearly two hundred paintings Poland was invaded, Stanislaus abdicated, and his kingdom was partitioned between Prussia, Austria, and Russia.

Desenfans, left with the collection on his hands, offered it to Russia as the nucleus of a national gallery, but was refused. He next approached the British government, which, pre-occupied with the threat of a French invasion, was equally unenthusiastic, though at the time there was a strong movement among artists and collectors for a public picture gallery in London, as one did not then exist. Desenfans continued to buy and sell pictures with great success until his death in 1807, often expressing the hope that the collection should not be dispersed but should remain intact.

He was an interesting man, one of the pioneers not only of a national gallery but also of the popularizing of art sale catalogues. He devised several of these, an early one advertising a sale at 'the Great Rooms, late the Royal Academy, Pall Mall, where the gentry and nobility may view the above pictures. The taste for this sublime art,' the catalogue continued, 'however coveted by the English at any time, did not effectually develop itself until the reign of Henry VIII . . . We now live in the reign of George III, by whose accession to the throne this, and all the other arts acquired new vigour, and new lustre . . . The whole kingdom hath caught the ardour of his royal example.'

Into the story there now comes Joseph Farington, a mediocre painter and topographical draughtsman who was an extremely influential figure in the affairs of the Royal Academy. He lived in Upper Charlotte Street, Fitzroy Square, so he was almost a neighbour of the Desenfans household in Charlotte Street (now Hallam Street), where there also lived a protégé of Desenfans, Sir Peter Francis Bourgeois. The diary which Farington kept between 1793 and 1821[1] contains many references to Desenfans and Bourgeois. On 20 November 1803 he writes:

> I sat a little time with Mr Desenfans who is much afflicted by nervous complaints, and has been for 7 or 8 years. His collection of pictures is now completely arranged in his house, and is very fine. Sir Francis told me that it was intended for the King of Poland; but that he, Mr D, has now resolved never to part with one of them. West[2] in conversation said Desenfans . . . has left his collection of pictures by will to Sir F. Bourgeois, as well as something besides. He says Sir Francis is son to a Swiss who came from near Yverdon in Switzerland, who married an English woman, and by her had two children, Sir Francis and a daughter. His wife dying he quitted England and left the two children here unprovided for. Desenfans was at this time a language master, and by some means became with others interested in the fate of these children to whom he was in no way related. He declared his resolution to take care of the boy, and the girl was sent to Switzerland to friends of her father.

[1] These fascinating memoirs, which have been compared to those of Pepys and Evelyn, disappeared after Farington's death. A century later they came to light in an attic in Northwood Lodge, where his descendants by marriage lived, and were put up for sale on 9 December 1921. Their importance was recognized by James Greig, the art critic of the *Morning Post*, who advised his paper to buy them. Selections from the diary were serialized for nearly two years (from January 1922 to October 1923), though originally it had been intended that the serialization should run for only six weeks.

[2] Benjamin West was American by birth. He set up in London in 1763 as a portrait painter and followed Reynolds as President of the Royal Academy, of which he was a founder member.

Bourgeois' title derived from a Polish order of merit conferred on him by Stanislaus, which George III ratified as being the equivalent of an English knighthood. The King also appointed him landscape painter to the court. But according to Farington the royal opinion of him could not have been very high, since when the possibility of making him President of the Royal Academy came up in conversation the King said, 'Ridiculous, Bourgeois President, why, he is a foolish man, I do not know that there is any harm in him, but he is an insignificant man.' West joined in with the remark that Desenfans was 'a spider who had his web fixed everywhere, and that Bourgeois scouted for information for him'.

Sir Francis, besides being a painter, also had a passion for buying pictures, as an undated letter from Desenfans to West, in the possession of the Pennsylvania Historical Society, shows:

> Sr. Francis promis'd that he never would propose buying another picture . . . especially as I had no more room to place them . . . Notwithstanding his promise, he has been since at every sale and every picture room, where, like a child who wishes for everything in a toy shop, he has been buying whatever he saw . . . One day, 'tis one hundred guineas for a Guercino, the next three hundred for a Van der Werft, then another sum for a Rubens, then for a Velasquez, then for a Guido, then for two Van Huysums, etc., etc. . . .

Nevertheless, Desenfans did bequeath the collection to Bourgeois, expressing the wish that he and Margaret Desenfans should continue to share the house in Charlotte Street, where the walls were lined with an astonishing collection of pictures—one visitor there during Desenfans' lifetime records that the dining-room contained no fewer than thirteen Poussins.[1] In 1813 they were catalogued room by room by John Britton, an antiquarian. He drew charts of the rooms to show where the pictures—by then numbering 371— were placed, and it is difficult to imagine private individuals living in the midst of such splendour, though several, Britton

---

[1] Only seven of the pictures now in the gallery are attributed to Poussin himself.

commented, were in bad condition, 'with the paint cracked, chipped, chilled and otherwise injured'. The small parlour, for instance, contained thirty pictures, including four by Rubens, three by Murillo, Titian's *Venus and Cupid*, Veronese's St Catherine, a Raphael, a Correggio, and a Hobbema, and the library walls were graced by twelve pictures by Cuyp. Of course, there have since been many reattributions, and many of the pictures catalogued by Britton would now be ascribed to other hands.

Bourgeois was much concerned about the eventual fate of the collection. He wanted to carry out Desenfans' wish that it should be kept together, and tried unsuccessfully to buy the freehold of his own house and its two neighbours so that he could establish a gallery there. Eventually he directed that after Mrs Desenfans' death the pictures should go to Dulwich College.

Over the years there has been much speculation as to the reason for his choice. There was certainly a theatrical connection, for Bourgeois and Desenfans were both friends of John Philip Kemble and Garrick, and Kemble was one of the art dealer's executors. So perhaps it was he who suggested to Bourgeois that Dulwich, founded by an actor, would be an appropriate beneficiary. There was another close link, too, for Launcelot Baugh Allen, the Master of Dulwich between 1811 and 1820 (when he married and so had to resign), was an intimate of the Desenfans household, and the schoolmaster at that time, Robert Corry, was their chaplain. The two men were often at Charlotte Street, and after Desenfans' death Corry conducted services in the mortuary chapel at the back of the house which contained Desenfans' body. Allen and Corry were also joint executors of Bourgeois' will.

However, there is a first-hand account by Farington of Bourgeois' final deliberations about the matter. On 13 December 1810 he was sent for by Bourgeois, then very ill, who said that he had thought of two recipients for the collection, the British Museum and Dulwich College. Farington wrote:

> On reading the laws and regulations respecting the [British Museum], he found that it was governed by an *Aristocracy*, to

which he had a great objection, but still more to a power vested in them, 'that in case of bequests being made to the Institution they might retain for the purpose of Exhibition to the public any part thereof, and might dispose of the remainder as they might think proper . . . Dulwich College, therefore,' said he, 'is most in my mind; the institution is for an excellent purpose; the distance from London moderate; and the country about it delightful. But were this collection to be placed there, I have had an apprehension of the pictures sustaining injury from being in the hands of people ignorant of art who might have them injudiciously cleaned and injured, but to guard against this I have thought of appointing that the President of the Royal Academy for the time being should be a Visitor to the College at stated periods, and that nothing should be done to the pictures but under his direction. I have further thought of annexing to this appointment the salary of £50 a year, and also a sum to defray the expense of an annual dinner to the members of the Royal Academy to be at Dulwich where they would assemble to see the collection and afterwards for a social purpose.

Less than a month afterwards Bourgeois died, and until her own death two years later Margaret Desenfans remained mistress of the house and its priceless contents. She must have been a woman of generosity and scrupulousness, for during this period she did everything in her power to carry out the wishes of her 'late dear husband' and her 'late dear friend', as she called them. So did Sir John Soane, another close member of the circle, who had designed the mortuary chapel which contained Desenfans' body.

It had been Bourgeois' wish that Soane should build a gallery at Dulwich to house the pictures, complete with a mausoleum where would be placed the bodies of himself and of the Desenfans. To this end he left £2,000 'for the repairing, improving and beautifying the west wing and gallery of the College for the reception of the pictures', and £10,000 to provide an income for the maintenance of the gallery. On the day after Bourgeois died Soane inspected the site (he had visited Bourgeois three days before his death, when no doubt plans were discussed), and reported to the Master that 'from the ruinous state of the present West Wing which contains the Picture Gallery and the Poor Sisters' Rooms the whole must be taken down'. His estimate for the rebuilding was £11,270. When it seemed unlikely that this sum would be forthcoming, Mrs Desenfans offered to make Bourgeois' legacy of £2,000 up to £6,000, and the remaining sum was provided out of the college endowment.

Soane produced an exceptionally large number of plans, and it seems that he regarded the commission as an act of homage and friendship, since there is no record that he charged either for the designs or for the supervision of the work.[1] Indeed he volunteered to make good out of his own pocket any financial deficiency, though this offer was not accepted. There are several references in his Notebooks to days when he stayed at home 'about Dulwich Gallery', and on 18 October 1811, together with his wife, he was on the site when the foundations were set out. The gallery was probably ready some time in 1813.

Soane's work was controversial in his day, and ten years after the Dulwich Gallery was built it inspired an attack in Knight's *Quarterly Magazine* which referred sneeringly to the 'dingy light', the 'sightless roof', and so on. One verse runs:

> The roofs unsham'd by slate or tile,
> The brick with Portland dress'd,
> The *stepless* door, the scorèd wall,
> Pillars *sans* base or capital,
> And curious antiques;
> The chimney groups that fright the sweeps,
> And *acroteria* fifty deep,
> And all thy mighty freaks . . .

Nowadays, however, it is regarded, as Sir John Summerson writes, as 'one of Soane's most individual buildings. It owes nothing to any building of his time or of a considerable period before it . . . I personally regard Dulwich as the quintessence of the Soane style and the apex of his achievements.'

---

[1] But there is a mystery. The accounts listing payments to him by the college between 1812 and 1815 for the work of building the gallery and the 'Poor Sisters' apartments, which amount to £10,217 15s 8d, include the unexplained item 'To cash, for Commission, £182.4.0.' Possibly this represents commission on Soane's work in connection with the poor sisters' apartments.

Margaret Desenfans died on 16 May 1813, and Soane records that he spent four hours with her on the 12th. It is not known exactly when the pictures were moved to the gallery, but from the records it appears as if this might have been in the latter part of June 1814. The *Bourgeois Book of Regulations* has a note that on the 10th of that month arrangements for the move were made with a Mr Morton, whose estimate for the job was £35. Another clue comes from the varying sums which from August 1813 onwards had been paid on a number of occasions to one Gill, the 'servant in charge of the pictures' since Mrs Desenfans' death. On 18 July 1814 there is an entry in the accounts 'To Gill in full on leaving . . .' Mr Morton's bill was eventually £58 5s, and it was paid on 7 September of the same year. The bodies of the Desenfans and of Bourgeois were moved in March 1815 to the mausoleum attached to the gallery which Soane had designed for the purpose, and which was similar to the one in Charlotte Street.

The date when the gallery was opened is also unrecorded, but on 31 August 1814 Farington writes that he had that day gone to see 'the Desenfans collection of pictures now arranged in the building erected from Soane's design . . . I remarked that there was a want of light in the gallery, and that the colour of the ground of the walls was heavy and unfavourable for the pictures, something like burnt ochre but heavier. Soane designed the building and [Benjamin] West recommended the colour of the ground. I told Cockburn[1] the small pictures could not be seen but imperfectly.' Lawrence (not yet knighted or President of the Royal Academy) went on the same day, and afterwards both men were dined by the college and treated with great hospitality.

On 1 December 1815 Farington has the following entry: 'A series of resolutions agreed to by the Council to establish a *School of Painting* in the Academy were also read, and agreed to. It arose from the Master and Fellows of Dulwich College having offered to lend any of the *Bourgeois* collection to the Academy for this purpose. A resolution was added after voting that this offer be accepted, that pictures obtained from other

---

[1] Ralph Cockburn, the first keeper of the gallery.

quarters should also be received for the students to copy.' As a result the Royal Academy School of Painting—in addition to the existing schools—came into being the following year, and four or five paintings (sometimes more, sometimes fewer) were borrowed every year from Dulwich for the purpose. Some of the more impecunious students complained if the pictures chosen were very big, because of the cost of canvas needed and the amount of work involved.

Just as forty years later the Governors of the newly constituted college were to meet for the purpose of creating a school, so in 1817 the Master, Warden, and fellows gathered together to draw up rules for the administration of their gallery and its funds. Admittance was free, but tickets had to be obtained in advance from a number of establishments in London, one of them being Colnaghi's, which was later to sell Pissarro's painting of the college for Lord Eccles. The fellows had absolute power over how and when the pictures should be shown, and were allowed to remove them from the gallery and hang them in their own rooms. One of the ushers, the Rev. John Lindsay, was particularly assiduous in this respect, borrowing amongst others a Van Dyck, a Poussin, and a Paggi.

As well as providing the additional £4,000 which made the building of the gallery possible, Margaret Desenfans had directed in her will that, in accordance with Bourgeois' wishes, the sum of £500 should be invested and the interest used to provide an annual dinner for the President and Academicians. To this end she left a quantity of silver and china, a tablecloth, a dining-table, glasses and decanters, 'which I direct shall be preserved by them and never be used on any other occasion or for any other purpose whatever'. The silver is still in the possession of the college, but the rest of her bequest has vanished with the passage of time. The dinner itself soon became a source of dispute, since the cost of the first one, which was held in 1818, was £62 18s 9d, whereas Mrs Desenfans' £500 yielded only £15 2s 4d per annum in interest. It was decided to hold the dinner triennially, which led to some acrimonious but gentlemanly correspondence between Launcelot Baugh Allen, the ex-Master, and his fellow executor Robert Corry on the one hand and the then Master, 'Holland House' Allen, on the other. The latter remained firm in his determination not to use Foundation funds for the dinner, and in the intervening summers the Royal Academicians came for an informal meeting and were treated to tea and strawberries.

The loan of pictures to the Royal Academy also caused some discontent. In 1865 three were returned in an unsatisfactory condition, two of them loose in their frames and one warped and with the varnish cracked. Two years later the privilege was temporarily withdrawn and the annual visits discontinued—later to be resumed, as were the controversial dinners. At about the same time one of the college Governors, J. C. Robinson, who had been asked to report on the pictures, remarked that they had 'suffered from neglect and timidity and over-scrupulousness' and expressed disapproval of the oil varnish which had been used. 'The greater part of the Dulwich pictures appear to have been covered with this deleterious mixture.' Worse still, Rubens' *Venus, Mars and Cupid* appeared to have been 'roughly cleaned or *scrubbed*'. However, one Royal Academician, visiting the gallery in 1871, complimented the Board on the very good state of preservation of the pictures, much work having been done on them meanwhile.

There were other early troubles, such as the 'steam apparatus' which had been installed, and which six years later led to dry rot. All the same, a visit to the Bourgeois Gallery, as it was generally called before the Reconstitution, became extremely popular. Until the National Gallery was opened in 1824 (for the first fourteen years in a private house), with only a modest number of pictures, the Dulwich Gallery was virtually the only, and much the most important, public gallery in the country. It was especially prized for the work of the Dutch painters who were so popular at the time.

Many eminent people came to see it. Lawrence was a frequent visitor, and others were Lord Holland, the Crown Prince of Germany, Flaxman, Sir Francis Chantrey, Sydney

Smith, the Archbishop of Canterbury, Landseer, and 'Mr Constable'. Ruskin, an assiduous visitor, was given permission to make water-colour drawings from the pictures, and as a student Holman Hunt haunted the gallery. In *Alton Lock* Kingsley's protagonist is taken first not to the National Gallery but to Dulwich, where there are 'much better pictures'. It was a favourite spot of Hazlitt's, and Robert Browning wrote to Elizabeth Barrett that when he was a child and living in Camberwell he was often taken to the gallery by his father, 'a good half-hour's walk over the fields'. George Eliot drove down for a visit, but admired the fresh spring green and the trees and buttercups more than the pictures.

In those early days many descriptions of the gallery and its contents were written, including one by Ruskin, and a long article by Hazlitt in the *London Magazine* in 1823. However, from the middle of the century they gradually dwindled, mainly because of the growing popularity and continual extension of the National Gallery, as well as its greater accessibility. In 1854, in fact, one newspaper referred to the gallery as being 'in a disgracefully neglected state, attracting to the spot a few stray visitors during the summer season'. But great numbers of students flocked there to copy the pictures— the Murillos were particular favourites—and after a while it was necessary to limit their number.

Over the years the gallery, which has acquired most of its possessions by gift rather than by purchase, has been enriched by some splendid bequests. One of the most interesting was a collection of portraits of the Linley family. The Linleys lived in Bath at the height of its popularity, when it was the musical centre of the country. The leading musician in the town was Thomas Linley. He had many children, most of whom died tragically young; one of them, Samuel, was nursed in his last illness by Mrs Linley's maid, the illiterate but lovely Emma Hart, later to become Lady Hamilton and Nelson's *inamorata*. There were also two daughters who were not only ravishingly beautiful but exquisite singers. The older, Elizabeth Ann, was famous far and wide as 'the Maid of Bath'. She subsequently married Sheridan, and a very unsatisfactory husband he proved to be.

Fig. 10.1 Dulwich Picture Gallery, 1849

Gainsborough was also living in Bath at this time, and he painted several portraits of this handsome and talented family. ('We are all geniuses here, sir,' one of the sons, as a small boy, is reputed to have told a visitor.) These pictures came to the college through another son, Ozias Linley, who was appointed organist at Dulwich, and who was the last of the fellows to be buried beneath the chapel.

The first mention of the portraits, and of others of the family by Lawrence, Oliver, and Lonsdale, in relation to the college is a note in the Art Gallery Records that on 23 March 1822 the Master, Warden, and two of the fellows 'ordered that a picture by Gainsborough of Elizabeth Ann Sheridan and Mary Tickle deceased, in the possession of William Linley Esq. [Ozias' brother], should be allowed at his request a place in the Picture Gallery till it shall be convenient for him to resume it.' Neither Ozias nor William had any children, and when they died they left their whole collection of family pictures to the gallery. There is a charming legend attached to the most famous of them, Gainsborough's picture of Elizabeth Ann and her sister Mary. Tradition has it that the music Mary is holding is 'A Song of Spring', the words by her husband and the music by her father.

Another interesting gift also concerns a painting by Gainsborough; this is the portrait of *Mrs Moody and her Children*, which in 1831 was given to the gallery by a Captain Thomas Moody. For nearly a century the reason for his generosity remained a mystery. However, in 1915 a picture dealer was asked to value the property of a Miss Sylvester, and amongst her goods he found a diary kept by Thomas Moody, one of the two children portrayed in the Gainsborough. The diary is full of bitter complaints about his father's second wife, Thomas' stepmother, who was Miss Sylvester's great-grandmother. She was many years younger than his father, and in seven years of boarding-school she never once had her two stepsons home for the holidays. Thomas seems to have disliked his stepbrothers and sisters as much as he did his stepmother, so he probably gave the portrait of his mother (who had died when she was twenty-six) to Dulwich in order that it should not fall into their hands. Why he chose Dulwich is still unexplained, but perhaps this was because in 1831 it was still almost the only picture gallery accessible to the public. There is also an interesting letter in which the curator acknowledged the gift, and referred to the 'satisfaction you have express'd as to the mode of preserving the pictures already in my custody'.

Constance Carver has a first-hand account of the gallery dating from the time when the Master and his family still lived in the old college:

> The Curator of the Gallery, a Mr Denning, painted one of the earliest portraits of our beloved Queen Victoria, this little picture has become well known as it appeared in pretty well every paper and magazine, at the time of the two Jubilees and at the end of her long and glorious reign. Mr Denning dearly loved children and we were often allowed in the gallery especially on wet days. I think that it was greatly due to his kindness that I developed in after years such an intense love of Art and Artistic tastes.
>
> Here I may say we have still in our possession some pictures from his hand, and it was only a few months ago, that an Artist of considerable note stood before one of these pictures, enraptured. Mr Denning, he said, 'Had made the flesh of the man alive. Why,' he said, 'it is all alive, it lives—it lives!' (This is the portrait of the old Dulwich Wood Cutter.)
>
> A yearly Banquet was given to the members of the Royal Academy in the Dulwich gallery in order that they might choose some pictures from the wonderful collection for the Academy students. At that time there was no public gallery in England, and so this may be said to have been the first of its kind, and it is rich in some of the choicest gems of the old Masters . . .
>
> Well I remember the faces of Mellais [sic], but most especially Sir Frederick Leighton with his grand head, good height and bearing, he was charming, a fine speaker, and for many years held the Office of President of the Royal Academy.

Stephen Poyntz Denning, who painted the portrait of Queen Victoria at the age of four to which Constance refers, was curator of the gallery for many years. This picture, one of the most popular of the collection, originally came up for sale in the 1880s, but the Governors did not buy it until 1891.

In 1870, when the school moved to the new buildings on Dulwich Common, and the old college buildings for a time housed the lower school (later to become Alleyn's), a home had to be found for the 157 pictures which were not part of the Bourgeois collection but had been left by Alleyn, Cartwright, and others. For the time being they were hung in the Master's house in the south block, but they were extremely crowded and many were hung in unsuitable places which made it impossible for the public to see them. When Carver resigned the pictures were taken down, with the idea of hanging them in the central block. This idea proved unsatisfactory for the same reason—lack of room, and the fact that the public would have only limited access to them. So it was decided to hang them in the picture gallery (which under the Act of 1857 was named the Dulwich College Picture Gallery), and in 1884 and 1886 two wings, used for many years as part of the almshouses, were adapted for this purpose. Mackenzie comments that Welldon made great efforts to retain some of the pictures in the Master's house, but 'his instances were smilingly set aside'. Several were placed in the boardroom of the new building, including the portrait of Edward Alleyn, which, Mackenzie said, 'has been so much painted over by unskilful hands as to have lost all look of life'. The *Alleynian* records that 'in the nineteenth century the walls of the Gallery were packed with pictures four levels high, going right up to the ceiling and down to within a foot of the floor.'

From the minutes of the Governors' meetings, intriguing glimpses are caught of what was happening in the gallery. In 1874, 1,508 visitors inspected the pictures in Easter week. Two years later the first complete catalogue was printed (there had been earlier ones, but none satisfactory) and sold at 1s a copy; it was by J. C. L. Sparkes, the master in charge of art at the college. In the same year 382 pictures were insured for £50,000 with the Hand-in-Hand Fire and Life Assurance Co. In 1889 the almsmen were debarred from having plots in the gallery grounds, in order that a pleasure garden could be laid out. Speech-days and prize-givings were at first held in the gallery, and on one of these occasions the face of St Catherine in the picture at that time attributed to Veronese, but now known to have been painted in his studio, was scratched. In 1903 it was recorded that 'the Royal Academicians would prefer holding their inspection in the afternoon and being entertained afterwards in the garden, to attending a luncheon in the middle of the day; and in as much as a luncheon is found to interfere with their professional callings we recommend that the annual entertainment be confined to the Garden Party'. Six years later it was decided to sell postcard reproductions of paintings in the gallery, and an estimate was accepted from a printer in Clifford's Inn for supplying 1,000 copies of each of twelve pictures for £23 10s. There were sold by the head porter, who was paid a commission of 1d in the shilling. By this time there were about 29,000 visitors annually.

In 1821, very soon after the gallery had come into existence, the keeper had been ordered to 'instruct such of the poor scholars in the art of drawing as may be recommended by the Trustees'. There is no indication that this was ever done, or that the twelve boys ever benefited from the Bourgeois legacy. However, when Carver became Master one of his earliest appointments to the staff was that of J. C. L. Sparkes, who was also head of the Lambeth School of Art and later of the National Art Training School of South Kensington. He and Carver collaborated in one of the early catalogues of the gallery, which came out in 1884. Sparkes was at Dulwich until 1881, and it is unquestionably on his teaching that the remarkable tradition of art at the school in the late nineteenth and early twentieth centuries was founded. When the Scheme of the Charity Commission came into force in 1882, £4,000 was allocated for building a School of Fine Art attached to the gallery. Plans were drawn up which would have involved adapting the almshouses to the use of this art school, but nothing came of the idea. Though a school of art of some kind seems to have been established in the old college in 1892—intended at first for the benefit solely of 'lady students'—it was closed three years later because of insufficient demand.

Nevertheless, many boys went from Dulwich to the Lambeth School of Art, where they were taught not only by Sparkes but also by Leighton and Millais, who, Mackenzie writes, was an inspiring teacher. Several of them, after leaving school, exhibited regularly at the Royal Academy; H. de T.

Glazebrook, H. H. La Thangue, S. Melton Fisher, Horace Fisher, P. Harland Fisher, Mouat Loudan, G. Atkinson, H. A. Bone, C. F. A. Voysey, and many others. In 1895 A. H. Gilkes wrote in his diary, 'In this term was won the principal distinction for young artists among my own pupils. H. R. Mileham won the Gold Medal for Historical Painting and the travelling studentship at the Royal Academy. He sent me an engraving of his picture. It represents the finding of Moses in the bulrushes; or rather the nursing of him when found by Pharaoh's daughter. The baby is very small.' The names of most of these painters have passed into oblivion, except that of the architect Voysey, who was at the college for only a very short time, but one of them is still remembered—Stanhope A. Forbes, who was the first Old Alleynian to be elected an R.A. He exhibited every year at the summer show between 1878 and 1946, missing only twice, and his pictures hang in several galleries round the country.

It was M. G. Glazebrook, later Canon of Ely, who wrote of his years at Dulwich, between 1867 and 1872, 'If the Sixth had little authority, they had one privilege for which I have never ceased to be grateful. We were allowed in all leisure hours to visit the Picture Gallery. Perhaps it was love of privilege more than love of pictures which led us to spend so many hours there: but I can still call up before my eyes all the main features of that delightful collection, and I am conscious that there I learned to feel the value of art.' When Sparkes left he wrote to Carver, 'I am happy in remembering that your boys have done more in Art than those of any other public school in England, thanks to the warm interest and support you have always given to all propositions I have made for their advantage.' A pupil of a later era, Adrian Hill, who was at the school from 1907–11, used virtually to live in the gallery—he would go there day after day to copy the pictures, and many years later, not having seen them for a very long time, he still remembered every one. During the 1914–18 war he became the first Official Serving War Artist, and 190 of his war pictures are in the Imperial Museum.

As the years passed the artistic tradition weakened, but in 1919 it was still strong enough for *The Observer* to write,

or money, so wire was procured instead. But each length had to be spliced at one end and tied off at the other, and who had the expertise to do that? 'Sailors, of course,' said Kelly. 'Go out and find half a dozen!' (Luckily a simpler method was found.) Hundreds of picture-hooks were needed, and were only obtained through the goodwill of Sir Francis Watson, then Assistant Keeper of the Wallace Collection.

By 1956 the deficit on the restoration account alone was £10,000, and Kelly, unrepentant, declared that he had landed the gallery 'in an ocean of debt'. But his boldness in going ahead with the restoration regardless of cost—and with the wholehearted support of the Governors, especially of their Chairman, Lord Soulbury—was a visionary act which has proved of inestimable value. Over the years, apart from a grant from the War Damage Commission, financial help came from various quarters to meet the £74,000 which it cost to restore the gallery, the main benefactors being the Pilgrim Trust, the Estates Governors, and the L.C.C. There was also a legacy from a Miss Mabel Alleyne, who in earlier days had visited the gallery to copy the pictures. She claimed to be a descendant of the founder, and in 1919 she had written to a member of Carver's family, 'I know how much we all owe Canon Carver, for the splendid work he did for the College, which will stand as a lasting memorial to *him*—for after all Alleyn was but the founder, Canon Carver created the masterpiece.'

In 1953 the gallery was reopened, and the Queen Mother came down for the occasion. *The Times*, reporting her visit, referred disparagingly to the 'funereal atmosphere' of the gallery before the war, 'the pictures getting more and more gloomy with the passage of time'. The transformation now was remarkable:

> The average visitor can now see, as was impossible before the war, the great Rubens of *Venus, Mars, and Cupid*, and the same artist's enchanting small portrait of Helene Fourment, the incomparable Poussins, the Claudes,[1] the Rembrandt of a young girl at a

---

[1] There is in fact only one Claude.

window, Watteau's *Ball*—Constable could hardly say today that this looked as if painted in honey—the superb Hobbema, the early Gainsborough, the three Murillos . . . and the splendid Veronese. The seicento paintings, and, above all, the marvellously operatic Guido Reni, have lost all their treacle; the two great Gainsboroughs and his smaller portraits look wonderfully fresh . . .

One reason why the gallery was particularly fortunate in having Sir Gerald Kelly as its adviser at this time was that he had very strong views about the correct approach to restoring pictures. Although these views went against the general tide of opinion in the art world, he was able to carry the Governors with him, and, in Dr Johann Hell, to engage for the work a man who was both sensitive and conservative in his technique. Hell died before the task was complete, and it was finished by John Brealey, later chief picture restorer to the Metropolitan Museum of Art in New York, who says:

> It was remarkable that there was this relationship between Hell and Kelly, who was violently opinionated, tough and outspoken, but who nevertheless had his heart in the right place. Almost every other gallery in the world has suffered from over-cleaning, and Dulwich is one of the few which have escaped. It's a question of aesthetics: if restoration affects the appearance of a picture, it affects the meaning too. You can always go back to a picture if it has been treated in a conservative way, but if it has been over-cleaned the damage is irreversible. Kelly served the best interests of the gallery at a time when no one else would have done so.

On new year's eve, 1966, eight of the pictures were stolen—three Rembrandts, three Rubens, a Gerard Dou, and an Elsheimer—their value variously put at anything between two and six million pounds. Three of them were discovered a few days later in a bed-sitter, and the others, carefully wrapped in several layers of newspaper, under a bush on Streatham Common, undamaged except for surface scratches on the varnish. About twelve people were initially held, but only one of them, who had considerately left his fingerprints behind, could be charged, and he was duly imprisoned for this and other misdemeanours. Some years afterwards he revisited the gallery—this time through the main entrance—and signed his name in the visitors' book, saying to the attendant as he did so, 'I'm the bloke who stole the pictures'. He then walked round the gallery like any respectable citizen and art-lover. The attempted *coup* was one of the biggest art robberies on record.

The gallery was once again in the news in 1971, when it was decided to sell one of the pictures. For many years there had been much discussion about how to make ends meet, which at that time was quite impossible from the available funds. Advice was sought from Professor Anthony Blunt, then Director of the Courtauld Institute; he advised against selling, and suggested that wealthy American foundations might be prepared to help. When this came to nothing, the proposal was made that the whole collection should be handed over to the Greater London Council or the nation, but to a man the Governors were against this. In the end the sale of one of the major works seemed inevitable, and the Department of Education and Science, whose permission it was necessary to seek, gave their consent. The picture chosen was Domenichino's *Adoration of the Shepherds*. It fetched £100,000, bringing some badly needed cash, but many people were—and still are—extremely unhappy about the whole affair, not least because this picture was the only nativity in the gallery, as well as the only painting by Domenichino, who is sparsely represented in this country.

Of recent years finances have been in a much sounder state, funds coming from an admission charge, grants from the Estates Governors, the gallery's own endowment from the Foundation, the local authorities, and the Friends of Dulwich Picture Gallery. The 'Friends' came into being in 1954, and are very active in raising money for such purposes as redecoration, and restoration of the beautiful antique furniture which the gallery possesses, as well as in arranging artistic, musical, and social functions there. In 1980 they provided the funds for a major refurbishing of the gallery, and for the rehanging of the pictures—an exciting venture which enticed a far greater number of people to come to admire all the treasures that the gallery had to offer.

For the first time for half-a-century or more the links are being strengthened between the gallery and the college—the only school in the country which can claim that it owns a famous picture gallery. The history of art is being taught to the boys in the gallery itself, and they are encouraged to take A-levels in this subject; talks on art are being given as part of the liberal studies course and there is an optional course on architecture; the lower school has an introductory course; an art scholarship is awarded annually; and the boys are being encouraged to visit the gallery on their own, as they were a century ago. An extension will provide a lecture room, a home for temporary exhibitions, and extra storage space. The staff of the National Maritime Museum at Greenwich have been called in to advise on the conservation of the pictures; and in 1978 it was decided that the gallery should in future be known simply as the Dulwich Picture Gallery.

The rich and varied collection contains paintings by Poussin and Claude, Rubens, Van Dyck and Teniers, Murillo, Rembrandt, Hobbema, and many other Dutch artists. The English painters include Hogarth, Reynolds, Gainsborough, and Laurence, and there are works by Watteau, Tiepolo, and Canaletto. It is hoped that other schools in the neighbourhood, as well as those of the Foundation, will be able to share in the enjoyment of all this beauty; that, as the gallery takes its place as one of the most important collections in the country, it will once more become a living and integral part of the life of the college; and that from far and wide people will flock to see its astonishing and little-known treasures.

Acknowledgements

M Y profound thanks are due to the Board of Governors of Dulwich College for authorizing me to write this history, and to their Chairman, Lord Wolfenden, for generously contributing the introduction.

I should like to have been able to thank by name all the people who have provided me with a wealth of information: among them are many Old Alleynians, who showed me much hospitality and kindness. It has been a particular pleasure to get to know them, as well as many past and present members of the teaching staff, whose reminiscences were especially valuable—what excellent memories they have! I enjoyed very much, also, various discussions with present Alleynians, who talked with such intelligence, interest, and engaging frankness. There are, alas, far too many of them to acknowledge individually, and I can only ask them to accept my immense gratitude for their help.

An exception must, however, be made in the case of three past members of the staff who went to much trouble to send me material: H. V. Styler, George Way, and especially Eric Handscomb. To the last I also owe a very considerable debt for his patience in answering my endless questions, and for the care with which he read the final typescript, as did the Deputy Master, Terry Walsh, and the Bursar, David Banwell. S. C. Griffith and David Knight helped me a great deal with Chapter 8—without them I should have been lost. Various other people were kind enough to read relevant portions of the book and make suggestions and corrections: Margaret Bryant, Arthur Bush, Ronald Groves, Charles Lloyd, Alan Morgan, Professor Peter Murray, and E. C. Shaw. I am exceedingly grateful to all of them for indispensable help. For any errors which still remain the responsibility is mine alone. Thanks are also due to Austin Hall, of the college library staff, to the Master's and the bursarial staff and to the Master's porters for their unfailing co-operation. Members of Canon Carver's and of the Gilkes families gave me a great deal of fascinating and invaluable material and information.

Mary Boast of the John Harvard Library of Local Studies; the staff of the Library of the Ministry of Education and Science; Professor David Layton of the Department of Education, University of Leeds; and Mr Neate, Keeper of the School Archives of the Greater London Council, provided much assistance. Deborah Deavin typed the manuscript with her usual care and intelligence: Old Alleynians will be interested to know that her grandfather, Sir Eric Conran-Smith, three of her great-uncles and a cousin were at the college at the end of the last century and the beginning of this one.

Mr and Mrs Maurice C. R. Taylor were particularly generous in allowing Pissarro's painting of Dulwich College to be used for the jacket illustration.

I am especially grateful to Pam Emms for her many kindnesses, and for all the warmth and hospitality which, in common with hundreds of masters, wives and other visitors, I have so often enjoyed at Elm Lawn; to Barry Viney, head of the Art Department at Dulwich College, for the many hours which, with characteristic generosity, he devoted to helping me with the illustrations and to designing the jacket; to my husband, John Bush, as always my best and most severe critic; and above all to David Emms, for his courage in backing such a singularly dark horse, and for the unfailing support and encouragement which made the writing of this book possible.

Bibliography

Unpublished Material

Abbott, Peter: *The Founding of Dulwich College and its Organisation During the Life of its Founder* (1974)

Account Books of Dulwich College, 1619–1857

Account Books of the Picture Gallery

Bourgeois Book of Regulations

Britton, J.: *A Brief Catalogue of Pictures, Late the Property of Sir Francis Bourgeois R.A.*

Broad, C. D.: *Autobiography*

Carver, A. J.: Miscellaneous Papers

Clee, W. R.: *The Hollingtonian Club: A Log of History* (1956)

Darby, William: *History of Dulwich College*

Daventry, June: *The 1944 Act, the Dulwich Experiment, and Its Demise* (Dip. Ed. Thesis)

Dulwich College School Association: *Abstract of Reports from the Formation to the Charity Commissioners' Enquiry* (1854)

Franks, D. L.: *The Stamford Brickworks and Dulwich College* (Dip. Ed. Thesis, 1972)

Gilkes, A. H.: Diary kept between August 1899 and Spring 1910

Hartley, Henry Joseph: *Petition to the Archbishop of Canterbury* (1844)

Hudson, Constance (Carver): *My Reminiscences*

Mackenzie, R. J.: *History of Dulwich College*

Minutes of the Board of Governors of Dulwich College, 1858–1980

Partington, J. A.: *The History of the System of Direct Grants to Secondary Schools* (Thesis submitted for M. Ed. Degree of the University of Durham, 1967)

Private Sittings of the Master, Warden and Fellows of Dulwich College, 1726–1857

Public Record Office: Secondary Education: Institution Files
Register of Admissions to Dulwich College, 1616–1857
Sheeran, J. N. G.: *Dulwich College Picture Gallery: A History of the College and the Building* (B.A. Thesis, Southampton University)
Stroud, Dorothy (compiled by): Soane Notebooks, Vol. VIII, *Catalogue raisonné*
Thompson, H. Y.: Dulwich Gallery Notes

Published Material

Abstract of Reports and Proceedings of the Dulwich College School Association (privately printed, 1854)
Addresses by the Worshipful Masters of the Old Alleynian Lodge at the Public Schools' Lodges Festival (privately printed, 1932 and 1976)
The Alleynian (1873–1980)
Anon: *The Charity of God's Gift College, Dulwich* (privately printed, 1853)
Bamford, T. W.: *Rise of the Public Schools* (Nelson, 1967)
Begbie, Harold: *Shackleton: A Memory* (Mills & Boon, 1922)
Bickley, Francis B.: *Catalogue of the Manuscripts and Muniments of Alleyn's College of God's Gift at Dulwich*, Second Series (published by the Governors, 1903)
Black, Clementina: *The Linleys of Bath* (Secker, 1911)
Blanch, W. H.: *Dulwich College and Edward Alleyn* (E. W. Allen, 1877)
        Ye Parish of Camberwell (E. W. Allen, 1875)
Brown, George: *A Wayfarer in Dulwich* (privately printed, undated)
Burford, E. J.: *Bawds and Lodgings* (Peter Owen, 1976)
Campbell, Rear-Admiral Gordon: *My Mystery Ships* (Hodder & Stoughton, 1928)
Campbell, Margaret: *Dolmetsch: The Man and His Work* (Hamish Hamilton, 1975)
Church Magazine Vol. V (1843)
Collier, J. Payne: *Memoirs of Edward Alleyn* (Shakespeare Society, 1841)
Coulton, C. G.: *Fourscore Years* (Cambridge University Press, 1943)
Curtis, S. J.: *History of Education in Great Britain* (University Tutorial Press, 1957)
Curtis, S. J. and Boultwood, M. E. A.: *An Introductory History of English Education since 1800* (University Tutorial Press, 1960)
Davies, Evan: *The Book of Dulwich* (Barracuda Books, 1975)
De Selincourt, Hugh: *Studies from Life* (Unicorn Press, 1934)

Desenfans, Noel: *Memoirs* (John Dean, 1810)
Dewhurst, Wynford: *Impressionistic Painting* (George Newnes, 1904)
Dictionary of National Biography
Dilke, Christopher: *Mr Moberly's Mint-Mark* (Heinemann, 1965)
Dulwich College Magazine for School News and General Reading (1864–5)
Dulwich College School Association: *Rules* (privately printed, April 1841)
Dulwich College Year Book 1903–1980 (privately printed)
Ellis, Havelock: *Introduction to Christopher Marlowe* (Vizetelly, 1887)
Endowed Charities: Report Made to the Charity Commissioners: Parish of Camberwell (1900)
Farington, Joseph: *Diary* (i) Edited by James Greig (Hutchinson, 1922), (ii) Edited by Kenneth Garlick and Angus Macintyre (Yale University Press, 1978)
Forester, C. S.: *Long Before Forty* (Michael Joseph, 1967)
Fraser, O.: *The World of the Public School* (Weidenfeld & Nicholson, 1977)
Gayford, A. W. P.: *History of Dulwich College* (privately printed, 1950)
Gilkes, A. H.: *Boys and Masters* (Longmans Green, 1887)
    The Modern Side of Public Schools (Board of Education Pamphlet, No. 10, 1907)
Goldthorpe, John H.: *Social Mobility and Class Structure in Modern Britain* (Clarendon Press, 1980)
Goodall, J.: *Dulwich College: The Story of a Foundation*, Part II (*Macmillan's Magazine*, June 1868)
Hall, E. T.: *Dulwich: History and Romance* (Bickers and Sons, 1922)
Halsey, A. H., Heath, A. F., and Ridge, J. M.: *Origins and Destinations* (Clarendon Press, 1980)
Highmore, A.: *Pietas Londinensis: The History of Public Charters in or near London* (1806–1810)
Honey, J. R. de S.: *Tom Brown's Universe* (Millington, 1977)
Hosking, G. L.: *The Life and Times of Edward Alleyn* (Cape, 1952)
Hovenden, Frederick: *The History of Dulwich College* (privately printed, 1873)
Jones, Paul: *War Letters of a Public School-Boy* (Cassell, 1918)
Kittermaster, A. N. C.: *School Songs*, etc (privately printed, 1918)
Latter, O. H.: *Report on Science Teaching in Public Schools represented on the Association of Public Schools Science Masters* (Board of Education Pamphlet No. 17, 1909)
Leake, W. R. M.: *Gilkes and Dulwich 1885–1914* (Alleyn Club, 1938)
Lester Smith, W. O.: *Education* (Penguin Books, 1957)

Lowndes, G. A. N.: *The Silent Social Revolution* (Oxford University Press, 1937)

Maclure, Stuart: *One Hundred Years of London Education, 1870–1970* (Allen Lane The Penguin Press, 1970)

Magnusson, Magnus: *The Clacken and the Slate* (Collins, 1974)

Marples, M.: *Public School Slang* (Constable, 1940)

Meadmore, W. S.: *Lucien Pissarro* (Constable 1962)

Memories of Dulwich College in the 'Sixties and the 'Seventies by Old Alleynians (privately printed, 1919)

Mill, H. R.: *The Life of Sir Ernest Shackleton* (Heinemann, 1924)

Newsome, David: *Godliness and Good Learning* (Murray, 1961)

   A History of Wellington College, 1859–1959 (Murray, 1959)

Norwood, Cyril: *The English Tradition of Education* (Murray, 1929)

Ormiston, T. L.: Dulwich College Register 1619–1926 (privately printed)

Percy, F. H. G.: *History of Whitgift School* (Batsford, 1976)

Peterson, A. D. C.: *A Hundred Years of Education* (Duckworth, 1971)

Public Schools and the General Education System, The (Fleming Report, H.M.S.O., 1944)

Rendle, W.: *Playhouses at Bankside in the Time of Shakespeare* (Walford's *Antiquarian,* 1877)

   The Stews on Bankside (*Antiquarian Magazine* Vol. 2, No. 8, 1882)

Rogers, William: *Reminiscences* (Kegan Paul, Trench, 1888)

Sargent, W. C.: '*Young England at School*' (*Ludgate Monthly*, April 1893)

Seaborne, Malcolm: *The English School: Its Architecture and Organization 1370–1870* (Routledge and Kegan Paul, 1971)

Simon, Brian, and Bradley, Ian: *The Victorian Public School* (Gill & Macmillan, 1975)

Sixth Report of the Royal Commission on Scientific Instruction and the Advancement of Science (The Devonshire Commission, 1875)

Staunton, Howard: *The Great Schools of England* (Sampson Low, Son and Marston, 1865)

Stevens, Auriol: *Clever Children in Comprehensive Schools* (Penguin Books, 1980)

Summerson, Sir John: *Sir John Soane* (Art and Technics, 1952)

Visit to Dulwich College (Journal of the London Society, September 1935)

Warner, George F.: *Catalogue of the Manuscripts and Muniments of Alleyn's College of God's Gift at Dulwich* (Longmans Green, 1881)

Webb, Sidney: *London Education* (Longmans Green, 1904)

Welldon, J. E. C.: *Forty Years On* (Nicholson & Watson, 1935)

Wells, H. G.: *The Story of a Great Schoolmaster* (Chatto & Windus, 1924)

Wheatley, Dennis: *Memoirs* (Hutchinson, 1977)

Wodehouse, P. G.: *The Gold Bat* (Souvenir Press, 1972)

                Performing Flea: A Self-Portrait in Letters, with an Introduction and Additional Notes by W. Townend (Herbert Jenkins, 1954)

                The Pothunters (A. & C. Black, 1902)

                A Prefect's Uncle (Souvenir Press, 1972)

                Over Seventy (Herbert Jenkins, 1957)

                Sunset at Blandings with Notes and Appendices by Richard Usborne (Chatto & Windus, 1977)

Wren, M. A., and Hackett, P.: *James Allen: A Portrait Enlarged* (Brown Knight & Truscott Ltd, 1968)

Wynne, Lewis: *Old South London* (1924)

Young, William: *The History of Dulwich College* (privately printed, 1889)

References

In order to keep the footnotes to a minimum I have listed below, rather than in the text itself, the origin of short quoted passages, giving the page number and the first few words for purposes of identification. Also included are a few other notes, sources, and references which may be of interest.

Frontispiece
> This print is a copy of the original portrait by an unknown artist. It was drawn by Sylvester Harding, who visited the college in 1790 and copied a number of the portraits in order to have them made into prints. Canon Carver bought the original pen-and-water-colour drawing in 1870. Two years after Sylvester Harding's visit the portrait was ruined, as R. J. Mackenzie complained, by extremely inept over-painting.

Preface
> ix Robert Jameson Mackenzie (1857–1912). He was a cousin of Canon Carver's son-in-law, J. R. M. Stuart, three of whose brothers had been at Dulwich. At the age of thirty-one he became Rector of the Edinburgh Academy, then in the doldrums, where he had to deal with problems not unlike those which bedevilled Carver at Dulwich. He wrote a history of Dr H. H. Almond, the great headmaster of Loretto, but because of ill-health had to resign from the Edinburgh Academy after ten years, having worn himself out in his work for the school.

Chapter 1
> 1 'able to make . . .' Thomas Nash, *Strange News*, 1592.

2 'Alleyn's purchase for fivepence . . .' This is recorded on the back of a letter from Thomas Bowker.
'with excellent action . . .' Thomas Dekker, *Magnificent Entertainment*, 1604.
3 'with mouthing words . . .' Anon, *The Return from Parnassus*, 1606.
4 'with full power and lawful . . .' The Letters Patent.
5 'I like well . . .' 18 August 1618.
7 'his life was one . . .' G. F. Warner, *Catalogue of the Manuscripts and Muniments.*
9 'not so much in respect . . .' Memorandum from Dr Love to Alleyn, undated.
11 'the fairest playhouse . . .' John Chamberlain to Sir Dudley Carleton, 15 December 1621.
12 'the college porch . . .' *Register of Dulwich College.*
14 The newspaper which reported the election, and which is in the archives of the John Harvard Library, is unidentifiable.
18 'a stout strong man . . .' The description is by Major-General Charles Richard Fox, to whom John Allen left a number of his journals and diaries.
20 'I went to see . . .' 2 September 1675.
There is a legend that Boswell accompanied Dr Johnson to the College in 1751, and recorded that the Doctor 'took the utmost interest in everything, and condescended to say that conditions had improved for both preceptors and taught since he was an usher', but I have been able to find no documentation of this. Certainly the expedition cannot have taken place in the supposed year, since the two men did not become acquainted until 1763.
'received by a smart Divine . . .' 8 June 1791.
25 'Alleyn's grammar school . . .' W. H. Blanch, *Dulwich College and Edward Alleyn.*
'the monkish restrictions . . .' Highmore, *Pietas Londinensis.*
26 'still the prettiest . . .' William Hone, *Table-book*, 1827.

Chapter 2
34 'I well remember . . .' Alleyn Club dinner, 1898.
36 'his object was . . .' *Alleynian*, 1909.
37 'introduced into another boy's desk . . .' F. S. Bone, in his contribution to *Memories of Dulwich College.*
'the opposition of the Governors . . .' Letter among Carver papers; signature illegible.

37 'I feel . . .' Carver papers.
38 'the introduction of two schools . . .' 10 July 1879.
   'he acted wisely . . .' Metcalf Hopgood, a Governor, to Mrs
   Carver, 20 November 1869.
42 'to submit to the addition . . .' *Macmillan's Journal*, June 1867.
44 'the most striking . . .' Malcolm Seaborne, *The English School*.
   '[Dulwich College] is the most . . .' D. L. Franks, *The Stamford
   Brickworks*.
45 Little is known about the early history of this painting; for such
   information as it has been possible to glean I am much in-
   debted to Michael Pantazzi, Assistant Research Curator of
   European Art, National Gallery of Canada. At one time it was
   in the possession of Joseph Hessel of Paris; no sale appears to
   have been recorded. It then passed into the collection of Emile
   Jouval and was sold, as part of this collection, in 1926. In
   1934 it was owned by Alex. Reid & Lefevre of London and
   was included in their exhibition of 'Renoir, Cezanne and their
   Contemporaries'. It was exhibited again in 1936 at the New
   Burlington Galleries in 'Maîtres Français du XIXe Siècle'. By
   then it was owned by Sir David (later Lord) Eccles. In the
   1940s Colnaghi's sold it to John Macaulay, C.C., Q.C., a
   Canadian lawyer of Hebridean descent and a former president
   of the League of Red Cross Societies, who owned one of the
   largest collections of French Impressionist paintings in Canada.
   It now belongs to his daughter, Mrs Maurice Taylor, and has
   at different times been on loan to the Toronto and Santa
   Barbara Galleries of Art.
   'living at Norwood . . .' Pissarro to Wynford Dewhurst, 1902.
   'the Prince looked bored . . .' R. B. Webber, in his contribution to
   Memories of Dulwich College.
46 'inasmuch as women . . .' Board Minutes, 1873.
   'we were allowed to choose . . .' *Memories of Dulwich College*.
   'would find it difficult . . .' Speech Day 1870.
49 'there are many boys here . . .' 31 July 1875.
50 'by degrees we became . . .' M. G. Glazebrook, in *Memories of
   Dulwich College*.
52 'few men . . .' George Way.
53 'the destructive zeal . . .' 4 November 1872.
   'so as to enable them to decide . . .' Board Minutes, 11
   December 1877.
55 'we have at Dulwich . . .' *South London Courier*, 6 November
   1872.
57 'the list of school honours . . .' 11 January 1883.

Chapter 3

58 'I think we are now . . .' *Gilkes and Dulwich*.
'I used to say . . .' *Forty Years On*.

59 'Beyond question the greatest man . . .' *The Story of a Great Schoolmaster*.

60 'While [Sanderson] was to Gilkes . . .' Sir C. D. M. Hindley, *Gilkes and Dulwich*.

62 'the most valuable . . .' *The Story of a Great Schoolmaster*.
'the engineering side . . .' April 1893.

64 'To a man . . .' E. D. Gibbon, *Gilkes and Dulwich*.
'rightly or wrongly . . .' *Fourscore Years*.

66 'he once said to me . . .' F. Griffin, Headmaster of Birkenhead School, quoted in *Gilkes and Dulwich*.
'an unpopular and nerve-destroying . . .' *The Gold Bat*.

68 'there was throughout the staff . . .' Deputation to Board of Education, 14 July 1905.

69 For a while the army class was in the charge of G. C. Coulton, who wrote in his autobiography that he had in it between twenty-five and thirty boys, 'some almost illiterate while others were already good enough to pass straight through into Woolwich or Sandhurst'.
'Alleynians carrying off . . .' At the school prize-giving, 1918.

69– Such scanty information as still exists regarding Dulwich's
71 participation in the L.C.C. scholarship scheme at the beginning of the century and in the Department of Science and Art grants scheme has been taken from the minutes of the Board of Governors of the college, the records of the Finance Committee and of the Higher Education and Scholarships Sub-committee of the L.C.C., the tantalizingly meagre files at the Public Record Office, and the *Statistics of Education in England and Wales* for the period in question. But the patchiness of the available statistics makes the whole subject fraught with question-marks and contradictions, as does the fact that in the records the college is so often confused with Alleyn's. The latter problem is illustrated by my experience when I went to see a very senior retired official of the L.C.C. who was closely involved with the Dulwich Experiment forty years later. He produced figures which, he said, showed the number of L.C.C. scholars who were at the college in 1946, and how much the L.C.C. was paying for them by way of fees—but even he had got it wrong, for the figures related to Alleyn's.

74 'the school permitted . . .' Margaret Campbell, *Dolmetsch*.

79 'the school by (more or less) . . .' *A Prefect's Uncle*.

80 'we never found you . . .' and 'some boys take . . .' Harold Begbie, *Shackleton*.
82 'under certain conditions . . .' *Performing Flea*.
83 'six years . . .' *Over Seventy*.
84 'I believe a boy . . .' The friend was S. C. Griffith.
    'the old man . . .' Aubrey Waugh to Charles Lloyd, 30 January 1972.
    'they have ruined it . . .' Wodehouse to McC. Christison, 1969.
    'if I do come to England . . .' Wodehouse to Charles Lloyd, 2 May 1972.
88 'a young man . . .' *Life of John Maynard Keynes*.
89 'I remember when I first went . . .' Sir Alwyne Ogden.
90 'besides doing away . . .' Gilkes' diary.
91 'there is sure to be an exodus . . .' H. I. Powell to Sir Alfred Lyall, the Chairman of the Board of Governors.
94 'I dreamed last night . . .' Letter to McC. Christison, 10 June (year not given).
    'everyone who teaches properly . . .' *The Modern Side of Public Schools*.
95 'we had for Master . . .' Sir F. A. Hirtzel, in *Gilkes and Dulwich*.

Chapter 4
97 'when I came to Dulwich . . .' Alleyn Club dinner, 1919.
    'it was part of his modesty . . .' 1957.
101 'he had a genius . . .' From the introduction to Gordon Campbell's *My Mystery Ships*.
    'as more and more boys . . .' and 'when the time came . . .' E. Finlason.
103 'I think it is quite inevitable . . .' Board of Education memorandum, 28 April 1919.
105 'at first the black coat . . .' G. H. Spinney.
    'I recall copying . . .' and 'I was the best . . .' Martin Tweed.
107 'the Council recognised . . .' W. H. Webbe, 15 February 1928.
110 'the apparatus is simple . . .' *South London Press*, undated cutting, probably early 1936
111 'a kind of limbo . . .' Eric Parsley, *Alleynian*, 1950.
113 'but he was a first-rate . . .' Professor C. D. Broad.
114 'he was slight and neat . . .' *An Essay on Teachers*.
    'one of three . . .' R. G. G. Price.
115 'had very little idea . . .' *Fourscore Years*.
124 'reeling from the effects . . .' H. I. Alexander.

Chapter 5

129 'there was complete devastation . . .' Alleyn Club dinner, 1945.
130 'it is a well-known trick . . .' Date of cutting 31 July 1944, but
   impossible to identify the German paper. Reproduced in *Crystal
   Palace District Time & Advertiser*, September 1944.
136 '[the project] enabled . . .' 10 September 1953.
138 'but I know from experience . . .' Letter to Governors, October
   1943.
140 'by the decline in its fortunes . . .' Memorandum to Governors,
   18 May 1945.
145 'a reversion . . .' Alleyn Club dinner, 1945.
   'anybody who has been connected . . .' Memorandum 4
   December 1965.
146 'the hideous row . . .' 1946.
147 'we have not surrendered . . .' Alleyn Club dinner, 1946.
148 'we need your sons . . .' Alleyn Club dinner, 1945.
150 'a completely home-made . . .' 10 June 1952.
153 'playing hard . . .' 1915.
   'what I admire most . . .' F. M. Powicke, Regius Professor of
   Modern History in the University of Oxford, 14 July 1941.
154 'the Old Man . . .' Letter to McC. Christison, 2 July 1941.
   'nothing could beat him . . .' Obituary in *Alleynian* by A. W. P.
   Gayford, 1953.

Chapter 6

157 'the greatest . . .' 1951.
168 'just as he had brought . . .' 11 September 1972.
169 'his performance . . .' The boy in question was J. E. Stoy.
   The brilliant mathematician was Eric Handscomb's son David.
   'he was one of the body of . . .' 1971.
170 'all sorts of programs . . .' 1972.
172 'glamour of pop music . . .' 1964.
175 'I wish there could be . . .' *Master's Notes on entry into and
   organisation at Dulwich*, 1964.
181 Doris Lloyd, Charles Lloyd's wife, played a considerable part
   in the reordering of the old library as a chapel, as indeed she
   did in the redecorating of the Great Hall.
188 'the absurd position . . .' Minutes of Governors' meeting 20
   April 1945.
190 'socially the school . . .' *Times Educational Supplement*, 17 June
   1949.
195 'to put it bluntly . . .' *Sunday Times*, 8 June 1980.

Chapter 7
197 'if I lived in the neighbourhood . . .' 1979.
199 'basically the atmosphere . . .' 1979.
210 'it would appear . . .' Memorandum to Governors, 7 December
      1948.

Chapter 8
220 'when you are forty . . .' *Gilkes and Dulwich.*
227 'this was originally . . .' Letter to R. J. Mackenzie, 4 September
      1911.
231 'for the very careful . . .' Board Minutes 1868.
      'I imagine sheep . . .' 1892.
232 'our great school match . . .' R. B. Webber, in *Memories of
      Dulwich College.*
      'only the very oldest . . .' Interview with *Evening News*, 22
      August 1928.
      'at Dulwich . . .' 21 December 1921.
234 'as a batsman . . .' 1967.
235 'the cable putting up the offer . . .' P. G. W. to S. C. Griffith,
      4 November 1947.
241 'throwing in an old shoe . . .' 1888.
      'a new name . . .' 30 May 1961.
242 'that the concession . . .' *Gilkes and Dulwich.*
243 'with head erect . . .' Reported in *Alleynian* 1881.
244 'how hot and red . . .' *Gilkes and Dulwich.*

Chapter 9
249 'in 1874 . . .' 12 July 1907.
250 'I put my foot . . .' Alleyn Club dinner 1894.
252 'a shy, gentle . . .' H. V. Styler.

Chapter 10
263 'the great Rooms . . .' The sale began on 8 April 1786 and
      continued for some days.
265 'Ridiculous . . .' 20 November 1803.
      'Sr. Francis promis'd . . .' Letter undated.
268 'the roofs unsham'd . . .' Vol. 2, January–April 1824.
271 'suffered from neglect . . .' and 'the greater part . . .' 1865,
      1866, and 1867.
272 'a good half hour's walk . . .' 1846.
      'in a disgracefully . . .' Cutting unidentifiable, date probably
      1854.

272 Hazlitt described Murillo's *Spanish Beggar Boys* as 'the triumph of this Collection, and almost of painting'.
275 'satisfaction you have expressed . . .' 1 September 1831.
276 'the Royal Academicians . . .' Minutes of Governors' meeting 6 June 1903.
277 'instruct such of the . . .' *Bourgeois Book of Regulations*, 26 January 1831.
278 'if the Sixth . . .' *Memories of Dulwich College*.
279 'probably there are . . .' 22 June 1919.
'the pictures will . . .' 23 February 1917.
280 'you may go there . . .' 14 June 1918.
283 'I know how much . . .' Letter to Rev. A. W. Carver, Canon Carver's son, dated 28 August 1919 and transcribed into a family copy of *Dulwich College and Edward Alleyn* by W. H. Blanch.
'the average visitor . . .' 28 April 1953.

Index